Phillip K. Trocki

Modern Curriculum Press

EXECUTIVE EDITOR   Wendy Whitnah

PROJECT EDITOR   Diane Dzamtovski

EDITORIAL DEVELOPMENT
DESIGN AND PRODUCTION   The Hampton-Brown Company

ILLUSTRATORS   Anthony Accardo, Joe Boddy, Harry Briggs, Roberta Collier-Morales,
Mark Farina, Meryl Henderson, Masami Miyamoto, Rik Olson, Doug Roy,
John Sandford, Rosalind Solomon.

PHOTO CREDITS   5, Ralph Nelson, Jr./Culver Pictures; 9, Uniphoto/Pictor;
13, Lawrence Migdale/Photo Researchers; 17, Long Beach Public Library
and Information Center; 20, Archive Photos;
29, Stuart Dee/Image Bank; 33, Jeff Spielman/Image Bank;
37, Karl H. Maslowski/Photo Researchers; 41, J. Cochin/Image Bank;
45, Bob Daemmrich/Uniphoto; 53, Michael Newman/Photo Edit;
57, John Spragens, Jr./Photo Researchers; 61, G. Colliva/Image Bank;
65, George Lepp/Comstock; 69, Images Unlimited/Image Bank;
77, Michael S. Thompson/Comstock; 85, Virginia P. Weinland/Photo Researchers;
89, The Bostonian Society/Old State House; 93, Gil C. Kenny/Image Bank;
101, D.O.E./Science Source/Photo Researchers; 105, Grant Huntington;
109, Courtesy of David Barry; 113, Steve Dunwell/Image Bank;
117, Peter Beck/Uniphoto; 125, Jim Mendenhall/Courtesy of the SimonWiesenthal
Center; 128, Courtesy of International Peace Garden; 129, Bruce Hands/Comstock;
133, Karl Hentz/Image Bank; 137, James L. Schaffer/Photo Edit.

COVER DESIGN   The Hampton-Brown Company
COVER PHOTO   Steve Satushek/Image Bank

Typefaces for the cursive type in this book were provided
by Zaner-Bloser, Inc., Columbus, Ohio, copyright, 1993.

ISBN 0-8136-2820-2
Printed in the United States of America
18 19 PO   06 05 04

1-800-321-3106
www.pearsonlearning.com

TABLE OF CONTENTS

Learning to Spell a Word...4
Making a Spelling Notebook..4
Lesson 1   /k/, /kw/, and /n/.......................................5
Lesson 2   Hard and Soft **c** and **g**; **dge**...................9
Lesson 3   /f/...13
Lesson 4   **gn, wr,** and **tch**.....................................17
Lesson 5   Silent Consonants..21
Lesson 6   Instant Replay..25
Lesson 7   /s/, /z/, and /zh/...29
Lesson 8   /sh/..33
Lesson 9   **sc**..37
Lesson 10   **ear, are,** and **air**......................................41
Lesson 11   /ē/..45
Lesson 12   Instant Replay..49
Lesson 13   /o/: **oa, oe, ou,** and **ow**.........................53
Lesson 14   **au** and **aw**..57
Lesson 15   **oo, ew, ue,** and **ui**...................................61
Lesson 16   **ai, ay, oi,** and **oy**.....................................65
Lesson 17   **ou** and **ow**..69
Lesson 18   Instant Replay..73
Lesson 19   **ei** and **ie**..77
Lesson 20   Prefixes **ir, in, il,** and **im**........................81
Lesson 21   Prefixes **de, pre, pro, con, com,** and **mis**........85
Lesson 22   Prefixes **em, en, fore, post,** and **over**.............89
Lesson 23   Prefixes **uni, mono, bi, tri,** and **mid**..........93
Lesson 24   Instant Replay..97
Lesson 25   Prefixes **anti, counter, super, sub,**
             ultra, trans, and **semi**...........................101
Lesson 26   Suffixes **or, er, ist, logy,** and **ology**.............105
Lesson 27   Suffixes **er, est,** and **ness**........................109
Lesson 28   Suffixes **able, ible, ful, hood, ship,**
             and **ment**...113
Lesson 29   Suffixes **ion, ation, ition, ance, ence,**
             ive, and **ity**..117
Lesson 30   Instant Replay...121
Lesson 31   Doubling Final Consonants;
             Adding Suffixes to Words Ending in **e**........125
Lesson 32   Adding Suffixes to Words Ending in **y**............129
Lesson 33   Plurals...133
Lesson 34   Homonyms and Hurdle Words.......................137
Lesson 35   Abbreviations 141
Lesson 36   Instant Replay...145
Writing and Proofreading Guide 149
Using Your Dictionary...150
Spelling Workout Dictionary 151

Learning to Spell a Word

1. Say the word.
   Look at the word and say the letters.

2. Print the word with your finger.

3. Close your eyes and think of the word.

4. Cover the word and print it on paper.

5. Check your spelling.

Making a Spelling Notebook

A Spelling Notebook will help you when
you write. Write the words you're having
trouble with on a sheet of paper. Add the
paper to a notebook or folder. Whenever
you need help to spell a word, look in
your Spelling Notebook.

/k/, /kw/, and /n/

Warm Up

What does it take to make a superstar?

Shaping a Superstar

You are the producer of a space adventure movie. Your script calls for a **unique** character. You know that because of the character's size or some special quality, you may have trouble casting a person for the part. There may be no one for the role that will **qualify**.

What will you do? In this **technical** age, you can build your own character! Be prepared to spend a few hundred thousand dollars, though. You will probably need to hire sculptors, painters, and puppeteers to help you create your new "star."

Many space adventure movie "stars" were made this way. Artists made **remarkable** numbers of sketches. Clay models were sometimes built. Then numbers of the final models, made of foam rubber, fiberglass, or plastic, were fit on metal frames.

People are usually surprised to learn how complicated these creatures really were. Some **required** three or four people to operate the controls. One person's entire job might have been moving one pair of eyes! A large creature might have had two or three people inside. Each had a different task. Together, the sounds and movements they made helped the creatures come "alive." **Knowledge** and technology have joined hands to shape superstars that can do almost anything but sign autographs!

Say each boldfaced word in the selection.
Listen for the /k/, /kw/, and /n/ sounds. What do you notice about the spellings for each sound?

On Your Mark

Take your Warm Up Test. Then check your spelling with the List Words on the next page.

Pep Talk

The /k/ sound can be spelled several different ways:
k, as in keyboard; **ck,** as in locksmith;
que, as in technique; **ch,** as in chorus.
The /kw/ sound is spelled **qu,** as in quantity and banquet.
The /n/ sound is sometimes spelled **kn,** as in knowledge and knelt.

LIST WORDS

1. echoes
2. chorus
3. chemistry
4. qualify
5. acknowledge
6. remarkable
7. locksmith
8. quantity
9. technical
10. banquet
11. knowledge
12. required
13. keyboard
14. chrome
15. antique
16. knelt
17. headache
18. unique
19. schedule
20. technique

Game Plan

Spelling Lineup

Write the List Words that contain the sound given. You will write one word twice.

/k/, as in king

1. _____
2. _____

/k/, as in chord

3. _____
4. _____
5. _____
6. _____
7. _____
8. _____
9. _____

/k/, as in deck

10. _____
11. _____

/k/, as in boutique

12. _____
13. _____
14. _____

/n/, as in knife

15. _____
16. _____
17. _____

/kw/, as in quite

18. _____
19. _____
20. _____
21. _____

Synonyms

Write a List Word that means the same or almost the same as the word or phrase given.

1. needed _____
2. feast _____
3. amount _____
4. one of a kind _____
5. admit _____
6. meet standards _____

7. timetable _____
8. old _____
9. wisdom _____
10. method _____
11. choir _____
12. repairs locks _____

Missing Words

Circle the List Word that belongs in each sentence.
Write the correct word on the line.

1. The cat tiptoed along the _____, making a little song.

   chorus   keyboard   chemistry   _____

2. Fred's beautiful paintings are proof of his _____ talent.

   qualify   remarkable   acknowledge   _____

3. The _____ of our voices bounced back from across the lake.

   quantity   technique   echoes   _____

4. Dad polished the _____ on his car with a soft cloth.

   chrome   technical   schedule   _____

5. Karen _____ down to play with the little puppy.

   required   knelt   echoes   _____

6. The loud music gave me a _____.

   keyboard   schedule   headache   _____

7. By studying computer science, he gained _____ knowledge.

   technical   chemistry   qualify   _____

8. Before she became a scientist, she received her degree in _____.

   chemistry   knowledge   technique   _____

Flex Your Spelling Muscles

Writing

Put yourself into a movie about a space adventure with a <u>remarkable</u> robot. Write the dialogue that takes place when you first meet this <u>unique</u> character. If you like, add descriptions that go with the actions.

Proofreading

This dialogue from the movie "My Friend Is a Robot" has ten mistakes. Use the proofreading marks to correct them. Then write the misspelled List Words correctly on the lines.

Proofreading Marks	
⬭	spelling mistake
≡	capital letter
⊙	add period

ROBOT: (*in a panicky voice*) I'm having tecnicle difficulties. I'm losing all of my knowlege. Now I know what a headake feels like! you must skeduel time to make the requyred repairs

IRMA: (*rolling her eyes in amusement*) Don't panic! All you need is to have your batteries recharged

ROBOT: (*more frantic*) Hurry up and recharge them! I'm quickly becoming a useless pile of krome

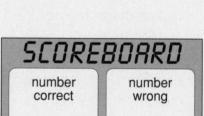

1. _____   4. _____

2. _____   5. _____

3. _____   6. _____

Now proofread your own dialogue. Correct any errors.

Go for the Goal

Take your Final Test. Then fill in your Scoreboard. Send your mistakes to the Word Locker.

SCOREBOARD

number correct	number wrong

★ ★ ★ ★ ★ ★ ★ ★ ★ **All-Star Words** ★ ★ ★ ★ ★ ★ ★ ★ ★

knothole   mechanic   plaque   quiz   kindling

Draw a simple sketch that gives a clue to the meaning of each All-Star Word. Then trade picture clues with a partner. Try to write the All-Star Word that fits each of your partner's sketches.

Hard and Soft c and g; dge

Warm Up

What is the hardest substance found on the earth?

Hard Rock

Have you ever heard the expression "diamonds are forever"? Diamonds can last as long as they take to make. They are made of **carbon**. That's the same substance as the graphite in your pencil. Nature, however, takes a longer time to create diamonds. Diamonds become **processed** over millions of years, and it all takes place nearly 100 miles below the earth's surface. Miners have to move tons of rock to dislodge a single ounce of diamonds.

A diamond is the hardest substance found on the earth. In fact, nothing can cut a **genuine** diamond except another diamond. Cutting a diamond is a very delicate process. To turn a rough diamond into a gem, flat surfaces called *facets* are carefully carved out of the stone. To increase the sparkle, each facet is ground at a certain **angle**.

Diamonds were first discovered in India more than 2,000 years ago. Ancient people thought this type of **crystal** had **magical** powers. They were thought to bring luck, power, good health, and long life. It has been a custom for a man to give a woman a diamond ring when they are **engaged** to be married. They are still used as symbols of love, but they also have other less romantic uses. Today we use diamonds to make phonograph needles and medical tools. The space program used diamonds in a window of a spacecraft that went to Venus. It was the only windowlike matter that would not be destroyed by the heat and atmospheric pressure of this far-off planet.

Look back at the boldfaced words in the selection. What do you notice about the sounds made with the letters **c** and **g**?

On Your Mark

Take your Warm Up Test. Then check your spelling with the List Words on the next page.

The letter **g** makes a hard sound, as in angle, and a soft sound, as in magical. The letters **dge** often spell the soft **g** sound, as in cartridge. The letter **c** makes a hard sound, as in carbon, and a soft sound, as in recipe. Be careful when spelling words with **c** or **g**, because their sounds can easily be confused with **s** or **j**.

LIST WORDS

1. crystal
2. angle
3. engaged
4. advantage
5. pledges
6. carbon
7. processed
8. medicine
9. celebration
10. icicles
11. language
12. budget
13. guesses
14. refrigerator
15. conjugate
16. magical
17. intelligent
18. cartridge
19. genuine
20. recipe

Game Plan

Spelling Lineup

Write each List Word under the correct heading. Some words are used more than once.

g, as in giant

1. _____
2. _____
3. _____
4. _____
5. _____
6. _____
7. _____
8. _____
9. _____
10. _____

g, as in gate

11. _____
12. _____
13. _____
14. _____
15. _____

c, as in card

16. _____
17. _____
18. _____
19. _____
20. _____
21. _____

c, as in cinema

22. _____
23. _____
24. _____
25. _____
26. _____

Alphabetical Order

Write this group of List Words in alphabetical order.

guesses	magical	crystal	conjugate
angle	engaged	carbon	advantage

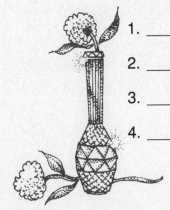

1. _____   5. _____

2. _____   6. _____

3. _____   7. _____

4. _____   8. _____

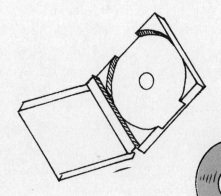

Definitions

Write a List Word to solve each definition clue.

1. container for CD or tape _____

2. directions for making food _____

3. real or true _____

4. cool place to keep food from spoiling _____

5. helps make sick people well _____

6. frozen spears of water _____

7. a party _____

8. promises or agreements _____

9. produced _____

10. spending plan _____

11. speech of a nation, tribe, etc. _____

12. having or showing intelligence _____

Flex Your Spelling Muscles

Writing

Write a magazine or newspaper advertisement for gemstones. Convince people that buying genuine gemstones instead of faux stones is an <u>intelligent</u> thing to do. Use List Words, such as <u>magical</u>, to make your advertisement positive and more effective.

Proofreading

This advertisement has ten mistakes. Use the proofreading marks to correct them. Then write the misspelled List Words correctly on the lines.

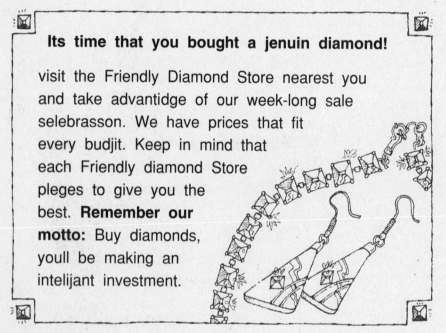

Its time that you bought a jenuin diamond!

visit the Friendly Diamond Store nearest you and take advantidge of our week-long sale selebrasson. We have prices that fit every budjit. Keep in mind that each Friendly diamond Store pleges to give you the best. **Remember our motto:** Buy diamonds, youll be making an intelijant investment.

Proofreading Marks	
spelling mistake
capital letter
add apostrophe

1. _____

2. _____

3. _____

4. _____

5. _____

6. _____

Now proofread your own advertisement. Fix any mistakes.

Go for the Goal

Take your Final Test. Then fill in your Scoreboard. Send your mistakes to the Word Locker.

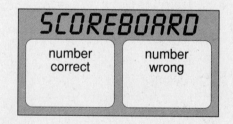

SCOREBOARD

number correct	number wrong

★ ★ ★ ★ ★ ★ ★ ★ ★ **All-Star Words** ★ ★ ★ ★ ★ ★ ★ ★ ★

foliage   gallery   recently   capacity   midget

Create a crossword puzzle that contains the All-Star Words. Write clues and draw a blank grid. Trade puzzles with a partner and try to solve each other's clues.

/f/

Warm Up

How many flowers does it take to cover a Tournament of Roses Parade float?

Flower Power

Every year in Pasadena, California, there's a parade called the Tournament of Roses. It is considered by many to be the only parade of its kind, as well as the most **photographed** event in the world. The focus of this parade, held every January 1st, is the display of hundreds of floats, all made of flowers. In one float, you might find a giant sun made of thousands of daffodils. In another, a ship made of **fragrant** carnations and roses parades by. Who is responsible for making these **magnificent** floats?

One of the parade's top floral float designers is Raul Rodríguez. He does not have an easy job. Floats are never reused, so he must create different designs every year. As soon as the parade ends, he begins his work for the next year. First, his designs are drawn and perfected. Next, the framework is constructed. This can take months. Finally, one week before the parade, millions of flowers are carefully attached to the frame. Fortunately, Rodríguez has a **sufficient** number of volunteers to help him.

Most artists **prefer** to see their work displayed in galleries and museums. Rodríguez, however, goes one step further. He rides his art as it parades for millions of viewers. Few artists can boast of that many admirers seeing their work!

Look back at the boldfaced words in the selection. How many different ways is the /f/ sound spelled?

On Your Mark

Take your Warm Up Test. Then check your spelling with the List Words on the next page.

Pep Talk

The /f/ sound can be spelled four different ways:
f, as in <u>fifteen</u>; **ff,** as in <u>coffee</u>;
ph, as in <u>photographed</u>; **gh,** as in <u>laughable</u>.

LIST WORDS

1. photographed
2. officer
3. triumphant
4. afford
5. toughen
6. fifteen
7. prefer
8. physician
9. fragrant
10. pamphlet
11. saxophone
12. effective
13. coffee
14. phrase
15. hyphenate
16. magnificent
17. sufficient
18. emphasize
19. hemisphere
20. laughable

Game Plan

Spelling Lineup

Write each List Word in the correct category to show how the /f/ sound is spelled.

/f/, as in <u>final</u>

1. _____
2. _____
3. _____
4. _____

/f/, as in <u>sheriff</u>

5. _____
6. _____
7. _____
8. _____
9. _____

/f/, as in <u>photo</u>

10. _____
11. _____
12. _____
13. _____
14. _____
15. _____
16. _____
17. _____
18. _____

/f/, as in <u>enough</u>

19. _____
20. _____

Missing Words

Write the List Word that completes each sentence.

1. Costa Rica, in Central America,

   is located in the Northern

   _____.

2. This Central American country is known

   for its _____,

   which is its most important crop.

3. Its rain forests, teeming with tropical trees, plants, and

   wildlife, are absolutely _____!

4. You can smell the more _____ flowers

   as you walk through the rain forests.

5. Camera buffs from around the world have _____

   the flora and fauna found in rain forests in Costa Rica.

6. If you don't bring a _____ amount of film, you will

   not be able to capture all the great photos.

7. Many concerned groups of people cannot _____

   enough the importance of protecting the rain forests all over the world.

8. Each group distributes a _____ with more

   information on how we can do our part to protect these resources.

Alphabetical Order

Write each group of List Words in alphabetical order.

hyphenate	1. _____	toughen	7. _____
fifteen	2. _____	triumphant	8. _____
effective		prefer	
afford	3. _____	saxophone	9. _____
officer	4. _____	phrase	10. _____
laughable		physician	
	5. _____		11. _____
	6. _____		12. _____

Flex Your Spelling Muscles

Writing

Write a newspaper article about a parade. Were the floats <u>effective</u> or <u>laughable</u>? Describe the sights, smells, and sounds. Were there any <u>fragrant</u> flowers?

Proofreading

Mayor Green's speech, to be given at a parade, has ten mistakes. Use the proofreading marks to correct them. Write the misspelled List Words correctly on the lines.

Proofreading Marks	
⬭	spelling mistake
≡	capital letter
⌃	add something

good day to all of my fellow citizens! Have you ever seen such a magniffisent parade I'm told that there are fiffteen more floats this year than at last year's parade. I can't enfasize enough how much this parade means to our town. That's why I'm surprised that my opponent thinks that we can't aforde a parade every year. what a lauphabel idea! I say that we can't afford not to hold a parade. our town needs to celebrate its triumfant history. Thank you.

1. _____   6. _____

2. _____

3. _____

4. _____

5. _____

Now proofread your newspaper article. Fix any mistakes.

Go for the Goal

Take your Final Test. Then fill in your Scoreboard. Send your mistakes to the Word Locker.

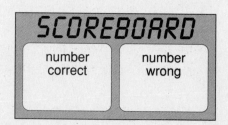

SCOREBOARD

number correct	number wrong

★ ★ ★ ★ ★ ★ ★ ★ ★ ★ **All-Star Words** ★ ★ ★ ★ ★ ★ ★ ★ ★ ★

affection   fender   phenomenon   roughen   orphanage

Divide the All-Star Words between you and a partner. Write both a real and a fake definition for your words. Trade papers. Can each of you match the All-Star Words with their correct meanings?

gn, wr, and tch

Warm Up

Do you know of any planes larger than today's jumbo jets?

The Spruce Goose

Do you think an airplane with a wingspan longer than a football field is far-fetched? An aviator named Howard Hughes imagined one. Because Hughes was also one of the world's richest men, he did more than just imagine it. He was the **designer** and builder of it.

Construction of this marvel began in 1942, during World War II. Hughes planned to use his giant plane to transport troops to foreign battlefields. Plans for his plane went **awry**. Metal was scarce in wartime, so he built the plane out of birch, a kind of wood. By the time his plane was completed, the war was over. The "Spruce Goose," as it was nicknamed, seemed like a dead duck. People said that if it ever got off the ground, little would be left but a **wreckage** of matchsticks. Hughes decided to prove them wrong. On November 2, 1947, he flew the plane on its one and only flight. The goose traveled for one mile. Future flights in this aircraft of **unmatched** size were cancelled.

For years, the Spruce Goose was on display in Long Beach, California. Recently, it has been moved to McMinnville, Oregon, for display at the Evergreen AirVenture Museum. Visitors will see how a modern "jumbo" jet could easily fit beneath the outstretched wooden wings of the goose. Maybe Hughes didn't lay an egg after all!

Look back at the boldfaced words in the selection. Say the words. Listen for the /n/, /r/, and /ch/ sounds. What do you notice about how these sounds are spelled?

On Your Mark

Take your Warm Up Test. Then check your spelling with the List Words on the next page.

Pep Talk

Sometimes you don't hear every letter in a word. The letters **gn** can spell the /n/ sound, as in <u>designer</u>, but the **g** is silent. The letters **wr** can spell the /r/ sound, as in <u>wrath</u>, but the **w** is silent. The letters **tch** can spell the /ch/ sound, as in <u>scratched</u>, but the **t** is silent.

LIST WORDS

1. stretches
2. designer
3. wristwatch
4. fetched
5. kitchen
6. wreckage
7. wrestling
8. crutches
9. hatchet
10. wrath
11. unmatched
12. cologne
13. scratched
14. resigned
15. sketching
16. foreigner
17. campaign
18. awry
19. gnarled
20. reigned

Game Plan

Spelling Lineup

Write each List Word under the correct heading. One word will be written twice.

/n/ spells gn

1. _____
2. _____
3. _____
4. _____
5. _____
6. _____
7. _____

/r/ spells wr

8. _____
9. _____
10. _____
11. _____
12. _____

/ch/ spells tch

13. _____
14. _____
15. _____
16. _____
17. _____
18. _____
19. _____
20. _____
21. _____

Word Clues

Fill in each mini-puzzle with a List Word. Use the word or words already filled in as a clue.

1.
C
R
E (row across)
A
T
O
R

2. S across ... C
   S
   M
   A
   L
   L

   C
   L
   O
   C
   K

3. A
   C
   C (row across)
   I
   D
   E
   N
   T

4. G
   O
   T (row across)

5. C across
   C
   A
   N
   E
   S

6. A
   X

7. I (row across)
   I
   T
   C
   H
   E
   D

8. W across
   W
   R
   O
   N
   G

9. E
   L
   E
   C (row across)
   T
   I
   O
   N

   P
   L
   A
   N

10. D
    R
    A
    W
    I (row across)
    N
    G

Dictionary

Write the List Words that would appear on a dictionary page that has the guide words below. Make sure the words are in alphabetical order.

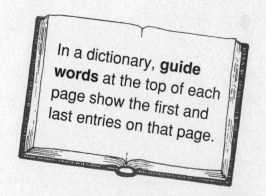

In a dictionary, **guide words** at the top of each page show the first and last entries on that page.

gnarled
foreigner
resigned
cologne
unmatched
wrath
wrestling
kitchen
stretches
reigned

collision/rein

1. _____

2. _____

3. _____

4. _____

5. _____

residue/wretch

6. _____

7. _____

8. _____

9. _____

10. _____

Flex Your Spelling Muscles

Writing

Write one or more journal entries that Howard Hughes might have written about the "Spruce Goose." How did he feel about inventing this type of aircraft? What were his future dreams for his flying machine?

Proofreading

This fictional journal entry has ten mistakes. Use the proofreading marks to correct them. Write the misspelled List Words correctly on the lines.

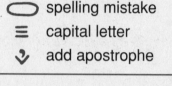

Proofreading Marks
- ⬭ spelling mistake
- ≡ capital letter
- ⌄ add apostrophe

june 18, 1983:

Its my first day in space and nothing has gone arye. The view of Earth from the Challenger is unmachd by anything I've ever seen. space streches on and on and on. I was wressling with the idea of staying awake to enjoy the view, but I need to be well-rested. I have one small complaint. I wish I could simply walk into a kichen for a snack. Im resined, however, to eating my freeze-dried grapefruit.

Sally K. Ride

1. _____   4. _____

2. _____   5. _____

3. _____   6. _____

Now proofread your journal entry. Fix any mistakes.

Go for the Goal

Take your Final Test. Then fill in your Scoreboard. Send your mistakes to the Word Locker.

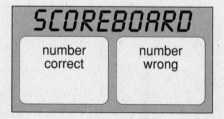

SCOREBOARD

number correct	number wrong

★ ★ ★ ★ ★ ★ ★ ★ ★ ★ **All-Star Words** ★ ★ ★ ★ ★ ★ ★ ★ ★ ★

gnomes   wring   wrench   twitch   stitched

Write a riddle for each All-Star Word leaving a space for the answer. Swltch riddles with a partner. See if you can write the correct answers.

Silent Consonants

Warm Up

How many sleeves are there in a coat of arms?

Coat of Arms

Imagine watching a football game where both teams wore the same uniforms and all players had the same number on their shirts. Even if you had excellent **eyesight**, it would be hard to tell who was who.

During the Middle Ages, when noble knights defended their kings' **castles**, there were no such things as uniforms. Each knight was dressed in a suit of armor that made him look like other knights. The knight's face was covered by a metal plate, too. How was one army of knights able to recognize who was on their side and who was the enemy? The knights came to solve the problem by wearing a "coat of arms" over their armor. The coat of arms was a shirt showing a symbol or shield. Often, the shield, too, bore the colors of the king who had hired the knight. Then, when each **column** of knights approached each other in battle, there was no **doubt** as to who was **fighting** for whom.

The days of knighthood are long past. Coats of arms, however, can still be found today. Many schools and organizations have special symbols called "seals." Families, too, may have their own shields called "family crests." Like the knights' shields, these crests contain symbols and colors that represent the family's history.

Say the boldfaced words in the selection. Do you hear all of the consonants in each word? What do you notice about some of the consonants?

On Your Mark

Take your Warm Up Test. Then check your spelling with the List Words on the next page.

1. doubt
2. knickers
3. tombstone
4. lightning
5. debt
6. softener
7. almighty
8. solemn
9. fasten
10. whistling
11. castles
12. column
13. hymns
14. eyesight
15. listening
16. plumber
17. playwright
18. condemn
19. moisten
20. crumbs

Pep Talk

Use the following rules to help you spell words with silent consonants:

- Silent **t** often comes before **en** or **le**, as in <u>fasten</u> and <u>castles</u>.
- Silent **b** often comes before **t**, as in <u>debt</u>, or after **m**, as in <u>crumbs</u>.
- Silent **n** often follows **m**, as in <u>hymns</u>.
- Silent **k** often comes before **n**, as in <u>knickers</u>.
- Silent **gh** often follows **i**, as in <u>eyesight</u>.

Game Plan

Spelling Lineup

Write each List Word in the category that tells what silent consonant or consonants it contains.

silent **b,** as in <u>thumb</u>

1. _____
2. _____
3. _____
4. _____
5. _____

silent **n,** as in <u>autumn</u>

6. _____
7. _____
8. _____
9. _____

silent **k,** as in <u>knife</u>

10. _____

silent **t,** as in <u>glisten</u>

11. _____
12. _____
13. _____
14. _____
15. _____
16. _____

silent **gh,** as in <u>flight</u>

17. _____
18. _____
19. _____
20. _____

Comparing Words

Study the relationship between the first two underlined words. Then write a List Word that has the same relationship with the third underlined word.

1. Poet is to poem as _____ is to play.

2. Birds are to nests as kings are to _____.

3. Peas are to vegetables as _____ are to songs.

4. Tie is to shoes as _____ is to seatbelts.

5. Huge is to big as _____ is to powerful.

6. Music is to hearing as colors are to _____.

7. Drops are to water as _____ are to bread.

8. Sandals are to shoes as _____ are to trousers.

9. Keep is to promise as pay is to _____.

10. Television is to watching as radio

    is to _____.

Missing Words

Write a List Word to complete each sentence.

1. Without a _____, Dan is the best singer in the chorus.

2. Use the cold water to _____ the towel.

3. Instead of calling a _____, mother fixed the leak herself.

4. The List Words appear in a long _____ on page 22.

5. They were _____ a tune as they raked the leaves.

6. The granite _____ of Paul Revere is in this graveyard.

7. The Health Department had to _____ the hotel due to unsanitary conditions.

8. Fabric _____ will make the towels soft and fluffy.

9. The thunder and _____ startled us.

10. I knew the man was worried when I saw his _____ look.

Flex Your Spelling Muscles

Writing

Write a mystery story titled "The Case of the Missing Coat of Arms." Use List Words to help you create an eerie mood. Perhaps you can add some <u>lightning</u> or <u>whistling</u> winds.

Proofreading

The book review has eight mistakes. Use the proofreading marks to correct them. Write the misspelled List Words correctly on the lines.

There are so many drawings in *The True Book of knights and Cassels* that you can spend hours looking at just one page. This book will take you to thirteenth century europe You'll see a solum knighthood ceremony You'll spot an unlucky knight who is in det after losing a joust and a lucky knight who gets to fassen his lady's scarf.

1. _____

2. _____

3. _____

4. _____

Now proofread your mystery story.
Fix any mistakes.

Proofreading Marks	
⬭	spelling mistake
≡	capital letter
⊙	add period

Go for the Goal

Take your Final Test. Then fill in your Scoreboard. Send your mistakes to the Word Locker.

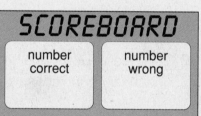

SCOREBOARD

number correct	number wrong

★ ★ ★ ★ ★ ★ ★ ★ **All-Star Words** ★ ★ ★ ★ ★ ★ ★ ★ ★

knuckles   thistle   numb   throughout   corps

Write an exclamatory sentence that includes each of the All-Star Words. Then erase the All-Star Words and switch papers with a partner. Fill in the missing words.

Name_____

Instant Replay • Lessons 1–5

LESSON 6

Time Out

Some words are spelled differently than you might expect. Some sounds, like /f/ and /k/, are spelled more than one way. The letters **g** and **c** have a hard and a soft sound. Some words contain silent letters.

Check Your Word Locker

Look at the words in your Word Locker. Write your most troublesome words from Lessons 1 through 5.

_____

_____

Practice writing your troublesome words with a partner. Say the words and point out to your partner what part of the word is spelled differently than you expected.

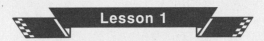

Sounds can be spelled in different ways. Keyboard, acknowledge, echoes, and antique all have the /k/ sound. Qualify has the /kw/ sound. Knelt has the /n/ sound.

List Words
chorus
schedule
keyboard
quantity
banquet
required
knowledge
antique
knelt
unique

Write a List Word that means the same or almost the same as the word given.

1. piano _____

2. necessary _____

3. timetable _____

4. amount _____

5. singers _____

6. feast _____

7. old _____

8. unequaled _____

9. bowed _____

10. understanding _____

The letter **g** makes a hard sound, as in <u>language</u>, and a soft sound, as in <u>budget</u>.
The letter **c** makes a hard sound, as in <u>magical</u>, and a soft sound, as in <u>celebration</u>.

List Words

crystal
engaged
medicine
icicles
language
guesses
intelligent
cartridge
genuine
recipe

Write a List Word to complete each sentence.

1. I like the way that _____ sounds when it is spoken.

2. Anna was _____ two years before she got married.

3. My doctor told me to take this _____.

4. The _____ requires two cups of flour.

5. So far, all your _____ have been wrong.

6. An _____ dog learns tricks easily.

7. Is that a _____ ruby or a fake?

8. Many fine goblets are made from _____.

9. This _____ does not fit my tape player.

10. Every winter, long _____ form.

The /f/ sound can be spelled with **f**, **ff**, **ph**, and **gh**, as in <u>prefer</u>, <u>afford</u>, <u>phrase</u>, and <u>toughen</u>.

List Words

officer
afford
toughen
fifteen
prefer
physician
fragrant
pamphlet
phrase
hemisphere

Write the List Word that belongs in each group.

1. catalog, booklet, _____

2. seven, thirteen, _____

3. sergeant, captain, _____

4. globe, planet, _____

5. word, sentence, _____

6. scented, perfumed, _____

7. save, spend, _____

8. like, desire, _____

9. strengthen, stiffen, _____

10. nurse, medic, _____

The /n/ sound can be spelled with **gn**, as in <u>gnarled</u>. The /r/ sound can be spelled with **wr**, as in <u>awry</u>. The /ch/ sound can be spelled with **tch**, as in <u>kitchen</u>.

List Words

stretches
fetched
wrath
wristwatch
gnarled
resigned
sketching
foreigner
awry
wreckage

Find List Words that mean the same as the underlined words in the sentences. Write the words on the lines.

1. By my <u>clock</u>, it's almost noon. _____

2. The apology ended my <u>fury</u>. _____

3. Tim <u>reaches</u> for the box on the top shelf. _____

4. That tree is so <u>twisted</u>! _____

5. Eileen <u>quit</u> after a week. _____

6. He is a <u>stranger</u> to our land. _____

7. Kirk <u>brought</u> the book I left behind. _____

8. The storm left <u>damage</u> everywhere. _____

9. Dad is <u>drawing</u> a boat. _____

10. Our plans for the trip went <u>wrong</u>. _____

Some words contain silent letters, such as the **t** in <u>softener</u>, the **b** in <u>plumber</u>, the **n** in <u>column</u>, the **k** in <u>knickers</u>, and the **gh** in <u>almighty</u>.

List Words

doubt
knickers
lightning
debt
solemn
fasten
hymns
condemn
moisten
crumbs

Write the List Word to match each clue.

1. short pants _____

2. declare unfit for use _____

3. make damp _____

4. comes with storms _____

5. something owed _____

6. be uncertain about _____

7. songs of praise _____

8. not laughing _____

9. bits of bread _____

10. attach or join _____

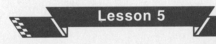

Write the List Word next to its dictionary sound-spelling.

List Words

recipe
intelligent
moisten
knowledge
chorus
prefer
fetched
wristwatch
genuine
knickers
medicine
sketching
wrath
hemisphere

1. (res´ə pe) _____

2. (mois´ən) _____

3. (kôr´əs) _____

4. (fech´t) _____

5. (jen´yo͞o in) _____

6. (med´ə sən) _____

7. (rath) _____

8. (in tel´ə jənt) _____

9. (nä´lij) _____

10. (prē fur´) _____

11. (rist´wäch) _____

12. (nik´ərz) _____

13. (skech´iŋ) _____

14. (hem'i sfir´) _____

Go for the Goal

Take your Final Replay Test. Then fill in your Scoreboard.
Send any misspelled words to your Word Locker.

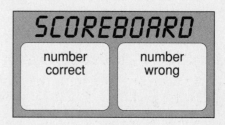

SCOREBOARD

number correct	number wrong

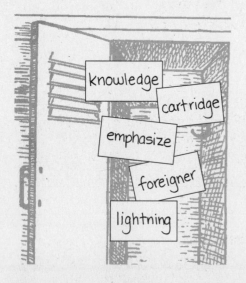

knowledge
cartridge
emphasize
foreigner
lightning

Clean Out Your Word Locker

Look in your Word Locker. Cross out each word you spelled
correctly on your Final Replay Test. Circle the words you're
still having trouble with. Add the words you circled to your
Spelling Notebook. What do you notice about the words?
Watch for those words as you write.

LESSON

7

/s/, /z/, and /zh/

Warm Up

What kind of career might require you to be a daredevil?

Double-duty Daredevils

A stunt performer and a race-car driver are **usually** thought of as daredevils. Either one of these could be considered a dangerous position. Some say that such people tempt danger on **purpose.**

There's a career field for those who find it **desirable** to have a bit of risk and danger in their work. It's not **casual** work, though. In fact, it's lifesaving work. A person who is this version of a "daredevil" is called a "firemedic."

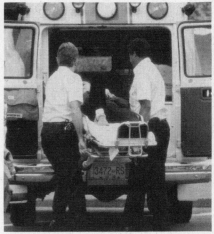

A firemedic really does the jobs of two people. He or she is a trained firefighter and a paramedic. This means that he or she can give medical help in an emergency. Both professions require a great deal of training. Becoming a firefighter requires many hours of **instruction** and practice. A paramedic learns information both in school and in a hospital. A person who is qualified in both of these areas is **deserving** of credit.

In many places it would be too expensive to hire firefighters as well as paramedics. A firefighter is often called to a scene where there's an injury. Having been trained in both medicine and firefighting, a firemedic is prepared for almost anything.

It takes a special kind of person to want to be a firemedic. It **usually** means giving up leisure time for the extra training. Months of study and practice are part of the program. However, firemedics claim that the feeling of satisfaction their careers offer is well worth the sacrifices.

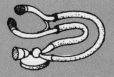

Say the boldfaced words in the selection. Notice the sound that the letter **s** makes in each word. How many different sounds for **s** do you hear?

On Your Mark

Take your Warm Up Test. Then check your spelling with the List Words on the next page.

Pep Talk

The letter **s** can stand for different sounds. For example, in the word <u>purpose</u>, the letter **s** spells the /s/ sound. In the word <u>resemble</u>, the letter **s** spells the /z/ sound. In the word <u>usually</u>, the letter **s** spells the /zh/ sound.

LIST WORDS

1. purpose
2. composure
3. diseases
4. casual
5. seasonal
6. resemble
7. measuring
8. husband
9. position
10. visual
11. trousers
12. instruments
13. desirable
14. instructor
15. leisurely
16. deserving
17. gymnasium
18. version
19. treasury
20. usually

Game Plan

Spelling Lineup

Write each List Word under the sound that **s** stands for. One word will be written twice.

/s/, as in <u>secure</u>

1. _____
2. _____
3. _____
4. _____

/z/, as in <u>music</u>

5. _____
6. _____
7. _____
8. _____
9. _____
10. _____
11. _____
12. _____
13. _____

/zh/, as in <u>pleasure</u>

14. _____
15. _____
16. _____
17. _____
18. _____
19. _____
20. _____
21. _____

Synonyms

Write a List Word that means the same or almost the same
as the word or phrase given.

1. reason _____

2. generally _____

3. worth wanting _____

4. teacher _____

5. informal _____

6. unhurried _____

7. self-control _____

8. look like _____

9. weighing _____

10. money or funds _____

11. ailments _____

12. placement _____

13. worthy _____

14. tools _____

15. variation _____

Puzzle

Fill in the crossword puzzle by writing a List Word to answer each definition clue.

ACROSS
1. place or location
3. finding the length or width
4. not formal
7. pianos and drums
10. almost always
11. related to sight
12. at a certain time of year
13. pants

DOWN
1. goal or aim
2. room for athletics
5. without hurry
6. one who teaches
8. wife's spouse
9. copy, variant

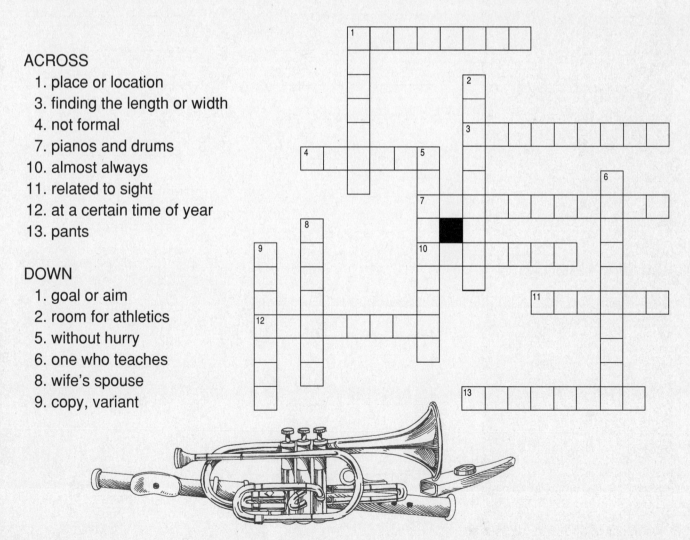

Flex Your Spelling Muscles

Writing

Write a brief speech praising people, such as firemedics, who perform an important job. Explain why those people are deserving of praise. Do they show <u>composure</u> in difficult situations?

Proofreading

This want ad has twelve mistakes. Use the proofreading marks to correct them. Then write the misspelled List Words correctly on the lines.

 **Gerry's Gymnassiem**
Hiring Now

We need an instruckter to work in our after-school program. the purpuse of our program is to help children become goodsports. Experience teaching team sports, such as baseball soccer, or basketball, is a must. Knowledge of first aid is dezirabul. Cazuall dress is okay. If you're interested in this posssion, pleasecontact: Sally O'Connell pauline Heaney, or Ari Geiger.
Telephone: **1-800-WRK-OUTS.**

1. _____

2. _____

3. _____

4. _____

5. _____

6. _____

Now proofread your speech. Fix any mistakes.

Go for the Goal

Take your Final Test. Then fill in your Scoreboard. Send your mistakes to the Word Locker.

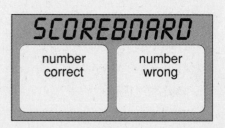

★ ★ ★ ★ ★ ★ ★ ★ **All-Star Words** ★ ★ ★ ★ ★ ★ ★ ★ ★

releases   resolve   foreclosure   intrusion   diffuse

Write a newspaper headline for each All-Star Word. Then, erase the All-Star Word. Trade headlines with a partner. Complete each other's headlines by writing the missing words.

/sh/

Warm Up

What can you wear to help you see better or to make a fashion statement?

Hocus Focus

Eyeglasses used to be called "spectacles" Before evolving to their present shape, they really were quite a spectacle.

No one is really sure who is responsible for the **invention** of eyeglasses. Using pieces of glass to enlarge the size of words on a printed page goes back to ancient times. Many scholars say that the first glasses were made in Italy around 1280.

Eyeglasses were first put in frames made of leather. They were held in place by tying the leather strips around the wearer's ears. This proved uncomfortable. Later, the Spanish invented frames made of silk ribbons. These, too, were uncomfortable and held the glasses too close tot he eyes. To avoid the problem of tightly tied frames, the Chinese found a **partial** solution to **assure** comfort. They added weights to the ribbons. Wearers draped the ribbons over their ears. This held the glasses comfortably–until the wearer turned his or her head too quickly. Then the weights swung around, hitting their owner in the head. Later came frameless glasses that stayed on with a clip over the wearer's nose. In this case, the wearer could see, but the clip interfered with breathing.

The big breakthrough in frames came in London, England, in 1730. An optician, Edward Scarlett, decided to attach the lenses to stiff side pieces.

Even after glasses became more practical, people were **ashamed** to wear them in **social** situations. Today glasses have become a fashion statement. To **appreciate** how things have changed, just take a long look around.

Say the boldfaced words in the selection. How many ways do you find to spell the /sh/ sound?

On Your Mark

Take your Warm Up Test. Then check your spelling with the List Words on the next page.

Pep Talk

The /sh/ sound can be spelled in several ways.

sh, as in <u>shoe</u>
su, as in <u>insure</u>
ti, as in <u>convention</u> and <u>partial</u>
ci, as in <u>facial</u>
ch, as in <u>machinery</u>

LIST WORDS

1. insure
2. information
3. exploration
4. ashamed
5. partial
6. nourish
7. social
8. brochure
9. invention
10. assure
11. facial
12. convention
13. official
14. machinery
15. parachute
16. negotiate
17. accomplish
18. potential
19. appreciate
20. quotient

Game Plan

Spelling Lineup

Write each List Word in the correct category to show how the /sh/ sound is spelled.

/sh/, as in <u>shoe</u>

1. _____
2. _____
3. _____

/sh/, as in <u>machine</u>

4. _____
5. _____
6. _____

/sh/, as in <u>glacial</u>

7. _____
8. _____
9. _____
10. _____

/sh/, as in <u>motion</u>

11. _____
12. _____
13. _____
14. _____
15. _____
16. _____
17. _____
18. _____

/sh/, as in <u>sure</u>

19. _____
20. _____

Balloon Popper

Classification

Write the List Word that belongs in each group.

1. news, facts, _____   5. do, complete, _____

2. sum, remainder, _____   6. search, adventure, _____

3. kite, balloon, _____   7. incomplete, in part, _____

4. book, pamphlet, _____   8. discuss, mediate, _____

Missing Words

Circle the List Word that belongs in each sentence. Write the correct word on the line.

1. Thank Alexander Graham Bell for the _____ of the telephone.

   convention   invention   brochure   _____

2. Plant food, rich soil, and water will _____ the seedlings.

   negotiate   appreciate   nourish   _____

3. The factory uses heavy _____ to produce aluminum cans.

   machinery   information   convention   _____

4. We knew she was happy because of her cheerful _____ expression.

   partial   facial   social   _____

5. I _____ you that this product will solve your problem.

   accomplish   nourish   assure   _____

6. The dance proved to be the most enjoyable _____ event of the year.

   ashamed   social   exploration   _____

7. Paul has the _____ to become a great musician.

   exploration   accomplish   potential   _____

8. Five interlocked circles are the _____ symbol of the Olympics.

   official   quotient   facial   _____

9. The company will _____ our business against fire and theft.

   negotiate   insure   appreciate   _____

10. She flew to Toronto for a _____ of sportswear designers.

    invention   machinery   convention   _____

Flex Your Spelling Muscles

Writing

You have a great idea for an invention. Write a letter to a friend naming and describing your invention and its benefits.

Proofreading

This letter to Benjamin Franklin has ten mistakes. Use the proofreading marks to correct them. Then write the misspelled List Words correctly on the lines.

Proofreading Marks

⬭ spelling mistake

≡ capital letter

✐ take out something

August 15, 1789

Dear benjamin,
   I apreshiate the the bifocals. I can ackomplis so much more work with your invenshon. I'm ashshamd that I haven't written sooner, but I have so many offishule duties. I ashure you you that George and I think of you often.

best regards,
Martha Washington

1. _____

2. _____

3. _____

4. _____

5. _____

6. _____

Now proofread your letter. Fix any mistakes.

Go for the Goal

Take your Final Test. Then fill in your Scoreboard. Send your mistakes to the Word Locker.

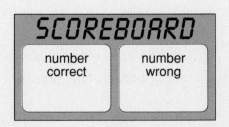

SCOREBOARD

| number correct | number wrong |

★ ★ ★ ★ ★ ★ ★ ★ **All-Star Words** ★ ★ ★ ★ ★ ★ ★ ★ ★

flourish   ensure   gracious   chagrin   regulation

Work with a partner to write one definition for each All-Star Word. Check your work in your dictionary. Are your definitions correct? Put a star next to any words that have more than one meaning.

SC

Warm Up

What kind of spider can dine on fish?

Something Fishy

Not all spiders are content to eat only bugs. There are some **fascinating** kinds of spiders that are "anglers," or fishers. They actually catch tadpoles and **miscellaneous** types of tiny fish!

In North America, there are more than a dozen types of fisher spiders. Their angling techniques vary. Most of them scamper swiftly across the water and wait patiently for a passing fish. A fisher spider may be seen **descending** upon a fish that is twice its own size. The capture itself is not the real problem for this eight-legged creature. Because the spider's digestive juices have litttle effect in the water, the spider has to haul its prey to land. Dragging its **luscious** little treat to land requires hard work, **discipline**, and **muscles**.

Two of these anglers are the raft spider and the nursery-web spider. The raft spider builds its own raft from leaves and its own silk threads. This spider sails out on its raft to wait for its prey. The nursery-web spider is named for the web it weaves to hold its egg sac. It gets a taste for fish now and then, too. Most of the time it stays with the eggs until all have hatched and the young spiders have **scattered.** Once in a while it may venture out across the water for a seafood supper. It may seem strange that a creature that is often eaten by fish can turn the tables and have a fish for lunch!

Say the boldfaced words in the selection. How many different sounds can you find made by the letters **sc**?

On Your Mark

Take your Warm Up Test. Then check your spelling with the List Words on the next page.

Pep Talk

The letters **sc** can make three different sounds:
the /sk/ sound, as in <u>escape</u>
the /s/ sound, as in <u>scissors</u>
the /sh/ sound, as in <u>conscience</u>

LIST WORDS

1. scented
2. adolescent
3. scattered
4. scissors
5. scientific
6. screaming
7. muscles
8. scalding
9. scenery
10. crescent
11. descending
12. sculpture
13. escape
14. scampered
15. scenic
16. miscellaneous
17. fascinating
18. luscious
19. discipline
20. conscience

Game Plan

Spelling Lineup

Write each List Word under the sound **sc** makes.

/s/, as in <u>scene</u>

1. _____
2. _____
3. _____
4. _____
5. _____
6. _____
7. _____
8. _____
9. _____
10. _____
11. _____
12. _____

/sk/, as in <u>scoop</u>

13. _____
14. _____
15. _____
16. _____
17. _____
18. _____

/sh/, as in <u>unconscious</u>

19. _____
20. _____

Alphabetical Order

Write this group of List Words in alphabetical order.

scented
scattered
scissors
scientific
screaming
scalding
scenery
sculpture
scampered
scenic

1. _____

2. _____

3. _____

4. _____

5. _____

6. _____

7. _____

8. _____

9. _____

10. _____

Missing Words

Write the List Word that completes each sentence.

1. An _____ is a person between childhood and adulthood.

2. Your body moves by the stretching and tightening of

   your _____.

3. The bride looked lovely as she was _____ the stairway
   in her gown.

4. The moon is a _____

   shape in its first or last quarter.

5. Many people have a "junk drawer" where they store

   _____ household items.

6. She captured the attention of the entire audience with her

   _____ speech on an otherwise boring topic.

7. It takes a lot of _____ to practice the piano every day.

8. Reading is a great way to relax and _____ daily stress.

9. Otto, a gourmet chef, cooks _____, tasty meals.

10. Rely on your _____ when deciding whether something
    is right for you.

Flex Your Spelling Muscles

Writing

Write a nature poem. You can write about a <u>fascinating</u> creature such as a spider, your favorite season, or a <u>scenic</u> place. Use as many List Words as you can.

Proofreading

These nature poems have seven mistakes. Use the proofreading marks to correct them. Write the misspelled List Words correctly on the lines.

Proofreading Marks	
⬭	spelling mistake
⌄	add apostrophe
∧	add something

Work of Art

A spider web isa fassinating thing.
Its a skulptur made of silky string.

1. _____

2. _____

Hungry Night

Crecint Moon, Night has
Taken abite out of you.
What a lussious meal!

3. _____

4. _____

Now proofread your nature poem. Fix any mistakes.

Go for the Goal

Take your Final Test. Then fill in your Scoreboard. Send your mistakes to the Word Locker.

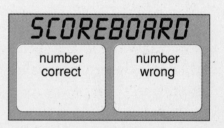

SCOREBOARD

number correct	number wrong

★ ★ ★ ★ ★ ★ ★ ★ ★ ★ **All-Star Words** ★ ★ ★ ★ ★ ★ ★ ★ ★ ★

scrimp   ascend   scour   conscious   scheme

Create a crossword puzzle that includes each of the All-Star Words. You'll need to draw a blank grid and write clues. Use your dictionary if you need help. Switch puzzles with a partner. Write the answers to solve each other's puzzle.

ear, are, air

Warm Up

How does luge racing differ from sledding?

Super Sledding

An exciting sporting event has **appeared** on the Winter Olympic scene. It's a race run on a fast, lightweight sled called a *luge*. This small, one-person sled has been **compared** to a bobsled. While they are both sleds, the comparison ends there.

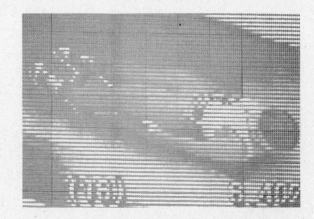

A luger lies on his or her back on the luge. When going down a run, the rider's head and feet extend past the length of the sled. In this position, an experienced luger can reach speeds of nearly 80 miles per hour! One of the most amazing things about the luge is the way it is steered. The rider **carefully** moves his or her thighs and upper arms to turn the luge. The movements are **barely** noticeable to spectators.

In luge racing, fearless riders wear little equipment. Their rubber suits are form-fitting with gloves and boots to match. The lugers wear a simple helmet with a face shield. The idea is to reduce the air friction that can slow a sled down.

The luge has been popular in Europe for many years. Many Americans were **unaware** of the sport until recently. Training camps give American athletes a chance to develop their racing skills. These Olympic hopefuls practice in **earnest** for the chance to compete with the world's best lugers.

Look back at the boldfaced words in the selection. Say the words. Compare the sounds made by the letters **ear**, **are**, and **air**.

On Your Mark

Take your Warm Up Test. Then check your spelling with the List Words on the next page.

Pep Talk

Sometimes the letters **ear** make the /ir/ sound, as in <u>years</u> and <u>appeared</u>.
The letters **ear** can also make the /ur/ sound, as in <u>earnest</u> and <u>earning</u>.
Sometimes the /er/ sound can be spelled **are**, as in <u>barely</u> or **air**, as in <u>stairway</u>.

LIST WORDS

1. searching
2. appeared
3. millionaire
4. silverware
5. compared
6. stairway
7. earthenware
8. carefully
9. barely
10. squares
11. gears
12. earning
13. unfairly
14. unaware
15. earrings
16. earnest
17. research
18. despair
19. questionnaire
20. rehearsal

Game Plan

Spelling Lineup

Write the List Words that contain the sound given. You will write one word twice.

/ur/, as in <u>earth</u>

1. _____
2. _____
3. _____
4. _____
5. _____
6. _____

/er/, as in <u>chair</u>

7. _____
8. _____
9. _____
10. _____
11. _____

/er/, as in <u>care</u>

12. _____
13. _____
14. _____
15. _____
16. _____
17. _____
18. _____

/ir/, as in <u>clear</u>

19. _____
20. _____
21. _____

Comparing Words

Study the relationship between the first two underlined words. Then write a
List Word that has the same relationship with the third underlined word.

1. Up is to down as _____ is to carelessly.

2. Wheels are to circles as boxes are to _____.

3. Bracelets are to wrists as _____ are to ears.

4. Turn is to return as search is to _____.

5. Peach is to fruit as fork is to _____.

6. Footbridge is to cross as _____ is to climb.

7. Happiness is to joy as sadness is to _____.

8. Review is to test as _____ is to performance.

Missing Words

Write the List Word that completes each sentence.

1. A rescue team is _____ for the lost boy.

2. Mountain bikes are equipped with several _____.

3. She is saving part of the money she is _____ every month.

4. Although the _____ pot was very old, it had no cracks.

5. The younger brother didn't appreciate being _____ to his older brother.

6. The sun was shining while it was showering, and a rainbow _____.

7. I was so sick I could _____ get out of bed.

8. She had no idea and was completely _____ that they were planning a

   surprise party for her.

9. The defendant was angry and felt that he was treated _____ by the judge.

10. He gave an _____ and moving speech about his fight with the disease.

11. Members will fill out a _____ to participate in the survey.

12. In today's economy, it is not easy to become a _____.

Flex Your Spelling Muscles

Writing

Research questionnaire formats (i.e., question-and-answer or multiple choice), and write a questionnaire about a new Olympic sport. Choose an event that you feel should be in the Olympics.

> **OLYMPICS QUESTIONNAIRE**
>
> **Instructions:** Darken the circle that indicates your response.
>
> 1. The Olympic Games should be held every year.
>   ○ strongly agree ○ agree ○ disagree ○ strongly disagree
> 2. The Summer Olympics should always be held in the same country.
>   ○ strongly agree ○ agree ○ disagree ○ strongly disagree

Proofreading

These how-to directions for a Trivia Olympics have eleven mistakes. Use the proofreading marks to correct them. Write the misspelled List Words correctly on the lines.

Proofreading Marks	
⬭	spelling mistake
⊙	add period
ℒ	take out something

1. You will need two teams and a a judge.
2. Each team has to reserch five questions for the other team to answer. Start by surching through reference books List the books where the information appaired. Work cairfully
3. Each correctly answered question is worth 50 points
4. Each incorrectly answered question results in the opposite team team erning a 25-point bonus.
5. At the end of the game, the scores are compard. The team with the most points wins.

1. _____
2. _____
3. _____
4. _____
5. _____
6. _____

Now proofread your questionnaire. Fix any mistakes.

Go for the Goal

Take your Final Test. Then fill in your Scoreboard. Send your mistakes to the Word Locker.

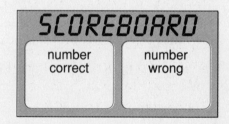

SCOREBOARD	
number correct	number wrong

★ ★ ★ ★ ★ ★ ★ ★ ★ **All-Star Words** ★ ★ ★ ★ ★ ★ ★ ★ ★

concessionaire   smeared   yearn   impair   welfare

Write a mystery story title for each All-Star Word. Then erase the All-Star Word from each title. Switch titles with a partner. Can you fill in the missing words correctly?

/ē/

Warm Up

Who are the competitors in the Special Olympics?

Olympic Gold

It takes a special kind of athlete to win an Olympic medal. There are some very special athletes who win every time they compete.

"Let me win, but if I cannot win, let me be brave in the attempt."

After reciting this official oath, each **athlete** is ready to **proceed**. This is no ordinary competition. It's called the Special Olympics.

The competitors are special, indeed. All are developmentally challenged. Yet all have developed the skills and the **esteem** it takes to make them winners.

The Special Olympics began over twenty years ago with a handful of athletes competing in a few track and field events. Today, over a million athletes compete annually in more than 75 events. Like the Summer and Winter Olympic Games that are **repeated** every four years, this series of competitions begins with a parade, during which all the hopeful competitors can be seen by their fans and families.

After every event, the top three athletes are presented with gold, silver, or bronze medals. All the competitors are recognized for their **achievement.** Each competitor, even the one who placed last, is awarded a well-deserved medal.

Most athletes only have to compete against one another. The participants in the Special Olympics go one step further. They compete against themselves—and win.

Say the boldfaced words in the selection. What vowel sound do you hear in each of these words? How many ways can you find to spell that sound?

On Your Mark

Take your Warm Up Test. Then check your spelling with the List Words on the next page.

Pep Talk

The /ē/ sound can be spelled different ways:

e, as in <u>ecology</u>　　　**ee**, as in <u>proceed</u>
ea, as in <u>repeated</u>　　**ie**, as in <u>nieces</u>
e_e, as in <u>athlete</u>　　**y**, as in <u>delivery</u>
ey, as in <u>trolley</u>

LIST WORDS

1. athlete
2. proceed
3. delete
4. extreme
5. repeated
6. esteem
7. reasonable
8. revealed
9. complete
10. greasy
11. achievement
12. squeezed
13. delivery
14. trolley
15. ecology
16. nieces
17. concealed
18. guarantee
19. believable
20. succeeded

Game Plan

Spelling Lineup

Write each List Word under the spelling of its /ē/ sound. Some List Words are used more than once.

ee, as in <u>succeed</u>

1. _____
2. _____
3. _____
4. _____
5. _____

ea, as in <u>speak</u>

6. _____
7. _____
8. _____
9. _____
10. _____

y, as in <u>apology</u>

11. _____
12. _____
13. _____

ey, as in <u>volleyball</u>

14. _____

e, as in <u>equal</u>

15. _____
16. _____
17. _____
18. _____
19. _____

ie, as in <u>piece</u>

20. _____
21. _____
22. _____

e_e, as in <u>scheme</u>

23. _____
24. _____
25. _____
26. _____

Respellings

Use the accent marks and the pronunciation key in the back of the book to say each respelling below. Then write the List Word that goes with each respelling.

In the dictionary, the respelling tells how to pronounce the word.
delete (dē lēt´)

1. (sək sēd´id) _____

2. (e stēm´) _____

3. (kən sēld´) _____

4. (dē liv´ər ē) _____

5. (rē vēld´) _____

6. (ri pēt´ əd) _____

7. (ath´ lēt) _____

8. (bē lēv´ə bəl) _____

9. (nēs´ iz) _____

10. (ē käl´ə jē) _____

11. (grē´ sē) _____

12. (trä´ lē) _____

13. (skwēzd) _____

14. (rē´ zən ə bəl) _____

15. (prō sēd´) _____

16. (ger ən tē´) _____

Classification

Write the List Word that belongs in each group.

1. omit, erase, _____

2. pressed, kneaded, _____

3. respect, admiration, _____

4. farthest, utmost, _____

5. total, whole, _____

6. train, bus, _____

7. uncles, cousins, _____

8. feat, accomplishment, _____

9. uncovered, exhibited, _____

10. biology, chemistry, _____

11. warranty, promise, _____

12. fair, sensible, _____

13. true, likely, _____

14. oily, slick, _____

15. advance, move, _____

16. hid, obscured, _____

Flex Your Spelling Muscles

Writing

Write a report about your favorite sports hero. Describe the way in which your hero has succeeded. Try to use as many List Words as you can.

Proofreading

This special message for an award has twelve mistakes. Use the proofreading marks to correct them. Then write the misspelled List Words correctly on the lines.

Proofreading Marks
⬭ spelling mistake
≡ capital letter
ℒ take out something

Most Improved Athleet of the Year

P. S. 321 recognizes Russ samuels for his acheivment in track. although Russ did not win any races, he suceded in winning our admiration. At at first, Russ could not even compleet a 100-yard dash. instead of quitting or giving up, Russ ran each day, even under the most extream weather conditions. At Field Day, Russ came in third in the the 3-mile race. He has truly earned our our highest esteam.

1. _____   4. _____

2. _____   5. _____

3. _____   6. _____

Now proofread your report. Fix any mistakes.

Go for the Goal

Take your Final Test. Then fill in your Scoreboard. Send your mistakes to the Word Locker.

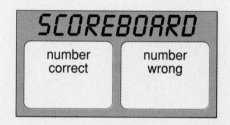

SCOREBOARD

number correct	number wrong

★ ★ ★ ★ ★ ★ ★ ★ ★ ★ **All-Star Words** ★ ★ ★ ★ ★ ★ ★ ★ ★ ★

precede   eastward   bleak   folly   siege

Write each List Word. Then, work with a partner to list at least one synonym and antonym for each All-Star Word. Use a thesaurus or an unabridged dictionary to check your work. How many additional synonyms and antonyms can you find?

Instant Replay • Lessons 7–11

Time Out

Some words are spelled differently than you expect. The letter **s**, the letters **sc**, and the letters **ear** can stand for more than one sound. In addition, one sound, like /er/ or /ē/ may be spelled in many different ways.

Check Your Word Locker

Look at the words in your Word Locker. Write your most troublesome words from Lessons 7 through 11.

_____

_____

Practice writing your troublesome words with a partner. Erase certain letters from the words, trade papers with your partner, and fill in the missing letters.

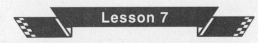

Lesson 7

The letter **s** can spell the /s/ sound, as in <u>instruments</u>; the /z/ sound, as in <u>husband</u>; and the /zh/ sound, as in <u>treasury</u>.

List Words
composure
diseases
casual
seasonal
resemble
husband
desirable
leisurely
deserving
usually

Write a List Word that means the opposite of the word given.

1. differ _____

2. never _____

3. health _____

4. year-round _____

5. quickly _____

6. unworthy _____

7. formal _____

8. wife _____

9. unwanted _____

10. nervousness _____

49

The /sh/ sound can be spelled with **sh**, as in <u>nourish</u>; **su**, as in <u>assure</u>; **ti**, as in <u>invention</u>; **ci**, as in <u>social</u>; and **ch**, as in <u>brochure</u>.

List Words

insure
ashamed
partial
nourish
brochure
invention
assure
facial
machinery
parachute

Write five List Words that could be found listed between each set of dictionary guide words given. Write the words in alphabetical order.

able/intact	interest/patio
1. _____	6. _____
2. _____	7. _____
3. _____	8. _____
4. _____	9. _____
5. _____	10. _____

The letters **sc** can stand for three different sounds: the /sk/ sound, as in <u>scalding</u>; the /s/ sound, as in <u>muscles</u>; and the /sh/ sound, as in <u>luscious</u>.

List Words

scented
scattered
scissors
screaming
muscles
scalding
crescent
descending
escape
luscious

Study the relationship between the first two underlined words. Then write a List Word that has the same relationship with the third underlined word.

1. <u>Throw</u> is to <u>catch</u> as <u>capture</u> is to _____.

2. <u>Draw</u> is to <u>sketch</u> as <u>tasty</u> is to _____.

3. <u>Sew</u> is to <u>needle</u> as <u>cut</u> is to _____.

4. <u>Reading</u> is to your <u>mind</u> as <u>exercise</u> is to your _____.

5. <u>Cool</u> is to <u>chilly</u> as <u>boiling</u> is to _____.

6. <u>Up</u> is to <u>down</u> as <u>climbing</u> is to _____.

7. <u>Whispering</u> is to <u>murmuring</u> as <u>yelling</u> is to _____.

8. <u>Whole</u> is to <u>part</u> as <u>full</u> moon is to _____ moon.

9. <u>Food</u> is to <u>flavored</u> as <u>flower</u> is to _____.

10. <u>Gathered</u> is to <u>spread</u> as <u>joined</u> is to _____.

The letters **ear** make the /ir/ sound, as in <u>earrings</u>, and the /ur/ sound, as in <u>research</u>. The /er/ sound is sometimes spelled **are**, as in <u>unaware</u>, or **air**, as in <u>unfairly</u>.

List Words
searching
appeared
millionaire
carefully
squares
gears
earning
unfairly
despair
rehearsal

Each word below is hidden in a List Word. Write the List Words.

1. mill _____

2. fully _____

3. earn _____

4. fair _____

5. hear _____

6. pair _____

7. ears _____

8. arch _____

9. pear _____

10. are _____

The /ē/ sound can be spelled several ways: **e**, **ee**, **ea**, **ie**, **e_e**, **y**, and **ey**, as in <u>ecology</u>, <u>esteem</u>, <u>revealed</u>, <u>believable</u>, <u>delete</u>, <u>delivery</u>, and <u>trolley</u>.

List Words
trolley
delivery
delete
greasy
revealed
concealed
squeezed
succeeded
repeated
achievement

Write a List Word to complete each sentence.

1. These dirty dishes are _____.

2. What an _____ it was to win first prize!

3. We can ride on the _____.

4. After many falls, my baby sister finally _____ in walking.

5. No one heard, so I _____ the question.

6. Send it by special _____.

7. Just _____ the extra names.

8. The magician _____ a rabbit that had been hiding under the hat.

9. Jon _____ the sponge dry.

10. The actor's face was _____ by a beard.

List Words

delete
scented
repeated
scalding
ashamed
resemble
partial
luscious
leisurely
appeared
usually
searching
brochure
scattered
nourish

Write a List Word to solve each definition clue. Then use the letters in the shaded box to solve the riddle.

1. a piece of
2. booklet
3. very hot
4. fragrant

5. looking for
6. without hurry
7. spread all over

8. did it again
9. not proud
10. look like

11. delicious
12. showed itself
13. feed
14. take out, erase

Riddle: What did the leopard say when the rain started?

Answer: _____ _____ _____ _____ !

Go for the Goal

Take your Final Replay Test. Then fill in your Scoreboard. Send any misspelled words to your Word Locker.

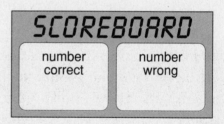

SCOREBOARD

number correct	number wrong

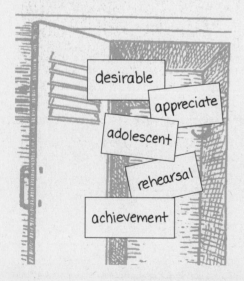

desirable
appreciate
adolescent
rehearsal
achievement

Clean Out Your Word Locker

Look in your Word Locker. Cross out each word you spelled correctly on your Final Replay Test. Circle the words you're still having trouble with. Add the words you circled to your Spelling Notebook. What do you notice about the words? Watch for those words as you write.

/ō/: o͟a, o͟e, o͟u, and o͟w

Warm Up

What musical instrument weighs very little but makes a big sound?

Your Own Kind of Music

A harmonica is **thoroughly** enjoyable to listen to, easy to play, and a lot easier to carry than a piano! You can keep it in your pocket and reach for it anytime you feel a song coming on.

This little music-maker was invented over one hundred years ago by a man named Sir Charles Wheatstone. **Although** no one is sure exactly why, Wheatstone named his instrument the *aeolina*. Since then, it has been known as a French harp, a mouth organ, and of course, a harmonica.

Its **growth** in popularity is certainly understandable. Depending upon how you play it, the sound of a harmonica **approaches** that of a bagpipe, piccolo, or **oboe**. Even though there are books on how to play, harmonica musicians usually learn by trial and error. With the harmonica, the errors generally aren't all that bad. With a little practice, you too can curve your hands around it and give it a sound all your own!

In his novel *The Grapes of Wrath*, John Steinbeck talks about the pride of harmonica ownership. Breaking or losing a harmonica "is no great loss," he says, "You can always buy another for a quarter." While that may not be true today harmonicas are still inexpensive. It's a small price to play to make your own kind of music.

Say the boldfaced words in the selection. What vowel sound do you hear in each word? How many ways can you find to spell that vowel sound?

On Your Mark

Take your Warm Up Test. Then check your spelling with the List Words on the next page.

Pep Talk

The /ō/ sound can be spelled many ways:

oa, as in <u>rowboat</u>
oe, as in <u>oboe</u>
ou, as in <u>doughnut</u>
ow, as in <u>growth</u>

LIST WORDS

1. borrower
2. doughnut
3. although
4. poultry
5. bowling
6. fallow
7. mistletoe
8. yellow
9. growth
10. approaches
11. boulders
12. stowaway
13. thoroughly
14. cocoa
15. oboe
16. bungalow
17. tiptoed
18. rowboat
19. cantaloupe
20. shoulders

Game Plan

Spelling Lineup

Write each List Word under the spelling of its /ō/ sound. One word will be used twice.

/ō/, as in <u>throw</u>

1. _____
2. _____
3. _____
4. _____
5. _____
6. _____
7. _____
8. _____

/ō/, as in <u>boat</u>

9. _____
10. _____
11. _____

/ō/, as in <u>dough</u>

12. _____
13. _____
14. _____
15. _____
16. _____
17. _____
18. _____

/ō/, as in <u>toe</u>

19. _____
20. _____
21. _____

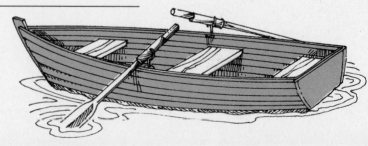

Vocabulary

The underlined word in each sentence does not make sense. Replace the word with a List Word that does make sense. Write that word on the line.

1. Would you like a steaming cup of <u>boulders</u>?   _____

2. Jim plays the <u>rowboat</u> in the high school band.   _____

3. The <u>tiptoed</u> is a melon with light orange flesh.   _____

4. The farmer made a wall out of <u>cocoa</u>.   _____

5. <u>Bungalow</u> is a sport the whole family enjoys.   _____

6. Stand back when the train <u>shoulders</u> the station.   _____

7. We hung <u>poultry</u> over the door during the holidays. _____

8. <u>Thoroughly</u> I tried, I couldn't lift the rock.   _____

9. The <u>doughnut</u> paid back the money I loaned her.   _____

10. He <u>shoulders</u> down the hall.   _____

Classification

Write the List Word that belongs in each group.

1. red, blue, _____

2. increase, development, _____

3. barren, unplanted, _____

4. ranch, townhouse, _____

5. watermelon, honeydew, _____

6. hen, rooster, _____

7. completely, totally, _____

8. holly, cactus, _____

9. elbows, knees, _____

10. bread, waffle, _____

11. flute, clarinet, _____

12. canoe, sailboat, _____

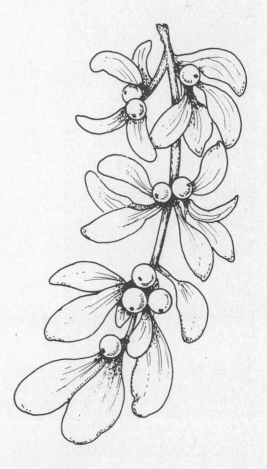

Flex Your Spelling Muscles

Writing

Create a silly song using as many List Words as you can. Write words to a familiar tune or create one of your own. Have a Silly Song Contest. Perhaps a partner would like to accompany you on a harmonica or other musical instrument.

Proofreading

The words to this silly song, sung to the tune of "On Top of Old Smokey," have ten mistakes. Use the proofreading marks to correct them. Then write the misspelled List Words correctly on the lines.

Proofreading Marks

◯ spelling mistake

≡ capital letter

∧ add something

1. on top of a doenut
    All filled with cream,
    I spilled myhot cocoe
    When I heard a scream.

2. I left my buhngalo
    And tiptowed around.
    I wanted to find out
    Who had made that sound.

3. i looked in a rouboat
    And what did I see?
    A stoaway owl
    Looking right back atme.

1. _____
2. _____
3. _____
4. _____
5. _____
6. _____

Now proofread your own lyrics. Fix any mistakes.

Go for the Goal

Take your Final Test. Then fill in your Scoreboard. Send your mistakes to the Word Locker.

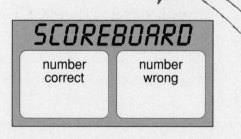

SCOREBOARD

number correct	number wrong

★ ★ ★ ★ ★ ★ ★ ★ ★ ★ **All-Star Words** ★ ★ ★ ★ ★ ★ ★ ★ ★ ★

overgrown   woeful   approach   borough   mellow

Write a sentence for each All-Star Word. Then, erase the letters that make the /ō/ sound in each word. Trade papers with a partner and fill in the missing letters in each other's words.

au and aw

Warm Up

For what sport do you need a board and a sail?

A New Wave

First, there was sailboating. Then there was surfboarding. Now, there's "boardsailing," or "windsurfing," a sport that combines the thrills and spills of both sailing and surfing.

On the water, boardsailors feel the **awesome** power of the wind and waves. They guide their boards by carefully adjusting the sail's mast. Steady, smooth movements allow the wind to catch the sail. Any quick, awkward movements could overturn the board.

Although boardsailing was **launched** only a few decades ago, it has risen in popularity due to a few dedicated boardsailors. One daredevil boardsailed across the Atlantic Ocean in just 37 days. Another, a 13-year-old, 103-pound boy, won the world championship.

For people who are afraid to try boardsailing on the water, there are schools for landlubbers where they can be **taught** to boardsail. Would-be boardsailors practice on a simulator. That's a surfboard mounted on a mechanical arm. The simulator duplicates the feel of ocean waves under a board. Although the waves aren't **authentic,** the excitement is real! The simulator has one big **drawback,** however. When a person falls, he or she "splashes" onto the floor. A few hard landings like that encourage people to take a chance and try the water!

Look back at the boldfaced words in the selection. What vowel sound do you hear in each word?

On Your Mark

Take your Warm Up Test. Then check your spelling with the List Words on the next page.

Pep Talk

The vowel digraphs **au** and **aw** sound alike. They both spell the /ô/ sound you hear in <u>paused</u> and <u>awesome</u>.

LIST WORDS

1. brawny
2. laundry
3. taught
4. paused
5. autumn
6. awning
7. awesome
8. launched
9. astronauts
10. squawking
11. drawback
12. exhausted
13. saucepan
14. automatically
15. dinosaur
16. authentic
17. withdrawal
18. thesaurus
19. precautions
20. applause

Game Plan

Spelling Lineup

Write the List Words in the correct category to show how the /ô/ sound is spelled.

au spells /ô/

1. _____
2. _____
3. _____
4. _____
5. _____
6. _____
7. _____
8. _____
9. _____
10. _____
11. _____
12. _____
13. _____
14. _____

aw spells /ô/

15. _____
16. _____
17. _____
18. _____
19. _____
20. _____

Vocabulary

A thesaurus is a reference book that contains synonyms and antonyms. Write a List Word to match the synonyms and antonyms given.

1. **synonyms**: instinctively, self-powered
   antonyms: mechanically, by hand

   _____

2. **synonyms**: real, genuine, true
   antonyms: fake, unreal

   _____

3. **synonyms**: took off, began, started
   antonyms: halted, stopped

   _____

4. **synonyms**: muscular, sturdy, strong
   antonyms: weak, delicate, frail

   _____

5. **synonyms**: tired, worn out, depleted
   antonyms: energetic, lively

   _____

6. **synonyms**: amazing, overwhelming
   antonyms: ordinary, unexceptional

   _____

7. **synonyms**: disadvantage, shortcoming
   antonyms: advantage, blessing

   _____

Puzzle

Fill in the crossword puzzle by writing a List Word to answer each definition clue.

ACROSS
1. clothes to be washed
4. safeguards
6. prehistoric reptile
9. instructed
10. space travelers
11. stopped momentarily
12. cooking pot
13. loud, harsh crying

DOWN
2. canvas covering
3. cheers or praise
5. book of synonyms and antonyms
7. the act of pulling out
8. fall

Flex Your Spelling Muscles

Writing

You have just been asked to interview a daredevil. Write a series of questions to ask during the interview. Find out as many details as possible about that person's most recent adventure.

Proofreading

The course description that follows has ten mistakes. Use the proofreading marks to correct them. Then write the misspelled List Words correctly on the lines.

Proofreading Marks
- spelling mistake
- ⊙ add period
- ∧ add something

Semester at Sea—Spend an entire semester aboard a sailboat Sail from Boston Massachusetts to the Bahamas aboard an awthentick 19th century sailing vessel. Students are tougt navigation, maritime history literature of the sea, and marine biology. You'll come back exshawsted but filled with stories about an awsume experience If you pass, you are outomaticaly enrolled in the advanced marine biology class. This course is available both awtum and spring terms. *15 credits*

1. _____
2. _____
3. _____
4. _____
5. _____
6. _____

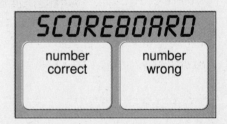

Now proofread your interview questions. Fix any mistakes.

Go for the Goal

Take your Final Test. Then fill in your Scoreboard. Send your mistakes to the Word Locker.

SCOREBOARD

number correct	number wrong

★ ★ ★ ★ ★ ★ ★ ★ ★ **All-Star Words** ★ ★ ★ ★ ★ ★ ★ ★ ★

clause   auction   law-abiding   nausea   gawk

Write a sentence for each All-Star Word. Then erase each All-Star Word. Trade papers with a partner. Can you correctly fill in each other's All-Star Words?

oo, ew, ue, and ui

Warm Up

What do animals do when they sense a storm coming?

Weather Report

Sea crabs are running along the beach, looking for a **suitable** hiding place. Fish are diving deeper and deeper into the sea, escaping into **smoother** waters. What are these sea creatures trying to tell us? A storm is coming!

Sea animals are not the only natural weather forecasters. Before a storm, field mice become more energetic. Rabbits eat more, and squirrels argue with one another. Raccoons and opossums remove their young from nests in carved-out logs. They seem to know that their homes are about to be flooded. Even indoor critters are good weather forecasters. Cockroaches scamper even more than usual before a storm.

Perhaps the best of nature's forecasters are birds. Birds are also the easiest to observe. Long before the first **gloomy** cloud appears overhead, you can see birds preparing for a storm. Since the air pressure always falls before a storm, you'll see birds flying close to the ground. They're trying to escape the low air pressure that is higher in the sky. Some birds will be **building** onto their nests, making sure the nests are strong enough. Though most birds eat early in the morning, some will catch insects even into the evening. Just before the rain begins to fall, you'll see few robins in the sky. They've all **pursued** a place to hide.

Say the boldfaced words in the selection. Which words have the /o͞o/ sound you hear in <u>poodle</u>? Which words have the /i/ sound you hear in <u>build</u>?

On Your Mark

Take your Warm Up Test. Then check your spelling with the List Words on the next page.

Pep Talk

The /yo͞o/ sound, as in <u>curfew</u>, can be spelled **ew**.
The /o͞o/ sound, as in <u>smoother</u>, can be spelled in the following ways:

      ew, as in <u>mildew</u>   **oo**, as in <u>gloomy</u>
      ue, as in <u>pursued</u>   **ui**, as in <u>fruitful</u>
The letters **ui** can spell the /i/ sound as in <u>biscuit</u>.

LIST WORDS

1. mildew
2. guitar
3. gloomy
4. cruise
5. guilty
6. curfew
7. pewter
8. juicy
9. smoother
10. bruised
11. quilted
12. building
13. fruitful
14. shampoo
15. soothing
16. suitable
17. pursued
18. biscuit
19. circuit
20. nuisance

Game Plan

Spelling Lineup

Write each List Word under the correct heading.

ew spells /o͞o/ or /yo͞o/

1. _____
2. _____
3. _____

ui spells /o͞o/

4. _____
5. _____
6. _____
7. _____
8. _____
9. _____

ue spells /o͞o/

10. _____

oo spells /o͞o/

11. _____
12. _____
13. _____
14. _____

ui spells /i/

15. _____
16. _____
17. _____
18. _____
19. _____
20. _____

Missing Words

Write the List Word that completes each sentence.

1. A _____ is an instrument that typically has six strings.

2. _____ is a grayish metal alloy made with tin and lead,

   brass, or copper.

3. He had no broken bones, but he was badly _____
   from the fall.

4. The lioness _____ her prey skillfully, never letting it out
   of her sight.

Puzzle

This is a crossword puzzle without definition clues. Use the length of the word
and the letters provided as clues to figure out which List Words fit in the
spaces. Then fill in the puzzle.

Flex Your Spelling Muscles

Writing

Write a script for a TV weather report that is both factual and entertaining. For example, you can give the temperature and describe what kinds of clothes would be suitable for viewers to wear. Use as many List Words as you can.

Proofreading

This naturalist's journal entry has nine mistakes. Use the proofreading marks to fix the mistakes. Write the misspelled List Words correctly on the lines.

Proofreading Marks	
⟳	spelling mistake
℮	take out something

March 13: I spotted a prairie dog being persooed by a a coyote. Warning barks could be heard all over the town. One prairie dog carrying grass sootable for a nest it was was bilding dove head-first into its burrow. Within seconds the the entire town was deserted as if a curfue had been set. I noticed that the soil is richer and more fertile in prairie dog towns. I must collect evidence to prove that prairie dogs are a help and not a a newsance to ranchers.

1. _____

2. _____

3. _____

4. _____

5. _____

Now proofread your weather report. Fix any mistakes.

Go for the Goal

Take your Final Test. Then fill in your Scoreboard. Send your mistakes to the Word Locker.

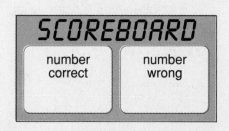

SCOREBOARD

number correct	number wrong

★ ★ ★ ★ ★ ★ ★ ★ ★ ★ **All-Star Words** ★ ★ ★ ★ ★ ★ ★ ★ ★ ★

steward   typhoon   undue   recruit   monsoon

Write a clue for each All-Star Word. Trade papers with a partner.
Write the All-Star Words that match the clues.

ai, ay, oi, and oy

Warm Up

What is the world's most naturally well-designed container?

A Half-Dozen Egg Facts

The world's most **praised** and well-designed **container** is not a gift-wrapped box from a department store. It's an eggshell. An eggshell may seem fragile, but it's able to withstand a lot of pressure. Try holding an egg in the palm of your hand and squeezing it tightly. It usually won't break.

Have you ever tried to balance an egg on its smaller end? Most of the time, you can't do it, but during the vernal equinox, the time in the spring when the sun crosses the equator, an egg will stand on end. A hard-boiled egg will spin on its side. An uncooked egg will barely spin.

Today's chickens are really super chickens. Two hundred years ago, before scientists got involved in egg breeding, an average chicken laid only about 15 eggs a year. Today they produce more than 300 yearly, which is what the average American eats every year. Therefore, one chicken provides enough eggs for one person. Not all the eggs are **boiled**, fried, or scrambled. Some are in soufflés, eggnog, **mayonnaise**, or baked into breads.

Egg breeding provides steady **employment** in the leading egg-producing states: California, Georgia, Arkansas, and Pennsylvania.

Say the boldfaced words in the selection. What vowel sound do you hear in each word? How are the vowel sounds alike? How are they different?

On Your Mark

Take your Warm Up Test. Then check your spelling with the List Words on the next page.

Pep Talk

The letters **ay** and **ai** make the /ā/ sound you hear in <u>crayons</u> and <u>praised</u>.

The letters **oy** and **oi** make the /ȯi/ sound you hear in <u>oysters</u> and <u>rejoicing</u>.

Game Plan

Spelling Lineup

Write each List Word under the spelling of its /ā/ or /ȯi/ sound. One word is used twice.

/ā/, as in <u>train</u>

1. _____
2. _____
3. _____
4. _____
5. _____
6. _____
7. _____
8. _____

/ā/, as in <u>play</u>

9. _____
10. _____
11. _____

/ȯi/, as in <u>oil</u>

12. _____
13. _____
14. _____
15. _____
16. _____
17. _____
18. _____
19. _____

/ȯi/, as in <u>toy</u>

20. _____
21. _____

RED
BLUE
YELLOW

Classification

Write the List Word that belongs in each group.

1. sewing, knitting, _____

2. repairs, improvements, _____

3. friend, neighbor, _____

4. enjoying, celebrating, _____

5. baked, fried, _____

6. cream, lotion, _____

7. stories, poems, _____

8. paints, pencils, _____

Antonyms

Write the List Word that means the opposite of the word or phrase given.

1. satisfaction _____

2. unemployment _____

3. criticized _____

4. grieving _____

5. looked for _____

6. calmness _____

Missing Words

Circle the List Word that belongs in each sentence. Write
the correct word on the line.

1. The knight set off on a daring ——.

   maintenance   acquaintance   exploit   _____

2. Drain the spaghetti in a ——.

   remainder   maintenance   strainer   _____

3. We keep the orange juice in a plastic ——.

   container   acquaintance   maintenance   _____

4. Put the —— of the sauce in the freezer.

   strainer   remainder   mayonnaise   _____

5. He has been a very —— friend.

   faithful   acquaintance   disappointment   _____

Flex Your Spelling Muscles

Writing

Write a recipe for a dish that contains eggs. Be sure that your directions for the cooking process are complete. Use as many List Words as you can.

Proofreading

This menu for Edna's Diner has ten mistakes. Use the proofreading marks to correct them. Write the misspelled List Words correctly on the lines.

Proofreading Marks	
⬭	spelling mistake
≡	capital letter
^	add apostrophe

All Lunch Specials Only $2.50

Our low, low prices are good for the remayndor of the week.

egg Salad—Its made with crunchy celery and maiyonayse.

Boiled Beef—Our most fathfull customers always enjoy this. order some and find out why.

Oyster Stew—Each bowl is made with a half-pint contaynor of milk. It's so thick with oisters, it wont go through a straynor!

---

1. _____   4. _____

2. _____   5. _____

3. _____   6. _____

Now proofread your recipe. Fix any mistakes.

Go for the Goal

Take your Final Test. Then fill in your Scoreboard. Send your mistakes to the Word Locker.

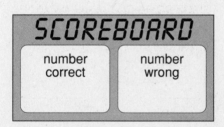

SCOREBOARD

number correct	number wrong

★ ★ ★ ★ ★ ★ ★ ★ ★ **All-Star Words** ★ ★ ★ ★ ★ ★ ★ ★ ★ ★

bail   attain   overjoyed   void   mainstay

Write a newspaper headline for each All-Star Word. Then erase the All-Star Word in each headline. Trade headlines with a partner and fill in each other's missing words.

ou and ow

Warm Up

What is the sea's most ferocious fish?

Great White

The white shark is known as a dangerous, man-eating monster. In fact, anyone who ran into one would probably feel like a **coward.** Much of what is said about this shark, however, isn't true. For one thing, the "white" shark is mostly grayish-brown. Only its underside is white. This shark isn't a man-eater, either. What is true about the white shark is that it's the sea's most ferocious fish.

Though not too smart, this fish seems programmed to rule the oceans. It can smell its prey—fish, squid, seals, sea lions, porpoises, and other sharks—in its **surrounding** area from as far as a quarter-mile away. Once attacked, few creatures can escape its steel-trap jaws. Its **mouthful** of teeth, serrated like a knife's blade, are as sharp as a razor's edge. When a tooth falls out, it is immediately replaced by another, equally powerful tooth.

Because few white sharks have been caught, no one is really sure how big they are. The smallest white shark ever found was just four feet long. The longest brought to shore was nearly 25 feet long and weighed more than an **outrageous** 7,000 pounds. That's larger than most houseboats. There has been more than one **account** of a white shark over 40 feet long. But that's probably just a fish story.

 Look back at the boldfaced words in the selection. Say the words. Compare the sounds made by the letters **ou** and **ow**.

On Your Mark

Take your Warm Up Test. Then check your spelling with the List Words on the next page.

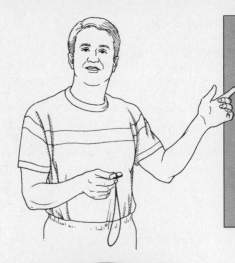

Pep Talk

The diphthongs **ou** and **ow** spell the /ᴏu/ sound you hear in <u>bough</u> and <u>coward</u>.

Listen for the /ᴏu/ sound in the List Words. Notice the letters that spell the /ᴏu/ sound in each word.

Game Plan

Spelling Lineup
Write the List Words in the correct category to show how the /ᴏu/ sound is spelled.

ou spells /ᴏu/

1. _____   9. _____
2. _____   10. _____
3. _____   11. _____
4. _____   12. _____
5. _____   13. _____
6. _____   14. _____
7. _____   15. _____
8. _____   16. _____

ow spells /ᴏu/

17. _____   19. _____
18. _____   20. _____

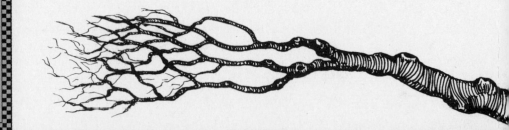

Missing Letters

Fill in the missing letters to form List Words. Then write the List Words on the lines.

1. d — — — sily _____

2. c — — — rd _____

3. b — — h _____

4. dis — — — nt _____

5. dr — — — ht _____

6. h — — — ehold _____

Puzzle

Fill in the crossword puzzle by writing a List Word to answer each definition clue.

ACROSS

1. made up of two parts
4. amount the mouth can hold
8. word that replaces a noun
10. loud and echoing
11. person or thing that closely resembles another
12. one who lacks courage
13. declare publicly
14. relax or be lazy
15. reduced price

DOWN

2. shocking
3. in the direction of the current of a stream
5. the base of a building
6. donate; to provide with
7. around all sides
9. said the sounds of a word
13. bank record

Flex Your Spelling Muscles

Writing

Write a tall tale that features a shark. Make yourself the hero. The more <u>outrageous</u> your exaggerations, the better your tale will be. Try to use as many List Words as you can.

Proofreading

This flyer for the Verne Aquarium has ten mistakes. Use the proofreading marks to correct them. Write the misspelled List Words correctly on the lines.

Proofreading Marks

⬭ spelling mistake

∧ add something

Where can you have your picture taken with a white shark a penguin, or a seal Where can everyone in your howshold have outrajous fun watching a dolphin do tricks? Where can you follow a river donstreem in a glass-bottomed boat Where can you lownge around and enjoy the ocean view? The answer is at the Verne Aquarium. We are pleased to announse that we now give a discownt to students senior citizens, and aquarium members.

1. _____   4. _____

2. _____   5. _____

3. _____   6. _____

Now proofread your tall tale. Fix any mistakes.

Go for the Goal

Take your Final Test. Then fill in your Scoreboard. Send your mistakes to the Word Locker.

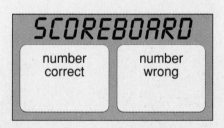

SCOREBOARD

| number correct | number wrong |

★ ★ ★ ★ ★ ★ ★ ★ ★ ★ **All-Star Words** ★ ★ ★ ★ ★ ★ ★ ★ ★ ★

profound   counsel   founder   cauliflower   scowl

Create a crossword puzzle using the All-Star Words. Write clues and draw an empty grid. Trade puzzles with a partner. Are you both able to solve the puzzles?

LESSON

18

Instant Replay • Lessons 13–17

Time Out

Look again at the spelling of vowel sounds in words. Some vowel sounds can be spelled many different ways.

Check Your Word Locker

Look at the words in your Word Locker. Write your most troublesome words from Lessons 13 through 17.

_____

_____

Practice writing your troublesome words with a partner. Write the words on slips of paper and put them in a container. Take turns drawing a word, illustrating it, and having the other person guess the word.

Lesson 13

The /ō/ sound can be spelled in more than one way: **oa**, as in <u>cocoa</u>; **oe**, as in <u>mistletoe</u>; **ou**, as in <u>boulders</u>; and **ow**, as in <u>bowling</u>.

List Words
bowling
yellow
growth
approaches
boulders
thoroughly
cocoa
oboe
rowboat
shoulders

Write a List Word to complete each sentence.

1. School buses are often _____.

2. That jacket is tight across your _____.

3. If a dog _____ with its tail wagging, you don't

   have to worry.

4. Wear a life jacket in the _____.

5. An _____ is a woodwind instrument.

6. These _____ are blocking the path.

7. Make sure the _____ is not too hot.

8. I'm getting better at _____ with our team.

9. Plant _____ depends upon light and water.

10. Mix the batter _____ to make it smooth.

The /ô/ sound can be spelled with **au**, as in <u>dinosaur</u>, and **aw**, as in <u>drawback</u>.

List Words

brawny
paused
autumn
awesome
exhausted
squawking
drawback
authentic
withdrawal
applause

Write a List Word that means the same or almost the same as the word given.

1. fatigued _____

2. waited _____

3. clapping _____

4. muscular _____

5. clucking _____

6. genuine _____

7. fall _____

8. removal _____

9. wonderful _____

10. shortcoming _____

The /yo͞o/ sound can be spelled **ew**, as in <u>pewter</u>. The /o͞o/ sound can be spelled in several ways: **ew**, as in <u>mildew</u>; **ue**, as in <u>pursued</u>; **oo**, as in <u>smoother</u>; **ui**, as in <u>juicy</u>. The /i/ sound can also be spelled with **ui**, as in <u>circuit</u>.

List Words

mildew
guitar
pewter
quilted
cruise
shampoo
biscuit
pursued
nuisance
soothing

Write the List Word that belongs in each group.

1. bother, annoyance, _____

2. copper, bronze, _____

3. mold, fungus, _____

4. soap, detergent, _____

5. sewed, stitched, _____

6. chased, followed, _____

7. banjo, mandolin, _____

8. muffin, toast, _____

9. calming, quieting, _____

10. voyage, trip, _____

Lesson 16

The /ā/ sound can be spelled with **ay**, as in <u>crayons</u>, and **ai**, as in <u>strainer</u>. The /oi/ sound can be spelled with **oy**, as in <u>employment</u>, and **oi**, as in <u>exploit</u>.

List Words

essays
boiled
oysters
maintenance
employment
ointment
praised
container
faithful
avoided

Write the List Words that fit each description.

1. What the people did who turned down every job:

_____ _____

2. What the teacher who liked my writing did:

_____ my _____

3. What you could call a jar for a creamy medicine:

an _____ _____

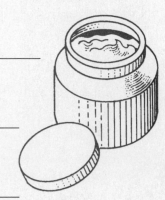

4. One kind of cooked shellfish:

_____ _____

5. What you could call regular painting of a house:

_____ _____

Lesson 17

The /ou/ sound can be spelled two ways: **ou**, as in <u>surrounding</u>, and **ow**, as in <u>drowsily</u>.

List Words

coward
bough
mouthful
compound
pronoun
discount
foundation
lounge
announce
outrageous

Write a List Word to match each clue.

1. tree part _____

2. a room to relax in _____

3. a bargain price _____

4. base of a house _____

5. shocking; excessive _____

6. proclaim, make known _____

7. don't talk with this _____

8. <u>he</u>, <u>she</u>, <u>it</u>, or <u>they</u> _____

9. mixture made of two or more parts _____

10. a person who lacks courage _____

List Words

Write a List Word to answer each definition clue.

maintenance
autumn
essays
guitar
thoroughly
exhausted
authentic
container
mouthful
shampoo
avoided
boulders
nuisance
cocoa
lounge

1. extremely tired _____

2. warm drink made with milk _____

3. hair cleaner _____

4. stayed away from _____

5. upkeep _____

6. a season of the year _____

7. real and genuine _____

8. lie around _____

9. completely _____

10. musical instrument _____

11. written works _____

12. big rocks _____

13. jar, box, carton _____

14. more than a taste _____

15. pest _____

Go for the Goal

Take your Final Replay Test. Then fill in your Scoreboard.
Send any misspelled words to your Word Locker.

SCOREBOARD

number correct	number wrong

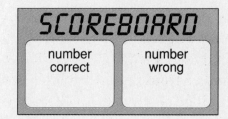

Clean Out Your Word Locker

Look in your Word Locker. Cross out each word you spelled
correctly on your Final Replay Test. Circle the words you're
still having trouble with. Add the words you circled to your
Spelling Notebook. What do you notice about the words?
Watch for those words as you write.

LESSON

19

ei and ie

Warm Up

What is the name of a tiny tree in Japan?

Tiny Trees

Japan is a small country, about the size of Montana. Yet 124 million people—the same number of people that live in America's ten most populated states combined—live there. Because of the limited space, the Japanese have developed smaller versions of many things. Japanese cars, for example, were among the first to come in compact sizes. Japanese houses, too, are small. Likewise, miniature gardens surround houses in Japan.

One of the most remarkable achievements in size reduction is the creation of the bonsai. The word *bonsai* means "trees in pots." When looking at a picture of a bonsai tree on a plain background, it may be **perceived** to be as large as a giant oak. It is perfectly formed. Its branches arch and drape just like a tree in a forest. Yet the picture may deceive you. A bonsai tree is usually no more than two feet in **height.** A bonsai cypress tree, for example, reaches just 19 inches tall. A bonsai maple tree grows red leaves smaller than your fingernail.

Growing bonsai trees is an **ancient** art. Some of the trees, too, are nearly ancient. It may seem **unbelievable,** but a bonsai can live in a small pot for 200 years or more. Some are handed down in families from parent to child. Each generation takes its turn bending and pruning the branches to keep the tree from growing larger. A grower's patience is rewarded with a forest that can fit in the palm of a hand.

Look back at the boldfaced words. Which words contain the vowel digraph **ei**? Which words contain the vowel digraph **ie**?

On Your Mark

Take your Warm Up Test. Then check your spelling with the List Words on the next page.

Here's a helpful rhyme you can use when spelling words that contain the vowel digraphs **ie** or **ei**:

I before E except after C
as in <u>retrieved</u> or <u>conceit</u>,
or when sounded like **A**
as in <u>neighborly</u> or <u>sleigh</u>.
There are exceptions to this rule, as in <u>weird</u> and <u>height</u>.

LIST WORDS

1. conceit
2. sleigh
3. height
4. veil
5. seized
6. yields
7. weird
8. mischief
9. neighborly
10. reindeer
11. fiercely
12. unbelievable
13. briefly
14. pierced
15. diesel
16. perceived
17. relieved
18. protein
19. ancient
20. retrieve

Game Plan

Spelling Lineup

Write each List Word under the correct heading.

ie spells /ē/

1. _____
2. _____
3. _____
4. _____
5. _____
6. _____
7. _____
8. _____

ei after **c** spells /ē/

9. _____
10. _____

ei spells /ā/

11. _____
12. _____
13. _____
14. _____

ie or **ei**—no rule

15. _____
16. _____
17. _____
18. _____
19. _____
20. _____

Comparing Words

Study the relationship between the first two underlined words or phrases. Then write a List Word that has the same relationship with the third underlined word.

1. Orange is to vitamin C as cheese is to _____.

2. Gave is to took as provided is to _____.

3. Water is to rowboat as snow is to _____.

4. Heavy is to weight as tall is to _____.

5. Young is to new as old is to _____.

6. Friend is to neighbor as friendly is to _____.

7. Knife is to sliced as arrow is to _____.

8. Generosity is to stinginess as modesty is to _____.

9. Happy is to content as strange is to _____.

10. Causing problems is to trouble as playing pranks is to _____.

11. Tusk is to elephant as antler is to _____.

12. Hear is to heard as perceive is to _____.

13. Furniture is to chair as covering is to _____.

Puzzle

Fill in the puzzle by writing a List Word to answer each definition clue. Then read across the shaded boxes to find out how these List Words are spelled.

1. for a short time
2. not likely
3. type of engine
4. wildly
5. fetch
6. gives way to
7. eased

Flex Your Spelling Muscles

Writing

You and your neighbors have received a notice that an <u>ancient</u> tree in your neighborhood is about to be cut down. Write a letter to the City Council to protest the action. Use as many List Words as you can.

Proofreading

This myth has eleven mistakes. Use the proofreading marks to correct them. Write the misspelled List Words correctly on the lines.

Proofreading Marks	
⬭	spelling mistake
᭓ ᭒	add quotation marks
¶	indent paragraph

"Your pointy leaves are weard," said Oak Tree.

"That's not very naighborley," said Pine Tree.

Mine are ever so much more beautiful, said Oak Tree. I'd be relived if you found another forest to live in. North Wind did not like Oak Tree's conseit. She blew feersely causing all of Oak Tree's leaves to fall. Oak Tree tried desperately to retreave his leaves, but he couldn't. That is why oak trees lose their leaves every autumn.

1. _____   4. _____

2. _____   5. _____

3. _____   6. _____

Now proofread your own letter. Fix any mistakes.

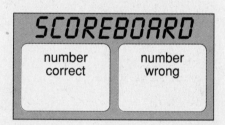

Go for the Goal

Take your Final Test. Then fill in your Scoreboard. Send your mistakes to the Word Locker.

SCOREBOARD

number correct	number wrong

★ ★ ★ ★ ★ ★ ★ ★ ★ **All-Star Words** ★ ★ ★ ★ ★ ★ ★ ★ ★

mischievous   receipt   freight   debrief   masterpiece

Write a tongue twister for each All-Star Word, leaving a blank where the word should go. Trade papers and fill in the missing words. Can you read the completed twisters aloud without twisting your tongue?

Prefixes ir, in, il, and im

Warm Up

Why do we make New Year's resolutions?

About Face

To the ancient Romans, Janus was an **immortal** god who represented new beginnings. Janus was portrayed as a bearded figure with two faces. One face looked west—toward the setting sun. The other face looked east—toward the new day. The face that looked at the past was old. The one facing the dawn was that of an **immature** youth. Janus inspired the Romans to review the past and to look toward the future with hope. We do not worship the god Janus today, but his inspiration, and even his name, are with us. January, the first month of the year, is named in honor of Janus. On January 1st, we, too, review the past and look forward to the new year with hope.

Though it may be **illogical,** people make New Year's resolutions every January 1st. On this day, we become **intolerant** of our imperfections, and we vow never to be **irresponsible** again. We may decide to stop being impolite or **impatient.** Deciding to be perfect is an **impractical** goal, however. No one, not even Janus, can do a complete about-face!

JANUARY						
S	M	T	W	TH	F	S
				1	2	3
4	5	6	7	8	9	10
11	12	13	14	15	16	17
18	19	20	21	22	23	24
25	26	27	28	29	30	31

Look back at the boldfaced words in the selection. These words have prefixes at the beginning of each word. How many prefixes can you find?

On Your Mark

Take your Warm Up Test. Then check your spelling with the List Words on the next page.

LIST WORDS

1. incredible
2. immortal
3. intolerant
4. immigrant
5. illogical
6. immature
7. illegal
8. improperly
9. incapable
10. irregular
11. impatient
12. impolitely
13. indirect
14. indefinite
15. immaterial
16. illiterate
17. impractical
18. irresponsible
19. irrational
20. illegible

Game Plan

Spelling Lineup

Add a prefix to each of these words. Then write each List Word under the correct heading.

1. legible

   _____

2. mature

   _____

3. capable

   _____

4. logical

   _____

5. properly

   _____

6. responsible

   _____

7. direct

   _____

8. practical

   _____

9. tolerant

   _____

10. politely

    _____

11. patient

    _____

12. credible

    _____

13. rational

    _____

14. migrant

    _____

15. material

    _____

16. legal

    _____

17. literate

    _____

18. definite

    _____

19. mortal

    _____

20. regular

    _____

Missing Words

Write a List Word to complete each sentence.

1. A person who acts childishly is _____ .

2. A person who has little patience is _____ .

3. An _____ person cannot read and write.

4. Something that is _____ is against the law.

5. A person who moves to a new country is an _____ .

6. Something that will never die is called _____ .

7. A piece of writing that is impossible to read is _____ .

8. A plan that will not work well is called _____ .

9. Something that is difficult to believe is _____ .

10. Something that really doesn't matter is _____ .

Alphabetical Order

Write the List Words in alphabetical order.

1. _____
2. _____
3. _____
4. _____
5. _____
6. _____
7. _____
8. _____
9. _____
10. _____
11. _____
12. _____
13. _____
14. _____

15. _____
16. _____
17. _____
18. _____
19. _____
20. _____

Flex Your Spelling Muscles

Writing

A resolution is something that you resolve or decide to do. Write one or more resolutions that you feel everyone should try to keep. Write an explanation saying why you feel these resolutions are important.

Proofreading

This magazine article has eight mistakes. Use the proofreading marks to correct them. Write the misspelled List Words correctly on the lines.

Proofreading Marks

⬭ spelling mistake
☰ capital letter
⊙ add period
∧ add something

> Are winter blues making you inpatiant for spring Don't just lie around and moan. Remember, january is a good month to do some new or different things.
> • Tutor someone who is iliterite.
> • Spend the day in bed reading an imcreditable adventure story
> • Clean out a closet and give away those inpractical gadgets that gather dust.
> • Try to master something that you assumed you were ircapible of learning.

1. _____

2. _____

3. _____

4. _____

5. _____

Now proofread your resolutions and explanation. Fix any mistakes.

Go for the Goal

Take your Final Test. Then fill in your Scoreboard. Send your mistakes to the Word Locker.

SCOREBOARD

number correct	number wrong

★ ★ ★ ★ ★ ★ ★ ★ ★ ★ **All-Star Words** ★ ★ ★ ★ ★ ★ ★ ★ ★ ★

inability   irrelevant   illuminate   imperfect   imprint

Divide the list of All-Star Words between you and a partner. Write a real and a made-up definition for each of your words. See if you can match each of your partner's words with its correct definition.

Prefixes de, pre, pro, con, com, and mis

Warm Up

What Olympic sport involves attacking your opponent with a foil, or sword?

Touché

Imagine yourself in a duel. A fencing sword is just inches from your body. You can't **predict** your opponent's next move. If you **propel** yourself toward your rival, you may catch him or her off guard. If you make a wrong move, however, you could be jabbed with the point of a foil, a 35-inch blade used in fencing.

Fencing is somewhat of a **misunderstood** sport. Those who **dedicate** their time to the sport do not want their fans to be **confused**. Some fans **presume** that the competitors get hurt. That is not the case today.

Fencing **competitors** used to engage in a duel to settle an argument. Only the winner survived. Today, however, fencing has endured **progress** and is now an Olympic sport; it is practiced just for show. Instead of dueling to the death, each fencer wears protective clothing. This includes a wired face mask, gloves, and a wired vest. If one fencer's foil touches the other's vest, the touch (called *touché*) is recorded electronically. A judge then determines if the touch is valid. The judge makes the decision based on whether or not the fencer used a proper defense, or parry. After all, had you left yourself open to attack while trying to touch your opponent, it wouldn't have been a good defense. The fencer must also be ready for a counterattack, or riposte. In other words, to score a point, your opponent must get the point!

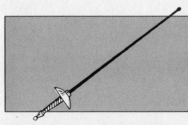

Say the boldfaced words in the selection. These words have prefixes at the beginning of each word. How many prefixes can you find?

On Your Mark

Take your Warm Up Test. Then check your spelling with the List Words on the next page.

Pep Talk

The prefixes **pre** and **pro** usually mean <u>before</u>. **Pro** can also mean <u>forward</u>.

The prefix **de** means <u>down</u>, <u>not</u>, or <u>reverse</u>. **De** can also mean <u>apart</u> or <u>aside</u>.

The prefixes **con** and **com** mean <u>with</u> or <u>together</u>.

The prefix **mis** usually means <u>bad</u> or <u>badly</u>.

LIST WORDS

1. propelling
2. competitors
3. provision
4. conference
5. previous
6. dedicate
7. deposited
8. complaint
9. depended
10. decreased
11. predicted
12. progress
13. misunderstood
14. confused
15. presume
16. prescription
17. mispronounced
18. prevented
19. compelled
20. confirmation

Game Plan

Spelling Lineup

Write the List Words under the correct category.

Words with the prefix pre or pro

1. _____
2. _____
3. _____
4. _____
5. _____
6. _____
7. _____
8. _____

Words with the prefix de

9. _____
10. _____
11. _____
12. _____

Words with the prefix con or com

13. _____
14. _____
15. _____
16. _____
17. _____
18. _____

Words with the prefix mis

19. _____
20. _____

complaints →

Word Parts

Write a List Word that contains the same root as the word given.

1. increase   _____
2. refuse   _____
3. invented   _____
4. devious   _____
5. compelling   _____
6. inference   _____
7. indicate   _____

8. division   _____
9. inscription   _____
10. announce   _____
11. assume   _____
12. suspended   _____
13. affirmation   _____
14. digress   _____

Missing Words

Write a List Word to complete each sentence.

1. The meteorologist _____ that it would rain today.

2. We are here to _____ this statue to the memory

of a great hero.

3. There were many _____ trying for first place.

4. Kathy filed a _____ against her employer when

he refused to pay her.

5. Jon _____ you and drove

to the wrong address.

6. They _____ all their

money into a joint savings account.

7. Louisa _____ on her

brother to drive her to work.

8. Manny felt _____ to

tell his mother about his low test grade.

Flex Your Spelling Muscles

Writing

Don't settle an argument by fencing. Instead, write a letter asking Consuelo, the advice columnist, to settle it for you. Once you write your letter, write Consuelo's answer. Use as many List Words as you can.

Proofreading

This letter has eleven mistakes. Use the proofreading marks to correct them. Write the misspelled List Words correctly on the lines.

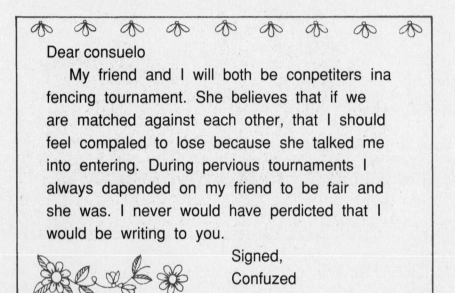

Dear consuelo

My friend and I will both be conpetiters ina fencing tournament. She believes that if we are matched against each other, that I should feel compaled to lose because she talked me into entering. During pervious tournaments I always dapended on my friend to be fair and she was. I never would have perdicted that I would be writing to you.

Signed,
Confuzed

Proofreading Marks
- ⬭ spelling mistake
- ≡ capital letter
- ∧ add something

1. _____

2. _____

3. _____

4. _____

5. _____

6. _____

Now proofread your letter. Fix any mistakes.

Go for the Goal

Take your Final Test. Then fill in your Scoreboard. Send your mistakes to the Word Locker.

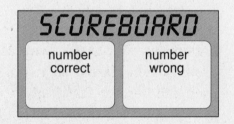

SCOREBOARD

number correct	number wrong

★ ★ ★ ★ ★ ★ ★ ★ ★ **All-Star Words** ★ ★ ★ ★ ★ ★ ★ ★ ★

miscalculate   commotion   provoke   prelude   decline

Write a definition for each All-Star Word. Then, write a question for each All-Star Word. Refer to your definitions if you need to. Trade papers with a partner. Answer each question repeating the All-Star Word in your response.

Prefixes <u>em</u>, <u>en</u>, <u>fore</u>, <u>post</u>, and <u>over</u>

Warm Up

How would you stop a flood of sticky molasses?

The Molasses Flood

It was a cold day in Boston, but not as cold as it usually was in January. The year was 1919. The city famous for its baked beans was about to become known for something else.

At around noontime, without any **forewarning,** a storage tank holding 14,000 tons of molasses began to split apart. The loose rivets that held the tank together popped out, and the molasses began to **overflow** onto the street. An enormous gooey wave nearly 15 feet high swept down the streets, traveling almost 35 miles per hour. It began to **endanger** everything in its path. It destroyed houses and even hit one of the supports for the elevated train. Luckily, the engineer saw the disaster ahead. The train screeched to a halt just before the tracks dropped down into the brown muck.

The cleanup effort lasted for weeks. Workers hired to **embattle** the sticky substance were knee deep in molasses and tracked the mess everywhere. Boots and clothing carried it as far as fifty miles away! Eventually nearby fireboats were employed to hose down the area. Boston Harbor turned a brown color as the syrup was washed into the bay. Wishing they had had the **foresight** to do it earlier, the streets were later covered with sand, so that people could walk without sticking to the ground.

Say the boldfaced words in the selection. Each boldfaced word has a prefix. How many prefixes can you find? How do the prefixes change the meanings of the root words?

On Your Mark

Take your Warm Up Test. Then check your spelling with the List Words on the next page.

Pep Talk

The prefixes **em** and **en** mean <u>in</u>, <u>into</u>, <u>cause to be</u>, or <u>to make</u>.
The prefix **fore** means <u>before</u>.
The prefix **post** means <u>after</u>.
The prefix **over** usually means <u>too much</u> or <u>above</u>.

LIST WORDS

1. forewarning
2. postscript
3. postwar
4. encourage
5. overweight
6. overflow
7. foresight
8. embellish
9. emblazon
10. engrave
11. endanger
12. foreground
13. embitter
14. overdue
15. foreknowledge
16. overprotect
17. embankment
18. embattle
19. enlistment
20. enlighten

Game Plan

Spelling Lineup

Write the List Word under the correct category.

Words with the prefix em or en

1. _____
2. _____
3. _____
4. _____
5. _____
6. _____
7. _____
8. _____
9. _____
10. _____

Words with the prefix fore

11. _____
12. _____
13. _____
14. _____

Words with the prefix post

15. _____
16. _____

Words with the prefix over

17. _____
18. _____
19. _____
20. _____

Comparing Words

Study the relationship between the first two underlined words. Then write a List Word that has the same relationship with the third underlined word.

1. Curb is to roadway as _____ is to river.

2. Underweight is to thin as _____ is to chubby.

3. Discourage is to hinder as _____ is to help.

4. Flood is to lake as _____ is to bathtub.

5. Careless is to careful as _____ is to protect.

6. Carve is to wood as _____ is to metal.

7. Period is to sentence as _____ is to letter.

8. Near is to far as _____ is to background.

Definitions

Write a List Word to answer each definition clue.

1. to make better or improve _____

2. to make bitter _____

3. to know beforehand _____

4. after war _____

5. being enrolled for service _____

6. warning ahead of time _____

7. to mark with an emblem _____

8. to make clear _____

9. power to look ahead _____

10. to protect more than necessary _____

11. delayed past expected date _____

12. to prepare to fight _____

Flex Your Spelling Muscles

Writing

What do you think people who were on the train that nearly plunged into the molasses flood might have said? Write quotations for several different people who may have experienced this train ride. Use as many List Words as you can.

Proofreading

This pamphlet on storm safety tips has ten mistakes. Use the proofreading marks to correct them. Write the misspelled List Words correctly on the lines.

Proofreading Marks

⬭ spelling mistake

≡ capital letter

∧ add something

⌄ add apostrophe

When a storm is coming, you cant overpertect yourself. With forsite and planning you can remain safe. If you don't have a portable radio, you're overdew to get one. Follow any forworning about flooding if you live in a low-lying area. Keep batteries bottled water, and candles on hand. During the storm, encaurage everyone to keep away from windows electrical appliances, and telephones. after the storm, don't emdanger yourself by going near downed wires.

1. _____

2. _____

3. _____

4. _____

5. _____

6. _____

Now proofread your quotations. Fix any mistakes.

Go for the Goal

Take your Final Test. Then fill in your Scoreboard. Send your mistakes to the Word Locker.

SCOREBOARD

number correct	number wrong

★ ★ ★ ★ ★ ★ ★ ★ ★ **All-Star Words** ★ ★ ★ ★ ★ ★ ★ ★ ★ ★

empower   encompass   foremost   oversensitive   overemotional

Write a question for each All-Star Word that you will use to interview a person who survived the molasses flood. With a partner, take turns role-playing the parts of interviewer and survivor.

Prefixes uni, mono, bi, tri, and mid

Warm Up

What does "barnstorming" mean?

Barnstorming

Picture yourself on a **midsummer** afternoon in the 1920s. It is more than a decade since the Wright brothers made their first airplane flight. You've just heard that some of those new flying machines would be landing at Farmer Jones' field. You've never seen an airplane, so you hop in your brand-new Model-T and drive off.

There they are—half a dozen biplanes sitting on the field. Then you hear an announcer's voice coming over the loudspeaker.

You take a seat on the newly built bleachers. The **biplane** speeds down the grassy "runway." It lifts off, carrying a pilot and one passenger. It seems impossible that this machine can travel in midair. Then, as you sit there in amazement, you see the passenger step out onto the wing. You're glad you brought your **binoculars** to get a close-up look. Everyone gasps in **unison** as the passenger, a stuntman, walks the length of the wing. He's holding on to nothing but a thin crossbar with a **triangular** shape.

Another plane takes off, and then another. They fly in a **uniform** pattern, zigzagging through the clouds. Then the engine of one of the planes starts to make a sputtering sound. It's losing power. It's falling in a spiral down toward the earth. The pilot leaps out and safely floats to the ground in his parachute. The plane, however, crashes through the farmer's barn. You've heard the word "barnstorming" before. Now you know what it means.

Look back at the boldfaced words in the selection. Find the different prefixes in the words. Try coming up with the meaning for each prefix.

On Your Mark

Take your Warm Up Test. Then check your spelling with the List Words on the next page.

Pep Talk

The prefixes **uni** and **mono** mean <u>one</u> or <u>single</u>.
The prefix **bi** means <u>two</u>, or <u>twice</u>.
The prefix **tri** means <u>three</u>, or <u>three times</u>.
The prefix **mid** means <u>in the middle of</u>.

Game Plan

Spelling Lineup

Write each List Word in the correct category to show the prefix it contains.

uni

1. _____
2. _____
3. _____
4. _____
5. _____

bi

11. _____
12. _____
13. _____
14. _____
15. _____

mono

6. _____
7. _____
8. _____

tri

16. _____
17. _____
18. _____
19. _____
20. _____

mid

9. _____
10. _____

Definitions

Write a List Word to solve each definition clue.

1. once every two weeks   _____

2. multiplied by three   _____

3. magnifying glasses   _____

4. twice a year   _____

5. having three sides   _____

6. train with one track   _____

7. flag with three stripes   _____

8. boring and repetitive   _____

9. in the middle of the west   _____

10. in three copies   _____

11. divides into two parts   _____

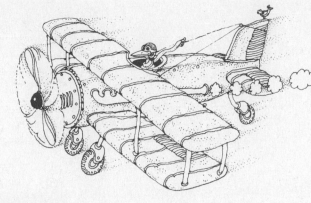

Alphabetical Order

Write this group of List Words in alphabetical order.

midsummer   unison   biplane   university   universal
trilogy   unicycle   uniform   monosyllable

1. _____   6. _____

2. _____   7. _____

3. _____   8. _____

4. _____   9. _____

5. _____

Flex Your Spelling Muscles

Writing

Write a paragraph comparing and contrasting the following means of transportation: a <u>biplane</u>, a <u>monorail</u>, a <u>unicycle</u>. Be sure to include the advantages and disadvantages of each of these.

Proofreading

This biography has ten mistakes. Use the proofreading marks to correct them. Write the misspelled List Words correctly on the lines.

> Bessie Coleman was the first African American woman to become a pilot. Tired of monotenus work, Coleman wanted to fly a a byplane. Prejudice nearly stopped her, but she earned a license in Europe. Her first exhibition was in a middwesdern city in 1922. Her stunts won her unaversil acclaim. Can you imagine Coleman in her her Pilot's unaforme standing before a cheering crowd If only we had a pair of magic binoculars that would enable us to see her as she bisecks the sky.

Now proofread your paragraph. Fix any mistakes.

Proofreading Marks

⬭ spelling mistake
∧ add something
℈ take out something
/ make small letter

1. _____
2. _____
3. _____
4. _____
5. _____
6. _____

Go for the Goal

Take your Final Test. Then fill in your Scoreboard. Send your mistakes to the Word Locker.

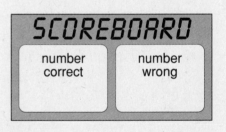

SCOREBOARD

| number correct | number wrong |

★ ★ ★ ★ ★ ★ ★ ★ ★ **All-Star Words** ★ ★ ★ ★ ★ ★ ★ ★ ★ ★

unilateral   monogram   bifocals   trilingual   midpoint

Write a definition or draw a simple sketch for each All-Star Word. Use your dictionary if you need help with a meaning. Then trade papers with a partner. Can you write the word that fits each clue?

Instant Replay • Lessons 19–23

LESSON
24

Time Out

Look again at the spelling of vowel sounds in words. Also look at the words with prefixes added to the root word. Think about what the prefixes mean.

Check Your Word Locker

Look at the words in your Word Locker. Write your most troublesome words from Lessons 19 through 23.

_____

_____

Practice writing your troublesome words with a partner. Say a sentence for each troublesome word and spell the word aloud for your partner.

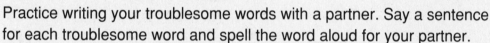
Lesson 19

Use the spelling rule you learned when spelling words with **ie** or **ei**. It will help you spell words, such as <u>pierce</u>, <u>ceiling</u>, and <u>weigh</u>. Remember that some words, such as <u>ancient</u>, are exceptions to the rule.

List Words
retrieve
yields
conceit
veil
height
fiercely
briefly
perceived
neighborly
weird

Write a List Word that means the opposite of the word given.

1. normal _____

2. expose _____

3. width _____

4. lengthily _____

5. throw _____

6. sweetly _____

7. unfriendly _____

8. modesty _____

9. overlooked _____

10. continues _____

The prefixes **ir**, **in**, and **im** usually mean not, as in <u>irresponsible</u>, <u>indirect</u>, <u>illogical</u>, and <u>immaterial</u>. The prefix **im** can also mean to, as in <u>immigrant</u>.

List Words

immortal
irregular
intolerant
indirect
illegal
illegible
immigrant
incapable
impatient
indefinite

Write the List Word that has the same root as the word given.

1. definitely _____

2. migrate _____

3. capability _____

4. mortality _____

5. legalize _____

6. tolerate _____

7. patience _____

8. regulate _____

9. direction _____

10. legibility _____

Prefixes and Their Meanings

pre, pro = <u>before</u>   con, com = <u>with</u> or <u>together</u>
pro = <u>forward</u>   mis = <u>bad</u> or <u>badly</u>
de = <u>down</u>, <u>not</u>, <u>reverse</u>, <u>apart</u>, <u>aside</u>

List Words

prevented
depended
confused
predicted
complaint
conference
prescription
decreased
progress
misunderstood

Write five List Words that could be found listed between each set of dictionary guide words given. Write the words in alphabetical order.

 comma/deposit    mistake/protect

1. _____   6. _____

2. _____   7. _____

3. _____   8. _____

4. _____   9. _____

5. _____   10. _____

Prefixes and Their Meanings
em, **en** = <u>in</u>, <u>into</u>, <u>cause to be</u>, <u>to make</u>
fore = <u>before</u>   **post** = <u>after</u>   **over** = <u>too much or above</u>

List Words

postscript
foresight
overweight
overdue
embattle
engrave
embitter
encourage
embankment
overflow

Make List Words by choosing a prefix from the chart above to add to each root or root word. Write the words on the lines.

1. sight _____

2. script _____

3. bitter _____

4. bankment _____

5. grave _____

6. weight _____

7. courage _____

8. flow _____

9. battle _____

10. due _____

Prefixes and Their Meanings
uni, **mono** = <u>one</u>, <u>single</u>   **bi** = <u>two</u>, <u>twice</u>
tri = <u>three</u>, <u>three times</u>   **mid** = <u>in the middle of</u>

List Words

unicycle
bisects
biplane
triangular
binoculars
monotonous
midsummer
triplicate
universal
trilogy

Write a List Word to match each clue.

1. <u>Wednesday</u> is to <u>midweek</u> as <u>July</u> is to _____.

2. <u>Unites</u> is to <u>joins</u> as <u>divides</u> is to _____.

3. <u>Balloon</u> is to <u>circular</u> as <u>pennant</u> is to _____.

4. <u>Pogo stick</u> is to <u>stilts</u> as _____ is to <u>bicycle</u>.

5. <u>Three artists</u> are to <u>trio</u> as <u>three books</u> are to _____.

6. <u>Double</u> is to <u>triple</u> as <u>duplicate</u> is to _____.

7. <u>1990s</u> are to <u>jet</u> as <u>1920s</u> are to _____.

8. <u>Telescopes</u> are to <u>astonomers</u> as _____

   are to <u>bird watchers</u>.

9. <u>Illegal</u> is to <u>unlawful</u> as <u>global</u> is to _____.

10. <u>Interesting</u> is to <u>captivating</u> as boring is to _____.

List Words

foresight
binoculars
conceit
irregular
predicted
overweight
monotonous
neighborly
indefinite
confused
encourage
retrieve
intolerant
complaint
incapable

Missing Words

Complete each sentence with a List Word.

1. We're not sure we'll move; our plans are _____.

2. Lena used _____ to see the animals up close.

3. If we _____ him to try harder, he will win the next race.

4. She can _____ the information from the computer.

5. My _____ was about the bad service.

6. No one had _____ the storm would be so intense.

7. The owner became _____ of his dog's bad behavior.

8. He does not show any _____ about his incredible talents.

9. We all wish for _____ to know what we're getting into.

10. He is _____ of doing that task until he is trained.

11. I'm _____ about this; the directions are unclear.

12. Being friendly and _____, she introduced herself.

13. The speaker's _____ voice bored us.

14. The shape of some volcanoes is _____.

15. The scale says he is _____, but he's in good shape.

Go for the Goal

Take your Final Replay Test. Then fill in your Scoreboard.
Send any misspelled words to your Word Locker.

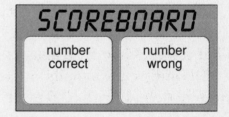

SCOREBOARD

number correct	number wrong

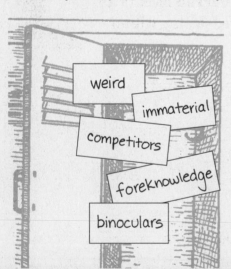

weird
immaterial
competitors
foreknowledge
binoculars

Clean Out Your Word Locker

Look in your Word Locker. Cross out each word you spelled correctly on your Final Replay Test. Circle the words you're still having trouble with. Add the words you circled to your Spelling Notebook. What do you notice about the words? Watch for those words as you write.

Prefixes <u>anti</u>, <u>counter</u>, <u>super</u>, <u>sub</u>, <u>ultra</u>, <u>trans</u>, and <u>semi</u>

LESSON 25

Warm Up

How can a robot improve your life?

Mechanical Marvel

The ultramodern robot is on its way. Although it is not yet a **substitute** for a human being, it can do some remarkable things. A personal robot can be programmed to teach you how to speak a foreign language. It can protect your house at night, wake you in the morning, and then do the housework. It can even follow you around and drill you on your spelling words. Unlike pets, you do not need to **supervise** a robot. It will even recharge itself.

One futuristic family attracted attention for being the first on the block with an android (robot). One day, the two teenaged sons decided to take the family robot for a walk. It was rush hour when they set the robot free on the freeway. The boys did not anticipate it, but traffic came to a halt. Drivers formed a **semicircle** around the machine. Eventually, the police arrived. The boys had planned on that. They had programmed their robot to run and shout, "Help me! Help me! They are trying to take me apart!" The boys were amused. The police weren't. They did **counteract** what the boys had done and carried the powerless robot off to jail.

The story ends happily, however. The android was **transferred** back to its owners. According to all reports, the robot has since managed to stay within the law.

Look back at the boldfaced words in the selection. Each word has a prefix at the beginning of the word. How many different prefixes can you find?

On Your Mark

Take your Warm Up Test. Then check your spelling with the List Words on the next page.

Pep Talk

Prefixes and Their Meanings

anti = against   **counter** = against
ultra = beyond   **super** = above; over
sub = below   **trans** = across; through
semi = half

LIST WORDS

1. antifreeze
2. supervise
3. semifinal
4. antiseptic
5. transparent
6. substitution
7. antidote
8. submarine
9. superficial
10. subscription
11. semicircle
12. counteract
13. counterattack
14. semicolon
15. supersonic
16. transistor
17. ultraviolet
18. transferred
19. counterfeit
20. antibodies

Game Plan

Spelling Lineup

Write each List Word under the correct heading.

words with the prefixes
anti and **counter**

1. _____
2. _____
3. _____
4. _____
5. _____
6. _____
7. _____

words with the prefix **super**

8. _____
9. _____
10. _____

word with the prefix **ultra**

11. _____

words with the prefix **sub**

12. _____
13. _____
14. _____

words with the prefix **trans**

15. _____
16. _____
17. _____

words with the prefix **semi**

18. _____
19. _____
20. _____

Word Parts

Add a prefix to each root given to form a List Word. Write the word on the line.

1. violet _____

2. colon _____

3. act _____

4. circle _____

5. final _____

6. marine _____

7. attack _____

8. sonic _____

9. freeze _____

10. septic _____

11. bodies _____

Definitions

Write a List Word to match each definition.

1. something that works against a poison _____

2. something that is false _____

3. limited to the surface area _____

4. electronic device that allows electrical impulses to travel across the air without any resistance _____

5. able to see through _____

6. to oversee or direct work _____

7. moved from one person, place, or thing to another _____

8. the act of putting one thing in place of another _____

9. agreement to receive and pay for magazines, books, theater tickets for a specified period of time _____

10. beyond the speed of sound _____

11. half of a round shape _____

12. something that acts against germs _____

13. to act directly against _____

Flex Your Spelling Muscles

Writing

A robot could be a handy thing to have around. What do you think it would be like to have a robot? Write a description of your robot and tell what jobs you would have it do.

Proofreading

The following poem has twelve mistakes. Use the proofreading marks to fix each mistake. Write the misspelled List Words correctly on the lines.

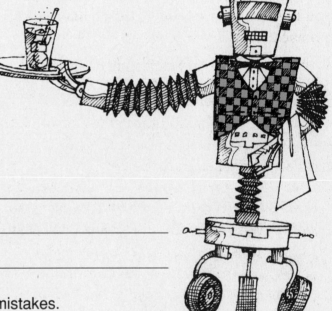

> Most robots appear official,
> But surely it is superfisial.
> Ive heard they can suppervize,
> And act in in ways most wise.
> But are they a a real solution
> As a human substitushon
> There's a transeestor in every space
> And less on a robots transparant face.
> Their anteseptic forms forms appear
> To lack a comfort some hold dear.

Proofreading Marks	
⬭	spelling mistake
ℛ	take out something
∧	add something
⌄	add apostrophe

1. _____

2. _____

3. _____

4. _____

5. _____

6. _____

Proofread your description of a robot. Fix any mistakes.

Go for the Goal

Take your Final Test. Then fill in your Scoreboard. Send your mistakes to the Word Locker.

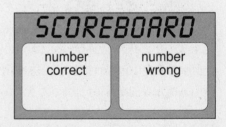

SCOREBOARD

number correct	number wrong

★ ★ ★ ★ ★ ★ ★ ★ ★ **All-Star Words** ★ ★ ★ ★ ★ ★ ★ ★ ★

antisocial   counterbalance   subcontract   transaction   semiprecious

Write a sentence for each All-Star Word. Then, erase the prefixes. Trade papers with a partner and rewrite each other's sentences, adding the prefixes. Talk about how the prefixes change the meanings of the words.

Suffixes <u>or</u>, <u>er</u>, <u>ist</u>, <u>logy</u>, and <u>ology</u>

LESSON

26

Warm Up

What mineral used to be as valuable as gold?

Salt of the Earth

You can preserve food with it. You can ease sore throat pain by gargling with it. You can even use it to melt snow or to flavor your popcorn. In case you haven't guessed, "it" is that marvelous mineral we call salt. As much as we need air and water, we need salt to live. If you are a **consumer** of packaged food, you probably get enough salt in your diet, so there's no need to sprinkle on any more. Besides, doctors warn that too much salt is just as bad as not enough.

Salt has played an interesting role in history. In ancient Rome, salt was so valuable that soldiers were paid handfuls of salt instead of money. Our word *salary* comes from the Latin word *sal*, which means *salt*. Salt also had a part in the American Civil War. The Northern forces had large supplies of salt. The Southern fighters, however, had very little. As a result, the Southerners could not preserve the food they needed.

Salt can be obtained by two different methods. Using modern **technology,** it can be mined from the earth, much like mining coal. It can also be collected by evaporating ocean water, which contains most of the world's salt. In fact, any **geologist** will tell you that there is enough salt in the sea to cover North America with a mile-thick layer of salt. Think of all the popcorn you could spice up with that!

Look back at the boldfaced words in the selection. These words have word parts, called suffixes, at the end of each word. How many suffixes can you find?

On Your Mark

Take your Warm Up Test. Then check your spelling with the List Words on the next page.

Pep Talk

The suffixes **or**, **er**, and **ist** mean <u>one who</u> or <u>something that</u>, as in <u>jeweler</u>, <u>typist</u>, <u>projector</u>, and <u>juror</u>.

The suffixes **logy** and **ology** mean <u>the study of</u>, as in <u>biology</u>.

LIST WORDS

1. juror
2. consumer
3. biology
4. jeweler
5. aviator
6. spectator
7. insulator
8. typist
9. transformer
10. projector
11. machinist
12. geologist
13. florist
14. divisor
15. journalist
16. technology
17. mythology
18. escalator
19. manufacturer
20. investigator

Game Plan

Spelling Lineup

Write a List Word that has the same root as the word given.

1. mythical

_____

2. consume

_____

3. geology

_____

4. escalate

_____

5. inspect

_____

6. aviation

_____

7. journal

_____

8. technique

_____

9. factory

_____

10. project

_____

11. biosphere

_____

12. machine

_____

13. investigate

_____

14. type

_____

15. jewel

_____

16. flower

_____

17. jury

_____

18. divide

_____

19. form

_____

20. insulate

_____

Comparing Words

Study the relationship between the first two underlined words. Then write a List Word that has the same relationship with the third underlined word or phrase.

1. Dishwasher is to sink as _____ is to stairs.

2. Poet is to poem as _____ is to news story.

3. Classroom is to student as courtroom is to _____.

4. CD is to CD player as film is to _____.

5. Pianist is to piano as _____ is to typewriter.

6. Listener is to radio as _____ is to sporting event.

7. Wood is to carpenter as gold is to _____.

8. Sailor is to boat as _____ is to plane.

9. Competing is to athlete as buying is to _____.

10. Wetsuit is to diver as _____ is to electric wire.

Classification

Write the List Word that belongs in each group.

1. legends, poetry, _____

2. dividend, quotient, _____

3. reporter, editor, _____

4. plants, animals, _____

5. science, industry, _____

6. maker, producer, _____

7. ramp, elevator, _____

Vocabulary

Write a List Word to name the person whose work involves the items given.

1. rocks and minerals _____

2. bracelets and pins _____

3. flowers _____

4. machines and wrenches _____

5. clues and fingerprints _____

Flex Your Spelling Muscles

Writing

Millions of Americans love spices. What is your favorite spice? Research how your favorite spice is made by the <u>manufacturer</u>. What kind of <u>technology</u> is used? Write a description of this process.

Proofreading

This article has twelve mistakes. Use the proofreading marks to fix each mistake. Write the misspelled List Words correctly on the lines.

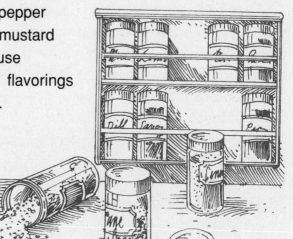

Proofreading Marks

⬭ spelling mistake

∧ add something

A manifackturer willuse many different spices to flavor food. Thesespices might include cinnamon garlic pepper and celery salt. They are used to flavor vinegar mustard sauces and pickles. Modern technolojy also can use current knowledge in biahlogy to produce artificial flavorings which a consumor cannot tell from natural spices.

1. _____

2. _____

3. _____

4. _____

Now proofread your description of your favorite spice. Fix any mistakes.

Go for the Goal

Take your Final Test. Then fill in your Scoreboard. Send your mistakes to the Word Locker.

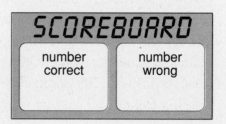

SCOREBOARD

| number correct | number wrong |

★ ★ ★ ★ ★ ★ ★ ★ ★ **All-Star Words** ★ ★ ★ ★ ★ ★ ★ ★ ★

counselor   zoology   lecturer   hypnotist   theology

Write a sentence for each All-Star Word. Underline each All-Star Word. Then, according to the meaning of the suffix, write either "person" or "field of study."

Suffixes er, est, and ness

Warm Up

If you were a storyteller, what kind of stories would you tell?

Storyteller

Joseph Bruchac is a storyteller. With just his voice, a drum, and a little dash of **cleverness,** he can turn the **simplest** tale into a fascinating event. His talents have taken him across the United States and Europe, spreading **happiness** through storytelling.

Joseph believes that a good storyteller helps people by getting them so involved in a story that they forget about their everyday problems and walk away with **healthier** outlooks. "When you hear a story for the first time," he says, "you often take it in with the mind of a child. You see things differently and you go away refreshed."

Joseph also thinks that old stories can give us answers to the problems we face in the future. He believes that we should look to the paths we followed when human beings were in harmony with the earth.

Storytelling events are held all over the country. Check with your local library. Who knows, maybe Joseph will be visiting your neighborhood library. Or you could read some of the folk tales in his book, *Thirteen Moons on Turtle's Back*, and maybe start to be a storyteller yourself.

Say the boldfaced words in the selection. These words have suffixes. What are the root words to which the suffixes are added? See if you notice any spelling changes in the root words when the suffixes are added.

On Your Mark

Take your Warm Up Test. Then check your spelling with the List Words on the next page.

Pep Talk

The suffix **er** means <u>more</u>. The suffix **est** means <u>most</u>. The suffix **ness** changes an adjective into a noun, as in <u>damp</u>— <u>dampness</u>.

For adding suffixes to words that end in **y**, change the **y** to **i**, as in <u>tiny</u>— <u>tinier</u>; <u>noisy</u>—<u>noisier</u>; <u>empty</u>— <u>emptiness</u>. For adding suffixes to words that end in **e**, drop the **e**, as in <u>simple</u>— <u>simplest</u>.

LIST WORDS

1. happiness
2. muddiest
3. tighter
4. cruelest
5. noisiest
6. crazier
7. stiffness
8. dampness
9. sharpness
10. strictest
11. brightest
12. thickest
13. emptiness
14. tinier
15. firmest
16. cleverness
17. healthier
18. simplest
19. cleanliness
20. promptness

Game Plan

Spelling Lineup

Write a List Word under the correct heading.

words with the suffix **er**

1. _____
2. _____
3. _____
4. _____

words with the suffix **est**

5. _____
6. _____
7. _____
8. _____
9. _____
10. _____
11. _____
12. _____

words that were changed from adjectives to nouns with the suffix **ness**

13. _____
14. _____
15. _____
16. _____
17. _____
18. _____
19. _____
20. _____

Word Parts

Add a suffix to each root word to form a List Word. Write the word on the line.

1. tight _____

2. empty _____

3. thick _____

4. clean _____

5. sharp _____

6. clever _____

7. tiny _____

8. muddy _____

9. stiff _____

10. noisy _____

11. bright _____

12. strict _____

13. prompt _____

14. crazy _____

Synonyms

On the spaces at the right, write a List Word that means the same as the word given. Then read the letters in the shaded box to solve the riddle.

1. shiniest   _ _ _ _ | _ _ _ _

2. heartier   _ _ | _ _ _ _ _

3. easiest   _ _ _ | _ _ _ _

4. moistness   _ _ _ | _ _ _ _

5. loudest   _ _ _ _ | _ _ _

6. smaller   _ _ | _ _ _

7. meanest   _ _ _ | _ _ _ _

8. dirtiest   _ _ _ _ _ | _ _

9. hardest   _ _ _ _ _ _ | _

Riddle: What is extremely precious, can't be bought, but can be found?

Answer: _____

Flex Your Spelling Muscles

Writing

Stories can take you anywhere, any time—even to places that do not exist. Do you have a favorite story? Perhaps you have an idea for a story. Write a paragraph that summarizes what your story is about.

Proofreading

This paragraph from a travel book has nine mistakes. Use the proofreading marks to fix each mistake. Then write the misspelled List Words on the lines.

Proofreading Marks
⬭ spelling mistake
⋀ add something
≡ capital letter

Hapyness mightbe listening to a story at the National Storytelling Festival in Jonesborough tennessee. This was the first such festival in the country and now it is the biggest. What happens there You can see the brietest storytellers make the simmplest of stories the most fascinating tales you've ever heard. You will be amazed by their clevarness.

1. _____

2. _____

3. _____

4. _____

Now proofread your story summary. Fix any mistakes.

Go for the Goal

Take your Final Test. Then fill in your Scoreboard. Send your mistakes to the Word Locker.

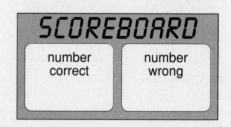

SCOREBOARD

number correct	number wrong

★ ★ ★ ★ ★ ★ ★ ★ ★ ★ **All-Star Words** ★ ★ ★ ★ ★ ★ ★ ★ ★ ★

bitterness   coarsest   filthier   gentler   painfulness

Write a paragraph using the All-Star Words. Then erase the suffixes. Trade papers with a partner. Read your partner's paragraph, adding the correct suffixes to the All-Star Words.

Suffixes able, ible, ful, hood, ship, and ment

LESSON
28

Warm Up

Do you think that freckles really help protect your skin?

Sun Spots

The chances are good that you or someone you know has freckles. Throughout history, freckles have been a mark of distinction. In the 1700s, a famous English poet named John Dryden referred to "sprinkled freckles" as a sign of beauty. At about the same time, some people in Great Britain were hoping for a "freckle-faced" king. They believed that such a king would provide the best leadership to conquer their enemies.

Freckles are spots of dark skin pigments that help protect the skin from the sun's harmful rays. They're most **noticeable** on the face and arms. These pigments absorb more of the sun's burning and tanning rays than the rest of the skin surrounding them.

You may think that getting freckles is **unavoidable.** That's not entirely true. A person who is prone to freckling can be somewhat **successful** in protecting skin with a sunscreen. Freckles are not fully **reversible.** People who have freckles but wish they didn't can wait for a natural **adjustment.** Freckles will often fade when people reach **adulthood.** What's more, a person who is over 20 probably won't get any new freckles, either.

Say the boldfaced words in the selection. Each boldfaced word has a prefix. What are the root words? What spelling changes in the root words occur when the suffixes are added?

On Your Mark

Take your Warm Up Test. Then check your spelling with the List Words on the next page.

Pep Talk

The suffixes **able** and **ible** usually mean <u>can</u>, or <u>able to be</u>. The suffix **ful** means <u>full of</u>. The suffix **hood** usually means <u>the state or condition of being</u>. The suffix **ship** means <u>having the qualities of</u>. The suffix **ment** means <u>act of</u>, <u>state of</u>.

Before adding the suffix to some words that end in **e** or **y**, drop the **e** or change **y** to **i**, as in <u>like</u> + **able** = <u>likable</u>, and <u>fancy</u> + **ful** = <u>fanciful</u>.

LIST WORDS

1. likable
2. appointment
3. parenthood
4. sportsmanship
5. changeable
6. adulthood
7. breakable
8. enrollment
9. fanciful
10. noticeable
11. successful
12. manageable
13. assignment
14. adjustment
15. argument
16. unavoidable
17. reversible
18. convertible
19. bountiful
20. scholarship

Game Plan

Spelling Lineup

Write each List Word in the correct category to show the suffix it contains.

able

1. _____
2. _____
3. _____
4. _____
5. _____
6. _____

ible

7. _____
8. _____

hood

9. _____
10. _____

ment

11. _____
12. _____
13. _____
14. _____
15. _____

ful

16. _____
17. _____
18. _____

ship

19. _____
20. _____

Missing Words

Write a List Word to complete each sentence.

1. With the loan and the _____ she received, she'll be able to afford the college tuition.

2. If you purchase a _____ shirt, it's like having two shirts in one.

3. Sometimes people raise their voices when they have an _____.

4. If the brakes are too tight, you'll need to make an _____.

5. After the animal trainer works with the lions, they will be _____.

6. She has a whimsical, _____ imagination.

7. The _____ has increased; the school has 500 more students.

8. That is a very _____ pitcher, please handle it with care.

9. When a bear cub reaches _____ , it can hunt on its own.

10. There are many magazines available to mothers and fathers that have articles about all

    aspects of _____.

Classification

Write the List Word that belongs in each group.

1. inescapable, unmistakable, _____

2. fairness, generosity, _____

3. visible, remarkable, _____

4. friendly, kind, _____

5. homework, book report, _____

6. date, meeting, _____

7. victorious, excellent, _____

8. unreliable, shifting, _____

9. sedan, station wagon, _____

10. abundant, rich, _____

Flex Your Spelling Muscles

Writing

Write a paragraph that tells how to take care of your skin. You may want to mention the importance of moisturizers and sunscreens.

Proofreading

This article has twelve mistakes. Use the proofreading marks to fix each mistake. Then write the misspelled List Words correctly on the lines.

Proofreading Marks
⬭ spelling mistake
⊙ add period
↷ add apostrophe

    The earths atmosphere can be changable The most noticeable change is the widening hole in the ozone layer. Pollutants are causing the ozone to break down. This exposes the earth to more ultraviolet radiation, which can harm peoples skin Some people feel this problem is unavoydable. Others believe it's reversable if theres an adjusment in the levels of pollution. Well be suksessful in doing so only if everyone makes this their own personal assienment.

1. _____

2. _____

3. _____

4. _____

5. _____

6. _____

Now proofread your paragraph about skin care. Fix any mistakes.

Go for the Goal

Take your Final Test. Then fill in your Scoreboard. Send your mistakes to the Word Locker.

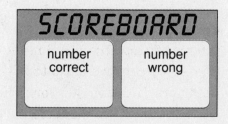

SCOREBOARD	
number correct	number wrong

★ ★ ★ ★ ★ ★ ★ ★ ★ **All-Star Words** ★ ★ ★ ★ ★ ★ ★ ★ ★

digestible   inflatable   livelihood   fellowship   ailment

Write a newspaper headline for each All-Star Word. Trade papers with a partner. Make up a brief story to go with one of the headlines.

Suffixes <u>ion</u>, <u>ation</u>, <u>ition</u>, <u>ance</u>, <u>ence</u>, <u>ive</u>, and <u>ity</u>

Warm Up

What is the best thing to do if you see dark clouds coiling like a snake in the sky?

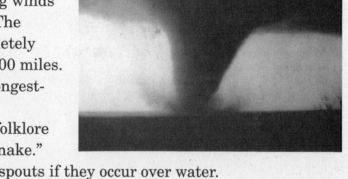

Twister!

The storm began near Havre, Montana, on February 23, 1925. For thirty days, swirling winds blew, destroying everything in their path. The winds didn't die down until they had completely circled the globe—a distance of nearly 22,000 miles. This was no ordinary tornado. It was the longest-lasting cyclone in **existence.**

The word *cyclone* is borrowed from the folklore of ancient India. Cyclone means "coil of a snake." Tornadoes are also called twisters or waterspouts if they occur over water.

A tornado is formed when a quantity of cool, dry air collides with a massive stream of warm, moist air. When the two air masses collide, the warm air rises rapidly and more warm air rushes in beneath it. The warm rushing air also rises and, in **addition,** may begin to rotate, or turn. The rotating air may form a tornado. Soon a funnel forms as the **combination** of cool and warm air actively changes position.

In North America the winds of a tornado spin in a counterclockwise direction. The winds may be whirling around the center of the storm at speeds of more than 300 miles per hour. Most tornadoes last just an hour or two. They can travel up to 200 miles before exhausting themselves. Despite the short duration of a tornado, these storms can be extremely **destructive.**

If you ever see dark clouds coiling like a snake, take cover. A twister is on its way!

 Look back at the boldfaced words in the selection. What are the root words? What spelling changes in the root words occur when the suffixes are added?

On Your Mark

Take your Warm Up Test. Then check your spelling with the List Words on the next page.

Pep Talk

Suffixes and Their Meanings

ion, **ation**, and **ition** = the act of or the condition of being, as in conversation and composition

ance, **ence**, and **ity** = quality or fact of being, as in resistance, experience, and activity

ive = likely to or having to do with, as in destructive and creative

LIST WORDS

1. difference
2. composition
3. electricity
4. abundance
5. conversation
6. existence
7. activity
8. communication
9. excellence
10. addition
11. combination
12. creative
13. explanation
14. passive
15. quotation
16. circulation
17. destructive
18. disturbance
19. experience
20. resistance

Game Plan

Spelling Lineup

Write the List Words that contain the suffixes given.

ence

1. _____
2. _____
3. _____
4. _____

ation

5. _____
6. _____
7. _____
8. _____

ance

9. _____
10. _____
11. _____

ion

12. _____
13. _____

ive

14. _____
15. _____
16. _____

ition

17. _____
18. _____

ity

19. _____
20. _____

❝Everybody talks about the weather, but nobody does anything about it.❞

—Mark Twain

Missing Words

Write the List Word that belongs in each sentence.

1. Soccer is a recreational _____.

2. The _____ storm caused heavy damage.

3. Anya's _____ as a tutor will help her to be a teacher.

4. The heart controls the _____ of blood.

5. The title of his _____ was "Sources of Energy."

6. The telephone is a _____ tool.

7. Winnie received an award for _____ in science.

8. Many people do not believe in the _____ of UFOs.

9. I memorized the _____ to the lock for my locker.

10. Our long-distance phone _____ lasted an hour!

11. We needed a more detailed _____ to fully understand how the machine worked.

12. That group was asked to leave because they were causing a _____.

13. We take _____ for granted until the power goes out.

14. I'm going to cite this famous _____ by Albert Einstein in my report.

Antonyms

Write the List Word that has the opposite meaning of the word given.

1. active _____

2. acceptance _____

3. subtraction _____

4. similarity _____

5. insufficiency _____

6. unimaginative _____

Flex Your Spelling Muscles

Writing

Tornadoes, hurricanes, and floods can all turn into a disaster for people who live in areas where they strike. What do you think people should do to prepare for a big storm? Write your advice in one or two paragraphs.

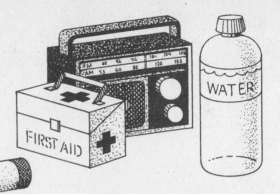

Proofreading

The news report below has ten mistakes. Use the proofreading marks to fix each mistake. Then write the misspelled List Words correctly on the lines.

The tornado that swooped through the area last night was quite a destruktive storm As one resident described it, I heard a roar like a huge freight train and then it hit." A conversashion with another witness resulted in this quoetasion: "My daughter Anna and I ran for the cellar as the electrisity flickered. The tornado tore off the roof.

It was a very frightening experience for many residents. Camunication systems were knocked out for several hours until the disturbence passed.

Now proofread your storm advice. Fix any mistakes.

Proofreading Marks	
⬭	spelling mistake
∧	add something
⸖ ⸷	add quotation marks
¶	insert paragraph

1. _____

2. _____

3. _____

4. _____

5. _____

6. _____

Go for the Goal

Take your Final Test. Then fill in your Scoreboard. Send your mistakes to the Word Locker.

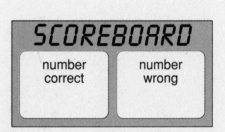

★ ★ ★ ★ ★ ★ ★ ★ ★ **All-Star Words** ★ ★ ★ ★ ★ ★ ★ ★ ★

legislation   inspection   correspondence   radiance   originality

Write a sentence for each All-Star Word. Then trade papers with a partner. Take turns saying what the entire word means, and then what the suffix means.

Instant Replay • Lessons 25–29

Time Out

Look again at the prefixes and suffixes added to words. Think about how they change the meanings and the spelling of some root words.

Check Your Word Locker

Look at the words in your Word Locker. Write your most troublesome words from Lessons 25 through 29.

_____

_____

Practice writing your troublesome words with a partner. Write sentences for each word. Trade papers, circle the prefixes, and tell the meaning of each prefix.

Lesson 25

Prefixes and Their Meanings

anti = against   **counter** = against   **super** = above, over

ultra = beyond   **semi** = half   **sub** = below   **trans** = across, through

List Words
antiseptic
supersonic
antifreeze
semifinal
semicolon
counteract
submarine
transparent
subscription
counterfeit

Write a List Word to complete each sentence.

1. Our team will play in the _____ match.

2. The bill was fake; it was _____.

3. We put _____ in the car in the winter.

4. Use this ointment to _____ the sting.

5. A _____ travels underwater.

6. Use a _____ to separate those clauses.

7. The nurse uses an _____ to kill germs.

8. Our _____ to that magazine is for one year.

9. That window is _____; you can see through it.

10. _____ aircraft exceeds the speed of sound.

121

Suffixes and Their Meanings

or, er, ist = one who or something that **counter** = against **logy, ology** = the study of

List Words

consumer
biology
jeweler
aviator
spectator
typist
journalist
technology
manufacturer
investigator

Write a List Word that means the same or almost the same as the word or phrase given.

1. maker _____

2. goldsmith _____

3. detective _____

4. reporter _____

5. pilot _____

6. onlooker _____

7. industrial science _____

8. buyer or user _____

9. keyboarder _____

10. life science _____

Suffixes and Their Meanings

er = more, as in healthier **est** = most, as in simplest **ness** changes an adjective into a noun

List Words

tighter
noisiest
dampness
brightest
thickest
emptiness
tinier
cleverness
simplest
cleanliness

Write the List Word that belongs in each group.

1. small, little, _____

2. loud, ear-splitting, _____

3. broad, wide, _____

4. easy, plain, _____

5. firm, snug, _____

6. abandoned, vacant, _____

7. wet, moist, _____

8. intelligence, wit, _____

9. dust-free, sanitary, _____

10. brilliant, shining, _____

Suffixes and Their Meanings

able, **ible** = can, able to be   **ful** = full of   **hood** = state or condition of being

ship = having the qualities of   **ment** = what is

List Words

likable
changeable
adulthood
enrollment
successful
assignment
argument
reversible
convertible
bountiful

Write the List Word that has the same root as the word given.

1. exchange _____

2. arguing _____

3. bounteous _____

4. irreversibly _____

5. unlikely _____

6. adultness _____

7. succeeding _____

8. reassign _____

9. enrolled _____

10. converter _____

Suffixes and Their Meanings

ion, **ation**, **ition** = the act of or the condition of being   **ance**, **ence**, **ity** = quality, fact of being

ive = likely to or having to do with

List Words

composition
destructive
conversation
communication
explanation
abundance
activity
excellence
addition
creative

Write a List Word to match each clue.

1. could describe an artist _____

2. involves action _____

3. something you might write _____

4. describes a fire or storm _____

5. a phone call or a letter _____

6. tells why it happened _____

7. more than enough _____

8. 2 plus 2 _____

9. talking between people _____

10. the best something can be _____

List Words

semicolon
technology
manufacturer
cleanliness
transparent
composition
typist
assignment
submarine
conversation
biology
tinier

Complete each sentence with a List Word.

1. Medical _____ has enabled us to cure many diseases.

2. Some windows in buildings are not _____.

3. My dad is concerned with _____; he's always straightening up things.

4. The pianist wrote the musical _____ for that piece.

5. One type of _____ can dive to a depth of over 30 meters in one minute.

6. In our field _____ class, we studied many native birds.

7. Some calculators are _____ than the palm of your hand.

8. The _____ of that product had to close down the factory.

9. He is a very fast _____; he can type over 100 words a minute.

10. That particular _____ involved a lot of research.

11. We try to keep each long-distance phone _____ brief.

12. A _____ is a cross between a period and a comma.

Go for the Goal

Take your Final Replay Test. Then fill in your Scoreboard.
Send any misspelled words to your Word Locker.

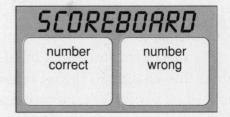

SCOREBOARD

number correct	number wrong

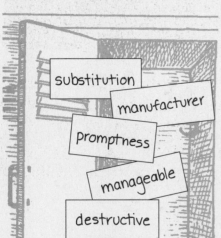

substitution
manufacturer
promptness
manageable
destructive

Clean Out Your Word Locker

Look in your Word Locker. Cross out each word you spelled correctly on your Final Replay Test. Circle the words you're still having trouble with. Add the words you circled to your Spelling Notebook. What do you notice about the words? Watch for those words as you write.

Doubling Final Consonants; Adding Suffixes to Words Ending in e

LESSON 31

Warm Up

What kind of displays do you think you would find in the Museum of Tolerance?

A Museum Built on Tolerance

There is an **exciting** new museum inLos Angeles, California, unlike any other in the world. It is not the kind of museum where you'll find display eases **crammed** with artifacts from bugone days. In fact, there are very few glass cases. The Museum of Tolerance is an unusual museum, **equipped** with special effects. It contains displays that will cause you to consider how you feel about others who are different than you. This museum will move you to think about prejudice, and its effect on your life.

During a 2 1/2 hour tour, **combining** audio-visual special effects and a learning center, you get a chance to witness the tragedies that intolerance can cause. For example, in the "Whisper Gallery," visitors are bombarded with recordings of slurs and lies people cansay about each other. The effect is chilling. Later in the tour, you hear firsthand accounts of people who have suffered becuase of prejudice and intolerance. The idea is to show what can happen when lies and ethnic slurs go unchallenged.

As one of the museum's creators said about the visitors to the museum., "We're calling on people to take responsibiity for their words and actions."

Look back at the boldfaced words in the selection. Find the root word in each word. What happened to the spelling of the root word when the suffixes were added?

On Your Mark

Take your Warm Up Test. Then check your spelling with the List Words on the next page.

When a short-vowel word or syllable ends in a single consonant, usually double the consonant before adding a suffix that begins with a vowel, as in **equip** + **ed** = equipped.

When you add a suffix that begins with a vowel to a word that ends with **e**, drop the **e** before adding the suffix, as in **unpave** + **ed** = unpaved and **combine** + **ing** = combining.

LIST WORDS

1. evaporated
2. combining
3. graduated
4. unpaved
5. approved
6. referred
7. advertising
8. crammed
9. produced
10. equipped
11. occurred
12. memorized
13. controlled
14. exciting
15. abbreviated
16. calculation
17. hesitation
18. organizing
19. disguised
20. realized

Game Plan

Spelling Lineup

Write the List Words in which the final consonant was doubled before the suffix was added.

1. _____
2. _____
3. _____
4. _____
5. _____

Write the List Words in which the final **e** was dropped before the suffix was added.

6. _____
7. _____
8. _____
9. _____
10. _____
11. _____
12. _____
13. _____
14. _____
15. _____
16. _____
17. _____
18. _____
19. _____
20. _____

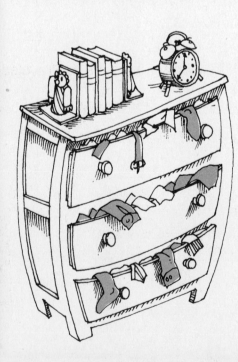

Word Parts

Add a suffix to each root word to form a List Word. Write the word on the line.

1. realize _____
2. occur _____
3. graduate _____
4. combine _____
5. calculate _____
6. excite _____
7. control _____
8. unpave _____
9. produce _____
10. organize _____

11. approve _____
12. refer _____
13. memorize _____
14. hesitate _____
15. cram _____
16. disguise _____
17. abbreviate _____
18. equip _____
19. advertise _____
20. evaporate _____

Missing Words

Write a List Word to complete each sentence.

1. Tony _____ the poem so he would not need notes.

2. The chef is _____ all the ingredients in a large bowl.

3. Without any _____, the firefighter rushed into the burning building.

4. He _____ his emotions well during the moving speech.

5. She _____ us to an excellent dentist.

6. We bounced up and down in the back seat as the car traveled

   down the _____ country road.

7. The audience laughed and cheered when they saw how

   many clowns had been _____
   into the tiny automobile.

8. Consuelo will be _____
   a new file system for the office files.

Flex Your Spelling Muscles

Writing

Write a paragraph telling what you think should be done about prejudice and intolerance and why your ideas would work.

Proofreading

The article below has eleven mistakes. Use the proofreading marks to fix each mistake. Write the misspelled List Words on the lines.

Proofreading Marks
- ⬭ spelling mistake
- / make small letter
- ∧ add something
- ⌄ add apostrophe

One of the worlds Longest borders along which conflict has rarely ockured is in North America. The lasting peace between Canada and the United States has prodused a beautiful place that is refared to as the International Peace Garden, which sits on the border in the Turtle Mountain Valley. Aprouved and built in 1932, the garden is a symbol of peace. Its the only one of its kind in the world, combineing beauty with a message. What kinds of things will you see there Youll see an exciteing stone tower made of rocks from both countries.

1. _____   4. _____

2. _____   5. _____

3. _____   6. _____

Now proofread your paragraph. Fix any mistakes.

Go for the Goal

Take your Final Test. Then fill in your Scoreboard. Send your mistakes to the Word Locker.

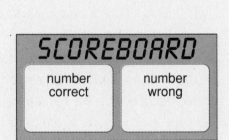

SCOREBOARD

number correct	number wrong

★ ★ ★ ★ ★ ★ ★ ★ ★ **All-Star Words** ★ ★ ★ ★ ★ ★ ★ ★ ★

challenged   relating   patrolling   tolerated   admitted

With your partner, write a story using the All-Star Words. Then erase and put the All-Star Words in the wrong places. Trade papers with another team and rewrite their paragraph, using the All-Star Words correctly.

Adding Suffixes to Words Ending in y

Warm Up

How are cranberries grown?

Ibimi

The word *ibimi* means "bitter berry." Ibimi is the name the Pequot Indians gave to a small red fruit that grew in Cape Cod.

When the Pilgrims reached Massachusetts, they, too, found the pink berries that bore pink blossoms. These flowers looked like the small delicate heads of cranes. The Pilgrims **identified** the berries that grew on these vines as crane-berries, which later became known as cranberries.

If you eat a cranberry right after it's been picked, you probably will be **dismayed** by its taste and spit it out. Its waxy coating and sour taste make this berry undelectable in its natural form. Nevertheless, more than half the households in America regularly consume cranberries produced by **companies.**

Cranberries are grown in bogs and marshy wetlands in the U.S. Northeast and Pacific Northwest. In mid-September growers flood the bogs and cover the berries with water. When the water is stirred, the berries come loose from their vines. The cranberries then float to the surface where they are harvested by a machine called an "egg beater." Next, they are transported to processing plants in refrigerated trucks that keep them from **decaying.** Then, cranberries are turned into juice, jams, and **jellies.**

Look back at the boldfaced words in the selection. Each of these words ends in a suffix. What happens to the root words that end in **y** when the suffixes are added?

On Your Mark

Take your Warm Up Test. Then check your spelling with the List Words on the next page.

Pep Talk

If a word ends in:
- a **vowel** and **y**, add **ed** or **s** without changing the base word, as in <u>disobeyed</u>.
- a **consonant** and **y**, change the **y** to **i** before adding **ed** or **es**, as in <u>occupied</u>.
- a **consonant** and **y**, change the **y** to **i** before adding **ly**, as in <u>sloppily</u>.
- **y**, add **ing** without changing the base word, as in <u>decaying</u>.

LIST WORDS

1. companies
2. jellies
3. sloppily
4. surveying
5. theories
6. steadily
7. waterways
8. identified
9. occupied
10. disobeyed
11. remedies
12. thirstily
13. decaying
14. modified
15. galaxies
16. industries
17. attorneys
18. dismayed
19. magnified
20. portrayed

Game Plan

Spelling Lineup

Add a suffix to each word to form a List Word. Write the List Word on the line.

1. attorney _____
2. modify _____
3. company _____
4. magnify _____
5. waterway _____
6. identify _____
7. industry _____
8. occupy _____
9. survey _____
10. galaxy _____

11. steady _____
12. theory _____
13. portray _____
14. dismay _____
15. jelly _____
16. decay _____
17. thirsty _____
18. sloppy _____
19. remedy _____
20. disobey _____

Vocabulary

Write a List Word to complete each sentence.

1. Things are _____ with these: telescopes, microscopes, binoculars.

2. These are used to make _____: grapes, strawberries, raspberries.

3. _____ work with these people: judges, juries, defendants.

4. These are _____ for a cold: fruit juice, warm clothes, bed rest.

5. These are _____: rivers, creeks, brooks.

6. You might see these through a telescope: planets, _____, asteroids.

7. These are words that mean changed: altered, adjusted, _____.

8. These are words that mean anxious: _____, saddened, worried.

9. These are different ways to be pictured: photographed, painted, _____.

10. These are businesses: industries, shops, _____.

Missing Words

Write a List Word to complete each sentence.

1. The surveyors are _____ the lot for a new building.

2. There are many _____ about where UFOs come from.

3. Place all the _____ leaves and twigs in the compost heap.

4. Many _____ are following strict guidelines regarding air pollution.

Antonyms

Write the List Word that means the opposite of the word or phrase given.

1. neatly _____

2. periodically _____

3. without thirst _____

4. empty, vacant _____

5. behaved _____

6. left unnamed _____

Flex Your Spelling Muscles

Writing

Harvesting cranberries is a job not many people do. Write a notice for cranberry bog workers. Be sure to include what the job requires. Try to use as many List Words as you can.

Proofreading

This article has eleven mistakes. Use the proofreading marks to fix the mistakes. Write the misspelled List Words correctly on the lines.

Proofreading Marks
- ⬯ spelling mistake
- / make small letter
- ^ add something
- ⟟ take something out

   Along the watewayes of the Great Lakes region a special harvest takes place in the summer. The Ojibway people begin survaying the Wild rice beds to plan their their harvest. Two people ride ride in each canoe, and one steedily pushes it through the water with a long pole. The Ojibway have occupyed thisarea and gathered wild rice for about 400 years. Their methods have not been modifyed very much over the years. They pull the stalks over, knock the tops and send the grains into the bottom of the canoe. Nothing isdone slaupily.

1. _____   4. _____

2. _____   5. _____

3. _____   6. _____

Now proofread your notice. Fix any mistakes.

Go for the Goal

Take your Final Test. Then fill in your Scoreboard. Send your mistakes to the Word Locker.

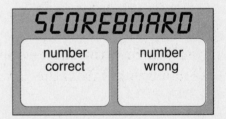

SCOREBOARD

| number correct | number wrong |

★ ★ ★ ★ ★ ★ ★ ★ ★ **All-Star Words** ★ ★ ★ ★ ★ ★ ★ ★ ★

jockeys   dictionaries   conveyed   glorified   greedily

Write a sentence with the root word for each All-Star Word. Trade papers with your partner. Add the suffixes to make the All-Star Words, and write new sentences.

LESSON

33

Plurals

Warm Up

Why do we call things by a certain name?

What's in a Name?

Did you ever wonder why we call a daisy a daisy? The names of many different **species** of flowers and plants that grow around our **patios** and yards come from other languages. For example, dandelion comes from the French, *dent de lion,* which means lion's tooth. You may well ask why the dandelion doesn't look like a lion's tooth. The name actually refers to the leaves of the plant itself. They are long and deeply indented, like a lion's tooth. Gladioli comes from the Latin word *gladiolus,* which means little sword, and a gladioli is long and slender like a sword. Chrysanthemum is the golden flower. It gets its name from the Greek word for gold, *crysos.*

Many of our foods get their names from other languages as well. We get a few food names from the Nahuatl peoples of Mexico and Central America. Tomato comes from its original Nahuatl name *tomatl.* The singular of **avocados**, avocado, can be traced back to the Nahuatl word *ahuacatl,* which means delicacy. **Broccoli** comes from the Italian word *broccolo,* which means cabbage sprout. And **spaghetti,** which certainly isn't a vegetable, is based on the Italian word *spago,* meaning string!

As for the daisy, its white petals open with the rays of sunshine that mark the beginning of a new day. Then in the evening, when the sun disappears, the daisy closes its petals. Its name comes from the Latin *daeges eage,* or "day's eye."

Look back at the boldfaced words in the selection. Say the singular form of each plural word. What do you notice about the spelling of some plural forms of words?

On Your Mark

Take your Warm Up Test. Then check your spelling with the List Words on the next page.

Some words remain the same in singular and plural form, as in species→species.

For most words that end in **f** or **fe**, change the **f** or **fe** to **v** and add **es** to form the plural. Sometimes, just add **s**, as in knife→knives and belief→beliefs.

When a word ends in **o**, sometimes form the plural by adding **es**. Other times just add **s**, as in mosquito→mosquitoes and stereo→stereos.

LIST WORDS

1. rodeos
2. kangaroos
3. tuxedos
4. patios
5. stereos
6. avocados
7. beliefs
8. thieves
9. tariffs
10. species
11. ponchos
12. dominoes
13. mementos
14. embargoes
15. broccoli
16. spaghetti
17. jackknives
18. handkerchiefs
19. Eskimos
20. mosquitoes

Game Plan

Spelling Lineup

Write the List Words under the correct headings.

words that do not change to form the plural

1. _____
2. _____
3. _____

words that change f or fe to v and add es to form the plural

4. _____
5. _____

words that end in o and add es to form the plural

6. _____
7. _____
8. _____

words that end in f or o and just add s to form the plural

9. _____
10. _____
11. _____
12. _____
13. _____
14. _____
15. _____
16. _____
17. _____
18. _____
19. _____
20. _____

Word Games

Write a List Word to match each definition clue.

1. suits worn by bridegrooms _____

2. cloths often used by people with a cold _____

3. areas where barbecues may be held _____

4. contests for cowboys _____

5. take what isn't theirs _____

6. bugs that won't quit biting _____

7. long strands of pasta _____

Puzzle

Fill in the crossword puzzle by writing a List Word
that is the plural form of the word given.

ACROSS
1. jackknife
4. broccoli
5. kangaroo
9. stereo
10. memento
13. Eskimo
14. species

DOWN
2. avocado
3. embargo
6. rodeo
7. thief
8. domino
11. tariff
12. poncho

Flex Your Spelling Muscles

Writing

Flowers have many different names. Think of a flower that you know of or like, or use one of the following: mosquito trap, Queen Anne's lace, buttercup, tiger lily, Johnny-jump-up, or snapdragon. Write a poem about its color, name, or shape.

Proofreading

The article below has ten mistakes. Use the proofreading marks to fix each mistake. Then write the misspelled List Words on the lines.

> **Proofreading Marks**
> ⬭ spelling mistake
> / make small letter
> ⌴ add apostrophe

Some spesies of plants are named after people. For Example, the bougainvillea flower comes from Louis Antonine de Bougainville, who was the first European to explore parts of the Pacific Ocean in 1766. He saw the Great Barrier Reef in Australia, but he missed seeing any kangarus. The red poinsettia is named for Joel Poinsett, a U.S. politician. When he became the countrys minister to Mexico, hed left behind tarifs and embargos but not his political belefs. Mexicos government resented his interfering in their affairs. Poinsett was also a botanist. One of the memeintoes he brought back from Mexico was the bright, red flower that was named for him.

1. _____

2. _____

3. _____

4. _____

5. _____

6. _____

Now proofread your flower poem. Fix any mistakes.

Go for the Goal

Take your Final Test. Then fill in your Scoreboard. Send your mistakes to the Word Locker.

SCOREBOARD

number correct	number wrong

★ ★ ★ ★ ★ ★ ★ ★ ★ **All-Star Words** ★ ★ ★ ★ ★ ★ ★ ★ ★

heroes   confetti   videos   sheaves   soprano

Write a sentence for each All-Star word. Compare sentences with your partner. Then work with your partner to write a spelling rule for each type of plural represented.

Homonyms and Hurdle Words

Warm Up

What is one form of identification that is unique to you?

One of a Kind Imprints

What is something you have that is unique, you carry it wherever you go, and it's right in your hand? It's your fingerprint! It is the only true form of **personal** identification. No two fingerprints are exactly alike.

Until recently, fingerprints were rarely used by police, **except** in really serious crimes, because of the cost and the time they take to process. Now, however, with the advances in computer technology, fingerprints are being used not only to solve, but to prevent crime as well.

Using the new technology, the fingerprint is first passed **through** a computer scanner. Every place where the **course** of a ridge line ends is noted by the computer and is then sorted by its type. This information is converted into a mathematical formula, which the computer can speedily compare to millions of others. The **principal** result is that some day in the near future, these mathematical formulas may be imbedded on credit cards and drivers licenses for identification purposes. We may even be able to unlock doors with just our fingerprints, making keys a thing of the past.

Say the boldfaced words in the selection. Can you think of another word that sounds the same, but is spelled differently and has a different meaning?

On Your Mark

Take your Warm Up Test. Then check your spelling with the List Words on the next page.

Pep Talk

Words that sound the same, but are spelled differently and have different meanings, are called homonyms, as in <u>through</u> and <u>threw</u>.

Some words have similar spellings and pronunciations, but different meanings, as in <u>personnel</u> and <u>personal</u>.

The best way to become familiar with these words is to practice using them.

Game Plan

Spelling Lineup

Write a List Word to match each clue. Then write another List Word that is its homonym or a List Word with a similar spelling.

1. rough _____ _____

2. school _____ _____

3. doctor _____ _____

4. private _____ _____

5. pitcher _____ _____

6. rain _____ _____

7. scale _____ _____

8. wall _____ _____

9. receive _____ _____

10. camel _____ _____

Missing Words

Complete each sentence with a List Word that is a homonym
for or sounds similar to the underlined word.

1. The principal discussed the _____ of honesty.

2. We are _____ the cracks in the ceiling.

3. I had to wait for the nurse to check my _____ .

4. The doctor showed _____ with his young patients.

5. _____ or not we go will depend on the weather forecast.

6. Except for two people, they all arrived to _____
their awards.

7. The boy threw the ball _____ the open window.

8. The personnel manager asked him some

very _____ questions.

Definitions

On the spaces at the right, write a List Word to solve each definition clue.
Then use the letters in the shaded box to solve the riddle.

1. served at the end of a meal   _ _ _ _ _ _ _

2. a school subject   _ _ _ _ _ _ _

3. not fine or delicate; harsh   _ _ _ _ _ _

4. head of a school   _ _ _ _ _ _ _ _ _

5. remain until something happens   _ _ _ _

6. top part of a room   _ _ _ _ _ _ _

7. people who need a doctor's care   _ _ _ _ _ _ _ _

8. employed persons   _ _ _ _ _ _ _ _ _

9. other than; but   _ _ _ _ _ _

Riddle: What's the best way to communicate with a fish?

Answer: _____ __ _____

Flex Your Spelling Muscles

Writing

In the future, people might also use their eyes or their voices as identification to unlock doors. Write a letter to a company in which you describe a security device that you have invented for use in the future.

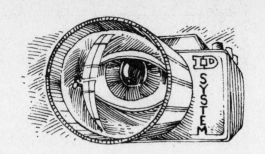

Proofreading

The book review below has fifteen mistakes. Use the proofreading marks to fix each mistake. Circle the misused List Words. Then write the List Words correctly on the lines.

Proofreading Marks
ᣐ ᣐ add quotation marks
∧ add something

> *The Principle Ate Desert* is such an exciting story There is nonstop action in this personnel story about a clever detective who has the patients to weight for the criminal tomake a mistake. One reviewer says, I read threw just the first ten pages, and I knew it was a book of principal. The author says, Of coarse, weather or not readers like it remainsto be seen."

1. _____

2. _____

3. _____

4. _____

5. _____

6. _____

7. _____

8. _____

Now proofread your letter. Fix any mistakes.

9. _____

Go for the Goal

Take your Final Test. Then fill in your Scoreboard. Send your mistakes to the Word Locker.

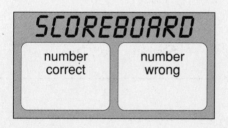

SCOREBOARD

number correct	number wrong

★ ★ ★ ★ ★ ★ ★ ★ ★ **All-Star Words** ★ ★ ★ ★ ★ ★ ★ ★ ★

capitol   chute   stationary   reign   martial

Make a list of the All-Star Words. Write a homonym for each word. Work with a partner. One of you write sentences for the first words, and the other write sentences for the homonym pairs. Then compare sentences.

Abbreviations

Warm Up

Can you figure out Joe Quick's message to Mrs. X?

Short and Sweet

Here's the letter that Mrs. X received from Joe Quick.

SPEEDY  **CO., INC.**
1001 Fast Blvd.   Velocity, NY 00240

Dear Mrs. X,

As **Pres.** of Speedy **Co., Inc.,** I have read your **biog.** along with those of a **no.** of other applicants. I am pleased that you have applied for a position with us **vs.** one with the **govt.**; however, I believe that an **oz.** of experience is worth more than a **lb.** of ability. Because the **vol.** of your experience is extremely limited, the only position I could possibly offer is an **asst.** to our **mdse. mgr.** in the shipping **dept.** As an **ex.** of what the job entails, you might be asked to ship a two oz. **pkg.** to Taiwan, or a three **lb.** pkg. to Timbuktu. Let me know what you think.

Sorry to change the **subj.** and cut this letter short, but I'm a very busy guy.

Sincerely,

Joe Quick, Pres.
Speedy Co., Inc.

Did Mrs. X get the job? What exactly was the job?

Look back at all the boldfaced abbreviations in the selection. Try to say all the words that the abbreviations stand for.

On Your Mark

Take your Warm Up Test. Then check your spelling with the List Words on the next page.

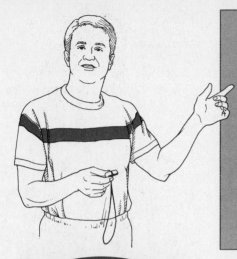

Pep Talk

An abbreviation is the shortened form of a word that ends with a period. Most are spelled with the first letters of the word, as in company → co. Some are spelled with a combination of letters from the word, as in package → pkg. Others are spelled with letters not found in the original word, as in ounce → oz. and pound → lb.

LIST WORDS

1. govt.
2. pres.
3. dept.
4. co.
5. inc.
6. subj.
7. ed.
8. vol.
9. biog.
10. no.
11. ex.
12. vs.
13. pt.
14. qt.
15. oz.
16. lb.
17. mgr.
18. asst.
19. pkg.
20. mdse.

Game Plan

Spelling Lineup

Write a List Word that is an abbreviation for the word given.

1. manager _____
2. incorporated _____
3. merchandise _____
4. versus _____
5. assistant _____
6. department _____
7. ounce _____
8. volume _____
9. subject _____
10. quart _____
11. number _____
12. biography _____
13. pound _____
14. company _____
15. government _____
16. example _____
17. package _____
18. pint _____
19. edition _____
20. president _____

Misspelled Words

In each set of words, circle the correct spelling of the
List Word. Then write the correct spelling on the line.

1. depa.   dep.   dept. _____

2. mang.   mgr.   mnr. _____

3. biog.   bio.   bphy. _____

4. pres.   prsd.   pdnt. _____

5. ver.   vs.   vrs. _____

6. no.   nu.   numb. _____

7. sub.   sbjt.   subj. _____

8. qut.   qt.   qrt. _____

9. mdse.   merc.   mrse. _____

10. pnd.   lnd.   lb. _____

11. inc.   in.   inct. _____

12. ou.   onc.   oz. _____

Abbreviations

Write a List Word that is the abbreviation for the underlined
word in each sentence.

1. The tour guide showed us an <u>example</u> of a fossil. _____

2. We found information about England in <u>volume</u> 6 of the encyclopedia. _____

3. The first <u>edition</u> of a classic would be priceless. _____

4. Martin wants to work for the <u>government</u> when he graduates. _____

5. Dr. Tripp introduced us to her young <u>assistant</u>. _____

6. The delivery service left the <u>package</u> on our doorstep. _____

7. The quiche recipe calls for a <u>pint</u> of heavy cream. _____

8. Carlos applied for a job at my aunt's <u>company</u>. _____

Flex Your Spelling Muscles

Writing

Why do you think people use abbreviations? Write your ideas in a paragraph. Be sure to explain why they are useful or why they create problems. Try to use as many List Words as you can.

Proofreading

The following recipe has nine mistakes. Use the proofreading marks to fix each mistake. Then write the misspelled List Words on the lines.

Golden Rich Bread

1 lb. butter   1 pakg. yeast
1 qrt. milk   6 cups flour
3 os. shredded coconut

Mix ingredients together and cover. Set the bowl bowl aside and allow the dough to to rise. Then punch knead, and push the dough. Put it in a loaf pan and bake for 1 hour. (Recipe from Cooks vs. Kitchens, Second edi., New Day Co., King Books, Ink., Rochester New York.)

Now proofread your paragraph about abbreviations. Fix any mistakes.

Proofreading Marks	
⬯	spelling mistake
∧	add something
℮	take out something

1. _____

2. _____

3. _____

4. _____

5. _____

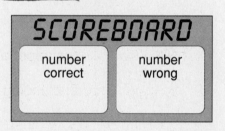

Go for the Goal

Take your Final Test. Then fill in your Scoreboard. Send your mistakes to the Word Locker.

SCOREBOARD

number correct	number wrong

★ ★ ★ ★ ★ ★ ★ ★ **All-Star Words** ★ ★ ★ ★ ★ ★ ★ ★

blvd.   mo.   tsp.   hwy.   etc.

Use your dictionary to find out what the abbreviations mean. Spell out each abbreviation as a complete word in a sentence. Trade papers with your partner. Replace the complete words in the sentences with the All-Star Words.

Instant Replay • Lessons 31–35

Time Out

Look again at how words are spelled when suffixes are added to words that end in **e** or **y**, how plurals are formed, homonyms, hurdle words, and abbreviations.

Check Your Word Locker

Look at the words in your Word Locker. Write your most troublesome words from Lessons 31 through 35.

_____

_____

Practice writing your troublesome words with a partner. Take turns saying the root words for words with suffixes, the singular form for plural words, homonyms, and the complete words for abbreviations.

Lesson 31

Before adding a suffix to a word, sometimes you need to double the final consonant, as in <u>referred</u>, or drop the final **e**, as in <u>organizing</u>.

List Words
combining
approved
referred
crammed
produced
occurred
controlled
exciting
hesitation
realized

Write a List Word that means the same or almost the same as the word given.

1. happened _____

2. blending _____

3. understood _____

4. thrilling _____

5. accepted _____

6. crowded _____

7. created _____

8. uncertainty _____

9. mentioned _____

10. managed _____

Before adding a suffix to a word that ends in **y**, sometimes you need to change the **y** to **i**, as in <u>jellies</u> and <u>magnified</u>.

List Words

jellies
theories
steadily
waterways
remedies
decaying
modified
industries
attorneys
magnified

Circle the correctly spelled List Word. Write the word on the line.

1. jellies   jellys _____

2. decaing   decaying _____

3. magnifyed   magnified _____

4. attorneys   attornies _____

5. waterways   waterwaies _____

6. theorys   theories _____

7. modified   modifyed _____

8. steadyly   steadily _____

9. industryes   industries _____

10. remedies   remedyes _____

Some words are the same in both the singular and plural form. To form the plural of most words that end in **f** or **fe**, change the **f** or **fe** to **v** and add **es.** Sometimes just add **s**. Some words that end in o take **es**, others just an **s**.

List Words

tuxedos
patios
stereos
thieves
tariffs
species
ponchos
mementos
spaghetti
mosquitoes

Write the List Words in alphabetical order.

1. _____   9. _____

2. _____   10. _____

3. _____

4. _____

5. _____

6. _____

7. _____

8. _____

Words that sound the same, but are spelled differently and have different meanings, are homonyms. Some words have similar spellings and pronunciations, but different meanings.

List Words

through
weight
principal
ceiling
weather
coarse
patients
accept
desert
personnel

Study the relationship between the first two underlined words. Then write a List Word that has the same relationship with the third underlined word.

1. Tall is to short as smooth is to _____.

2. Feet is to height as pounds is to _____.

3. Stairs is to up as tunnel is to _____.

4. Ship is to crew as office is to _____.

5. Sell is to buy as give is to _____.

6. Side is to top as wall is to _____.

7. Wet is to lake as dry is to _____.

8. Team is to captain as school is to _____.

9. Population is to people as climate is to _____.

10. Lawyer is to clients as doctor is to _____.

Abbreviations are shortened forms of words formed with the first letters of the word or with a combination of letters in the word. Others are formed with letters that are not in the original word.

List Words

pres.
inc.
no.
oz.
asst.
dept.
vol.
qt.
lb.
pkg.

Write the List Word or List Words to complete each sentence.

1. Please give me a 1 _____, 1 _____ _____ of beef.

2. Make an appointment to see the _____ with her _____.

3. Please buy one _____ of skim milk.

4. She works in the manufacturing _____ of Speedy Co., _____.

5. What _____ is _____ S of the encyclopedia?

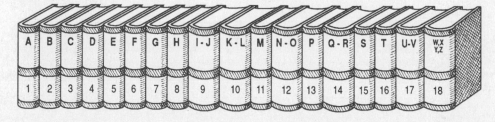

Write a List Word to solve each definition clue.

List Words

controlled
decaying
weather
personnel
inc.
exciting
industries
asst.
stereos
magnified
theories
spaghetti
modified
patients
tuxedos

1. thrilling _____

2. made larger _____

3. big businesses _____

4. kind of pasta _____

5. unproven ideas _____

6. dressy kinds of suits _____

7. under a doctor's care _____

8. incorporated (abbreviation) _____

9. sleet, snow, rain _____

10. changed in some way _____

11. regulated or operated _____

12. staff of people _____

13. assistant (abbreviation) _____

14. sound systems _____

15. spoiling _____

Go for the Goal

Take your Final Replay Test. Then fill in your Scoreboard.
Send any misspelled words to your Word Locker.

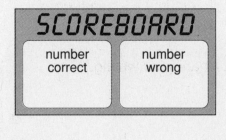

SCOREBOARD

number correct	number wrong

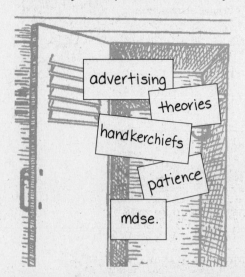

advertising
theories
handkerchiefs
patience
mdse.

Clean Out Your Word Locker

Look in your Word Locker. Cross out each word you spelled
correctly on your Final Replay Test. Circle the words you're
still having trouble with. Add the words you circled to your
Spelling Notebook. What do you notice about the words?
Watch for those words as you write.

Writing and Proofreading Guide

1. Choose a topic to write about.
2. Write your ideas. Don't worry about mistakes.
3. Now organize your writing so that it makes sense.
4. Proofread your work.

    Use these proofreading marks to check your work.

Proofreading Marks

◯	spelling mistake
≡	capital letter
⊙	add period
∧	add something
⋁	add apostrophe
ℛ	take out something
¶	indent paragraph
/	make small letter
⌄ ⌄	add quotation marks

---

the electronic keyboard is a (remarkible) musical
instrument that can can produce the sounds
of drums, pianos, or violins ⊙

5. Write your final copy.

    The electronic keyboard is a remarkable musical
    instrument that can produce the sounds of drums,
    pianos, or violins.

6. Share your writing.

Using Your Dictionary

The Spelling Workout Dictionary shows you many things about your spelling words.

The **entry word** listed in alphabetical order is the word you are looking up.

The sound-spelling or **respelling** tells how to pronounce the word.

The **part of speech** is given as an abbreviation.

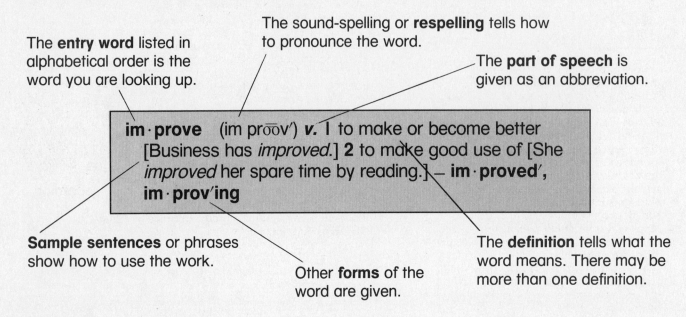

im·prove (im prōōv′) **v. 1** to make or become better [Business has *improved*.] **2** to make good use of [She *improved* her spare time by reading.] — **im·proved′, im·prov′ing**

Sample sentences or phrases show how to use the work.

Other **forms** of the word are given.

The **definition** tells what the word means. There may be more than one definition.

Pronunciation Key

SYMBOL	KEY WORDS	SYMBOL	KEY WORDS	SYMBOL	KEY WORDS	SYMBOL	KEY WORDS
a	ask, fat	o͝o	look, pull	b	bed, dub	t	top, hat
ā	ape, date	ōō	ooze, tool	d	did, had	v	vat, have
ä	car, lot	ou	out, crowd	f	fall, off	w	will, always
				g	get, dog	y	yet, yard
e	elf, ten	u	up, cut	h	he, ahead	z	zebra, haze
ē	even, meet	u̇	fur, fern	j	joy, jump		
				k	kill, bake	ch	chin, arch
i	is, hit	ə	a in ago	l	let, ball	ŋ	ring, singer
ī	ice, fire		e in agent	m	met, trim	sh	she, dash
			e in father	n	not, ton	th	thin, truth
ō	open, go		i in unity	p	put, tap	*th*	then, father
ô	law, horn		o in collect	r	red, dear	zh	s in pleasure
oi	oil, point		u in focus	s	sell, pass		

An Americanism is a word or usage of a word that was born in this country. An open star before an entry word or definition means that the word or definition is an Americanism.

Aa

ab·bre·vi·ate (ə brē′vē āt) *v.* to make shorter by cutting out part [The word "Street" is often *abbreviated* to "St."] —**ab·bre′vi·at·ed, ab·bre′vi·at·ing**

ab·stract (ab strakt′ *or* ab′strakt) *adj.* **1** thought of apart from a particular act or thing [A just trial is a fair one, but justice itself is an *abstract* idea.] **2** formed with designs taken from real things, but not actually like any real object or being [an *abstract* painting].

a·bun·dance (ə bun′dəns) *n.* a great supply; an amount more than enough [Where there is an *abundance* of goods, prices are supposed to go down.]

ac·cel·er·a·tor (ak sel′ər āt′ər) *n.* a thing that accelerates an action; especially, the foot pedal that can make an automobile go faster by feeding the engine more gasoline.

ac·cept (ak sept′) *v.* **1** to take what is offered or given [Will you *accept* $20 for that old bicycle?] **2** to answer "yes" to [We *accept* your invitation.] **3** to believe to be true [to *accept* a theory.]

ac·cess (ak′ses) *n.* **1** a way of approach [The *access* to the park is by this road.] **2** the right or ability to approach, enter, or use [Do the students have *access* to a good library?]

ac·com·plish (ə käm′plish) *v.* to do; carry out [The task was *accomplished* in one day.]

ac·cor·di·on (ə kôr′dē ən) *n.* a musical instrument with keys, metal reeds, and a bellows. It is played by pulling out and pressing together the bellows to force air through the reeds, which are opened by fingering the keys.

ac·count (ə kount′) *v.* **1** to give a detailed record of money handled [Our treasurer can *account* for every penny spent.] **2** to give a satisfactory reason; explain [How do you *account* for your absence from school?] ◆*n.* **1** *often* **accounts,** *pl.* a statement of money received, paid, or owed; record of business dealings. **2** a report or story [The book is an *account* of their travels.]

a·chieve·ment (ə chēv′mənt) *n.* **1** the act of achieving something [his *achievement* of a lifelong dream]. **2** something achieved by skill, work, courage, etc. [The landing of spacecraft on the moon was a remarkable *achievement*.]

ac·knowl·edge (ak näl′ij) *v.* **1** to admit to be true [I *acknowledge* that you are right.] **2** to recognize the authority of [They *acknowledged* him as their king.] **3** to recognize and answer or express one's thanks for [She *acknowledged* my greeting by smiling. Have you written to your uncle to *acknowledge* his gift?] —**ac·knowl′edged, ac·knowl′edg·ing**

ac·quaint·ance (ə kwānt′ns) *n.* **1** knowledge of a thing or person got from one's own experience [She has some *acquaintance* with modern art.] **2** a person one knows but not as a close friend.

ac·tiv·i·ty (ak tiv′ə tē) *n.* **1** the condition of being active; action; motion [There was not much *activity* in the shopping mall today.] **2** normal power of mind or body; liveliness; alertness [His mental *activity* at age eighty was remarkable.] **3** something that one does besides one's regular work [We take part in many *activities* after school.] —*pl.* **ac·tiv′i·ties**

ad·di·tion (ə dish′ən) *n.* **1** an adding of numbers to get a sum or total. **2** a joining of one thing to another thing [The lemonade was improved by the *addition* of sugar.] **3** a thing or part added [The gymnasium is a new *addition* to our school.]

ad·just·ment (ə just′mənt) *n.* **1** a changing or settling of things to bring them into proper order or relation [She made a quick *adjustment* to her new job.] **2** a way or device by which parts are adjusted [An *adjustment* on our television set can make the picture brighter.]

ad·mit (ad mit′) *v.* **1** to permit or give the right to enter [One ticket *admits* two persons.] **2** to accept as being true; confess [Lucy will not *admit* her mistake.] —**ad·mit′ted, ad·mit′ting**

ad·o·les·cent (ad′ə les′ənt) *adj.* growing up; developing from a child to an adult. ◆*n.* a boy or girl between childhood and adulthood; teen-age person.

a·dult (ə dult′ *or* ad′ult) *adj.* grown up; having reached full size and strength [an *adult* person or plant]. ◆*n.* **1** a man or woman who is fully grown up; mature person. **2** an animal or plant that is fully developed. —**a·dult′hood** *n.*

ad·van·tage (ad van′tij) *n.* **1** a more favorable position; better chance [My speed gave me an *advantage* over them.] **2** a thing, condition, or event that can help one; benefit [What are the *advantages* of a smaller school?]

ad·ver·tise (ad′vər tīz) *v.* **1** to tell about a product in public and in such a way as to make people want to buy it [to *advertise* cars on television]. **2** to announce or ask for publicly, as in a newspaper [to *advertise* a house for rent; to *advertise* for a cook]. —**ad′ver·tised, ad′ver·tis·ing** —**ad′ver·tis′er** *n.*

accordion

alligator

ad·ver·tis·ing (ad′vər tīz′ iŋ) *n.* **1** an advertisement or advertisements. **2** the work of preparing advertisements and getting them printed or on radio and TV [*Advertising* is a major industry in this country.]

ad·vise (ad vīz′) *v.* **1** to give advice or an opinion to [The doctor *advised* me to have an operation.] **2** to notify; inform [The letter *advised* us of the time of the meeting.] —**ad·vised′, ad·vis′ing**

af·fec·tion (ə fek′shən) *n.* fond or tender feeling; warm liking.

af·ford (ə fôrd′) *v.* **1** to have money enough to spare for: *usually used with can or be able* [Can we *afford* a new car?] **2** to be able to do something without taking great risks [I can *afford* to speak frankly.]

ag·ri·cul·tur·al (ag′ri kul′chər əl) *adj.* of agriculture; of growing crops and raising livestock; farming.

ail·ment (āl′mənt) *n.* an illness; sickness.

al·li·ga·tor (al′ə gāt′ər) *n.* a large lizard like the crocodile, found in warm rivers and marshes of the U.S. and China.

al·might·y (ôl mīt′ē) *adj.* having power with no limit; all-powerful.

al·though (ôl *th*ō′) *conj.* in spite of the fact that; even if; though [*Although* the sun is shining, it may rain later.]

an·a·lyze (an′ə līz) *v.* to separate or break up any thing or idea into its parts so as to examine them and see how they fit together [to *analyze* the causes of war]. —**an′a·lyz′er** *n.*

an·cient (ān′chənt *or* ān′shənt) *adj.* **1** of times long past; belonging to the early history of people, before about 500 A.D. **2** having lasted a long time; very old [their *ancient* quarrel].

an·gle (aŋ′gəl) *n.* **1** the shape made by two straight lines meeting in a point, or by two surfaces meeting along a line. **2** the way one looks at something; point of view [Consider the problem from all *angles*.] ◆*v.* to move or bend at an angle. —**an′gled, an′gling**

an·nounce (ə nouns′) *v.* **1** to tell the public about; proclaim [to *announce* the opening of a new store]. **2** to say; tell [Mother *announced* she wasn't going with us.] —**an·nounced′, an·nounc′ing**

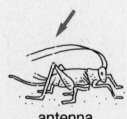

antenna

an·ten·na (an ten′ə) *n.* **1** either of a pair of slender feelers on the head of an insect, crab, lobster, etc. —*pl.* **an·ten·nae** (an ten′ē) *or* **an·ten′nas 2** a wire or set of wires used in radio and television to send and receive signals; aerial. —*pl.* **an·ten′nas**

an·ti·bod·y (an′ti bäd′e) *n.* a specialized protein that is formed in the body to neutralize a particular foreign substance that is harmful, making the body immune to it. —*pl.* **an′ti·bod′ies**

an·tic·i·pate (an tis′ə pāt′) *v.* to look forward to; expect [We *anticipate* a pleasant trip.] —**an·tic′i·pat·ed, an·tic′i·pat·ing** —**an·tic′i·pa′tion** *n.*

an·ti·dote (an′ti dōt) *n.* **1** a substance that is taken to work against the effect of a poison. **2** anything that works against an evil or unwanted condition [The party was a good *antidote* to the sadness we felt.]

☆**an·ti·freeze** (an′ti frēz′) *n.* a liquid with a low freezing point, such as alcohol, put in the water of automobile radiators to prevent freezing.

an·tique (an tēk′) *adj.* very old; of former times; made or used a long time ago. ◆*n.* a piece of furniture or silverware, a tool, etc. made many years ago [They sell *antiques* of colonial America.]

an·ti·sep·tic (an′ti sep′tik) *adj.* **1** preventing infection by killing germs. **2** free from living germs; sterile [an *antiseptic* room]. ◆*n.* any substance used to kill germs or stop their growth, as alcohol or iodine.

an·ti·so·cial (an′ti sō′shəl) *adj.* not liking to be with other people [Are you so *antisocial* that you never have visitors?]

ap·par·el (ə per′əl) *n.* clothing; garments; dress [They sell only children's *apparel*.] ◆*v.* to dress; clothe [The king was *appareled* in purple robes.] —**ap·par′eled** *or* **ap·par′elled, ap·par′el·ing** *or* **ap·par′el·ling**

ap·pear (ə pir′) *v.* **1** to come into sight or into being [A ship *appeared* on the horizon. Leaves *appear* on the tree every spring.] **2** to seem; look [He *appears* to be in good health.] **3** to come before the public [The actor will *appear* on television. The magazine *appears* monthly.]

ap·plause (ə plôz′ *or* ə pläz′) *n.* the act of showing that one enjoys or approves of something, especially by clapping one's hands.

ap·point·ment (ə point′mənt) *n.* **1** the act of appointing or the fact of being appointed [the *appointment* of Jones as supervisor]. **2** an arrangement to meet someone or be somewhere at a certain time [an *appointment* for lunch].

ap·pre·ci·ate (ə prē′shē āt′) *v.* **1** to think well of; understand and enjoy [I now *appreciate* modern art.] **2** to recognize and be grateful for [We *appreciate* all you have done for us.] —**ap·pre′ci·at·ed, ap·pre′ci·at·ing** —**ap·pre′ci·a′tion** *n.*

ap·proach (ə prōch′) *v.* to come closer or draw nearer [We saw three riders *approaching*. Vacation time *approaches*.] —**ap·proach′a·ble** *adj.*

ap·prove (ə prōōv′) *v.* **1** to think or say to be good, worthwhile, etc.; be pleased with: *often used with of* [She doesn't *approve* of smoking.] **2** to give one's consent to [Has the mayor *approved* the plans?] —**ap·proved′, ap·prov′ing**

ar·gu·ment (är′gyōō mənt) *n.* **1** the act of arguing; discussion in which people disagree; dispute. **2** a reason given for or against something [What are your *arguments* for wanting to study mathematics?]

ar·range·ment (ə rānj′mənt) *n.* **1** the act of arranging or putting in order. **2** the way in which something is arranged [a new *arrangement* of pictures on the wall]. **3** a preparation; plan: *usually used in pl.*, **arrangements** [*Arrangements* have been made for the party.]

as·cend (ə send′) *v.* to go up; move upward; rise; climb [The procession *ascended* the hill.]

a·shamed (ə shāmd′) *adj.* feeling shame because something bad, wrong, or foolish was done [They were *ashamed* of having broken the window.]

as·sign·ment (ə sīn′mənt) *n.* **1** the act of assigning. **2** something assigned, as a lesson.

asst. *abbreviation for* **assistant**.

as·sure (ə shoor′) *v.* **1** to make a person sure of something; convince [What can we do to *assure* you of our friendship?] **2** to tell or promise positively [I *assure* you I'll be there.] **3** to make a doubtful thing certain; guarantee [Their gift of money *assured* the success of our campaign.] —**as·sured′, as·sur′ing**

as·ter·isk (as′tər isk) *n.* a sign in the shape of a star (*) used in printing and writing to call attention to a footnote or other explanation or to show that something has been left out.

as·ter·oid (as′tər oid) *n.* any of the many small planets that move in orbits around the sun between the orbits of Mars and Jupiter.

as·tro·naut (as′trə nôt *or* as′trə nät) *n.* a person trained to make rocket flights in outer space.

ath·lete (ath′lēt) *n.* a person who is skilled at games, sports, or exercises in which one needs strength, skill, and speed.

at·tain (ə tān′) *v.* to get by working hard; gain; achieve [to *attain* success].

at·tor·ney (ə tur′nē) *n.* a lawyer. —*pl.* **at·tor′neys**

auc·tion (ôk′shən *or* äk′shən) *n.* a public sale at which each thing is sold to the person offering to pay the highest price. ◆ *v.* to sell at an auction [They *auctioned* their furniture instead of taking it with them.]

Aus·tral·ia (ô strāl′yə *or* ä strāl′yə) **1** an island continent in the Southern Hemisphere, southeast of Asia. **2** a country made up of this continent and Tasmania.— **Aus·tral′ian** *adj., n.*

au·then·tic (ô then′tik *or* ä then′tik) *adj.* **1** that can be believed; reliable; true [an *authentic* news report]. **2** that is genuine; real [an *authentic* antique]. —**au·then′ti·cal·ly** *adv.*

au·to·mat·ic (ôt′ə mat′ik *or* ät′ə mat′ik) *adj.* **1** done without thinking about it, as though by a machine; unconscious [Breathing is usually *automatic*.] **2** moving or working by itself [*automatic* machinery].—**au′to·mat′i·cal·ly** *adv.*

au·tumn (ôt′əm *or* ät′əm) *n.* the season of the year that comes between summer and winter; fall. ◆ *adj.* of or like autumn. —**au·tum·nal** (ô tum′n'l) *adj.*

a·vi·a·tor (ā′vē āt′ər) *n.* a person who flies airplanes; pilot.

☆**av·o·ca·do** (av′ə kä′dō *or* äv′ə kä′dō) *n.* a tropical fruit that is shaped like a pear and has a thick, green or purplish skin and a single large seed. Its yellow, buttery flesh is used in salads, sauces, dips, etc. —*pl.* **av′o·ca′dos**

a·void (ə void′) *v.* **1** to keep away from; get out of the way of; shun [to *avoid* crowds]. **2** to keep from happening [Try to *avoid* spilling the milk.] —**a·void′a·ble** *adj.* —**a·void′ance** *n.*

awe·some (ô′səm *or* ä′səm) *adj.* **1** causing one to feel awe [The burning building was an *awesome* sight.] **2** showing awe [He had an *awesome* look on his face.]

awn·ing (ôn′iŋ *or* än′iŋ) *n.* a covering made of canvas, metal, or wood fixed to a frame over a window, door, etc. to keep off the sun and rain.

a·wry (ə rī′) *adv., adj.* **1** twisted to one side; askew [The curtains were blown *awry* by the wind.] **2** wrong; amiss [Our plans went *awry*.]

ax·le (ak′səl) *n.* **1** a rod on which a wheel turns, or one connected to a wheel so that they turn together. **2** the bar joining two opposite wheels, as of an automobile.

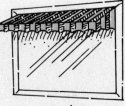
awning

Bb

back·gam·mon (bak′gam ən) *n.* a game played on a special board by two people. The players have fifteen pieces each, which they move after throwing dice to get a number.

bad·min·ton (bad′mint'n *or* bad′mit'n) *n.* a game like tennis, in which a cork with feathers in one end is batted back and forth across a high net by players using light rackets.

bail (bāl) *n.* money left with a law court as a guarantee that an arrested person will appear for trial. ◆ *v.* to have an arrested person set free by giving bail.

bail·iff (bāl′if) *n.* **1** a sheriff's assistant. **2** an officer who has charge of prisoners and jurors in a court.

bank·rupt (baŋk′rupt) *adj.* not able to pay one's debts and freed by law from the need for doing so [Any property a *bankrupt* person may still have is usually divided among those to whom the person owes money.]

ban·quet (baŋ′kwət) *n.* a formal dinner or feast for many people. Banquets, during which speeches are made, are often held to celebrate something or to raise money.

a	ask, fat
ā	ape, date
ä	car, lot
e	elf, ten
ē	even, meet
i	is, hit
ī	ice, fire
ō	open, go
ô	law, horn
oi	oil, point
oo	look, pull
o͞o	ooze, tool
ou	out, crowd
u	up, cut
u	fur, fern
ə	a in ago
	e in agent
	e in father
	i in unity
	o in collect
	u in focus
ch	chin, arch
ŋ	ring, singer
sh	she, dash
th	thin, truth
th	then, father
zh	s in pleasure

bare·ly (ber′lē) *adv.* **1** only just; no more than; scarcely [It is *barely* a year old.] **2** in a bare way; meagerly [a *barely* furnished room, with only a bed in it].

be·lief (bē lēf′) *n.* **1** a believing or feeling that certain things are true or real; faith [You cannot destroy my *belief* in the honesty of most people.] **2** trust or confidence [I have *belief* in Pat's ability.] **3** anything believed or accepted as true; opinion [What are your religious *beliefs*?]

be·lieve (bē lēv′) *v.* **1** to accept as true or real [Can we *believe* that story?] **2** to have trust or confidence [I know you will win; I *believe* in you.] —**be·lieved′, be·liev′ing** —**be·liev′a·ble** *adj.* —**be·liev′er** *n.*

bi·an·nu·al (bī an′yoo əl) *adj.* coming twice a year. —**bi·an′nu·al·ly** *adv.*

bi·fo·cals (bī′fō kəlz) *pl.n.* eyeglassses in which each lens has two parts, one for reading and seeing nearby objects and the other for seeing things far away.

bil·lion (bil′yən) *n., adj.* a thousand millions (1,000,000,000).

bin·oc·u·lars (bi näk′yə lərz) *n.pl.* a pair of small telescopes fastened together for use with both eyes [Field glasses are a kind of *binoculars*.]

binoculars

biog. *abbreviation for* **biographical** *or* **biography.**

bi·ol·o·gy (bī äl′ə jē) *n.* the science of plants and animals; the study of living things and the way they live and grow. —**bi·ol′o·gist** *n.*

bi·plane (bī′plān) *n.* the earlier type of airplane with two main wings, one above the other.

bis·cuit (bis′kit) *n.* ☆a small bread roll made of dough quickly raised with baking powder.

bi·sect (bī sekt′ *or* bī′sekt) *v.* **1** to cut into two parts [Budapest is *bisected* by the Danube River.] **2** to divide into two equal parts [A circle is *bisected* by its diameter.]

bit·ter (bit′ər) *adj.* **1** having a strong, often unpleasant taste [The seed in a peach pit is *bitter*.] **2** full of sorrow, pain, or discomfort [Poor people often suffer *bitter* hardships.] —**bit′ter ·ness** *n.*

bi·week·ly (bī wēk′lē) *adj., adv.* once every two weeks.

bleak (blēk) *adj.* **1** open to wind and cold; not sheltered; bare [the *bleak* plains]. **2** cold and cutting; harsh [a *bleak* wind]. **3** not cheerful; gloomy [a *bleak* story]. **4** not hopeful or promising [a *bleak* future].

Blvd. *abbreviation for* **Boulevard.**

boil (boil) *v.* **1** to bubble up and become steam or vapor by being heated [Water *boils* at 100°C.] **2** to heat a liquid until it bubbles up in this way [to *boil* water]. **3** to cook in a boiling liquid [to *boil* potatoes].

bor·ough (bur′ō) *n.* **1** in some States, a town that has a charter to govern itself. **2** one of the five main divisions of New York City.

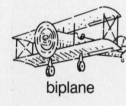

biplane

bor·row (bär′ō *or* bôr′ō) *v.* **1** to get to use something for a while by agreeing to return it later [You can *borrow* that book from the library.] **2** to take another's word, idea, etc. and use it as one's own [The Romans *borrowed* many Greek myths.] —**bor′row·er** *n.*

bough (bou) *n.* a large branch of a tree.

boul·der (bōl′dər) *n.* any large rock made round and smooth by weather and water.

boun·ti·ful (boun′tə fəl) *adj.* **1** giving much gladly; generous [a *bountiful* patron]. **2** more than enough; plentiful [a *bountiful* harvest]. —**boun′ti·ful·ly** *adv.*

bowl·ing (bōl′iŋ) *n.* a game in which each player rolls a heavy ball along a wooden lane (**bowling alley**), trying to knock down ten wooden pins at the far end.

brave (brāv) *adj.* willing to face danger, pain, or trouble; not afraid; full of courage. —**brav′er, brav′est** ◆*n.* a Native American warrior. ◆*v.* to face without fear; defy [We *braved* the storm.] —**braved, brav′ing** —**brave′ly** *adv.* —**brave′ness** *n.*

brawn·y (brôn′ē *or* brän′ē) *adj.* strong and muscular. —**brawn′i·er, brawn′i·est** —**brawn′i·ness** *n.*

break·a·ble (brāk′ə bəl) *adj.* that can be broken or that is likely to break.

brief (brēf) *adj.* **1** not lasting very long; short in time [a *brief* visit]. **2** using just a few words; not wordy; concise [a *brief* news report]. —**brief′ly** *adv.* —**brief′ness** *n.*

bright (brīt) *adj.* **1** shining; giving light; full of light [a *bright* star; a *bright* day]. **2** very strong or brilliant in color or sound [a *bright* red; the *bright* tones of a cornet]. **3** lively; cheerful [a *bright* smile]. **4** having a quick mind; clever [a *bright* child]. ◆*adv.* in a bright manner [stars shining *bright*]. —**bright′ly** *adv.* —**bright′ness** *n.*

broc·co·li (bräk′ə lē) *n.* a vegetable whose tender shoots and loose heads of tiny green buds are cooked for eating.

bro·chure (brō shoor′) *n.* a pamphlet, now especially one that advertises something.

bronze (bränz) *n.* **1** a metal that is an alloy of copper and tin. **2** a reddish-brown color like that of bronze. —**bronzed, bronz′ing** *v.*

bruise (brooz) *v.* **1** to hurt a part of the body, as by a blow, without breaking the skin [Her *bruised* knee turned black-and-blue.] **2** to hurt the outside of [Some peaches fell and were *bruised*.] —**bruised, bruis′ing** ◆*n.* an injury to the outer part or flesh that does not break the skin but darkens it in color.

budg·et (buj′ət) *n.* a careful plan for spending the money that is received in a certain period. ◆*v.* **1** to plan the spending of money; make a budget. **2** to plan in detail how to spend [I *budget* my time as well as my money.]

buf·fet (bə fā′ *or* boo fā′) *n.* platters of food on a buffet or table from which people serve themselves.

build·ing (bil′diŋ) *n.* **1** anything that is built with walls and a roof; a structure, as a house, factory, or school. **2** the act or work of one who builds.

bun·ga·low (buŋ′gə lō) *n.* a small house with one story and an attic.

Cc

cal·ci·um (kal′sē əm) *n.* a chemical element that is a soft, silver-white metal. It is found combined with other elements in the bones and teeth of animals and in limestone, marble, chalk, etc.

cal·cu·late (kal′kyoo lāt′) *v.* **1** to find out by using arithmetic; compute [*Calculate* the amount of cloth you will need for the skirt.] **2** to find out by reasoning; estimate [Try to *calculate* the effect of your decision.] —**cal′cu·lat·ed, cal′cu·lat·ing**

cal·cu·la·tion (kal′kyoo lā′shən) *n.* **1** the act of calculating. **2** the answer found by calculating. **3** careful or shrewd thought or planning.

cam·er·a (kam′ər ə) *n.* **1** a closed box for taking pictures. The light that enters when a lens or hole at one end is opened by a shutter forms an image on the film or plate at the other end. **2** that part of a TV transmitter which picks up the picture to be sent and changes it to electrical signals.

cam·paign (kam pān′) *n.* a series of planned actions for getting something done [a *campaign* to get someone elected]. ◆*v.* to take part in a campaign. —**cam·paign′er** *n.*

Ca·na·di·an (kə nā′dē ən) *adj.* of Canada or its people. ◆*n.* a person born or living in Canada.

can·ta·loupe or **can·ta·loup** (kan′tə lōp) *n.* a muskmelon, especially a kind that has a hard, rough skin and sweet, juicy, orange-colored flesh.

can·vas (kan′vəs) *n.* **1** a strong, heavy cloth of hemp, cotton, or linen, used for tents, sails, oil paintings, etc. **2** an oil painting on canvas.

ca·pac·i·ty (kə pas′i tē) *n.* **1** the amount of space that can be filled; room for holding [a jar with a *capacity* of 2 quarts]. **2** the ability to be, learn, or become; skill or fitness [the *capacity* to be an actor]. —*pl.* —**ca·pac′i·ties**

cap·i·tal (kap′it′l) *adj.* where the government is located [a *capital* city]. *See also* **capital letter**. ◆*n.* **1** same as **capital letter**. **2** a city or town where the government of a state or nation is located.

capital letter the form of a letter that is used to begin a sentence or a name [THIS IS PRINTED IN CAPITAL LETTERS.]

Cap·i·tol (kap′it′l) the building in which the U.S. Congress meets, in Washington, D.C. ◆*n. usually* **capitol** the building in which a State legislature meets.

car·bo·hy·drate (kär′bō hī′drāt) *n.* any of a group of substances made up of carbon, hydrogen, and oxygen, including the sugars and starches. Carbohydrates are an important part of our diet.

car·bon (kär′bən) *n.* a chemical element that is not a metal, found in all plant and animal matter. Diamonds and graphite are pure carbon, while coal and charcoal are forms of impure carbon.

car·bu·ret·or (kär′bə rāt′ər) *n.* the part of a gasoline engine that mixes air with gasoline spray to make the mixture that explodes in the cylinders.

care·ful (ker′fəl) *adj.* **1** taking care so as not to have mistakes or accidents; cautious [Be *careful* in crossing streets.] **2** done or made with care [*careful* work]. —**care′ful·ly** *adv.* —**care′ful·ness** *n.*

car·i·ca·ture (kar′i kə chər) *n.* a picture or imitation of a person or thing in which certain features or parts are exaggerated in a joking or mocking way. ◆*v.* to make or be a caricature of [Cartoonists often *caricature* the President.] —**car′i·ca·tured, car′i·ca·tur·ing** —**car′i·ca·tur·ist** *n.*

car·ni·val (kär′ni vəl) *n.* an entertainment that travels from place to place, with sideshows, amusement rides, refreshments, etc.

car·tridge (kär′trij) *n.* **1** the metal or cardboard tube that holds the gunpowder and the bullet or shot for use in a firearm. **2** a small container used in a larger device, as one holding ink for a pen. **3** a roll of camera film in a case. **4** a unit holding the needle for a phonograph.

cas·tle (kas′əl) *n.* a large building or group of buildings that was the home of a king or noble in the Middle Ages. Castles had thick walls, moats, etc. to protect them against attack.

cas·u·al (kazh′oo əl) *adj.* **1** happening by chance; not planned [a *casual* visit]. **2** not having any particular purpose [a *casual* glance; a *casual* remark]. **3** for wear at times when dressy clothes are not needed [*casual* sports clothes]. —**cas′u·al·ly** *adv.* —**cas′u·al·ness** *n.*

ca·ter (kā′tər) *v.* to provide food and service [Smith's business is *catering* for large parties.] —**ca′ter·er** *n.*

cau·li·flow·er (kôl′ə flou ər *or* käl′ə flou ər) *n.* a kind of cabbage with a head of white, fleshy flower clusters growing tightly together.

ceil·ing (sēl′iŋ) *n.* the inside top part of a room, opposite the floor.

bungalow

a	ask, fat
ā	ape, date
ä	car, lot
e	elf, ten
ē	even, meet
i	is, hit
ī	ice, fire
ō	open, go
ô	law, horn
oi	oil, point
oo	look, pull
ōō	ooze, tool
ou	out, crowd
u	up, cut
u	fur, fern
ə	a in ago
	e in agent
	e in father
	i in unity
	o in collect
	u in focus
ch	chin, arch
ŋ	ring, singer
sh	she, dash
th	thin, truth
th	then, father
zh	s in pleasure

cello

cel·e·brate (sel′ə brāt) *v.* **1** to honor a victory, the memory of something, etc. in some special way [to *celebrate* a birthday with a party; to *celebrate* the Fourth of July with fireworks]. **2** to have a good time: *used only in everyday talk* [Let's *celebrate* when we finish painting the garage.] —**cel′e·brat·ed, cel′e·brat·ing** —**cel′e·bra′tion** *n.*

cel·lo (chel′ō) *n.* a musical instrument like a violin but larger and having a deeper tone. *Its full name is* **violoncello**. —*pl.* **cel′los** or **cel·li** (chel′ē)

cha·grin (shə grin′) *n.* a feeling of being embarrassed and annoyed because one has failed or has been disappointed. ◆ *v.* to embarrass and annoy [Our hostess was *chagrined* when the guest to be honored failed to appear.]

chal·lenge (chal′ənj) *v.* **1** to question the right or rightness of; refuse to believe unless proof is given [to *challenge* a claim; to *challenge* something said or the person who says it]. **2** to call to take part in a fight or contest; dare [He *challenged* her to a game of chess.] **3** to call for skill, effort, or imagination [That puzzle will really *challenge* you.] —**chal′lenged, chal′leng·ing** ◆ *n.* **1** the act of challenging [I accepted his *challenge* to a race.] **2** something that calls for much effort; hard task [Climbing Mt. Everest was a real *challenge.*]

change·a·ble (chān′jə bəl) *adj.* changing often or likely to change [*changeable* weather].

check·ers (chek′ərz) *n.pl.* a game played on a checkerboard by two players, each of whom tries to capture all 12 pieces of the other player: *used with a singular verb.*

chem·is·try (kem′is trē) *n.* the science in which substances are examined to find out what they are made of, how they act under different conditions, and how they are combined or separated to form other substances.

chess (ches) *n.* a game played on a chessboard by two players. Each has 16 pieces (called **chess′men**) which are moved in trying to capture the other's pieces and checkmate the other's king.

chisel

chis·el (chiz′əl) *n.* a tool having a strong blade with a sharp edge for cutting or shaping wood, stone, or metal. ◆ *v.* to cut or shape with a chisel. —**chis′eled** or **chis′elled, chis′el·ing** or **chis′el·ling** —**chis′el·er** or **chis′el·ler** *n.*

chives (chīvz) *n.pl.* a plant related to the onion, having slender, hollow leaves that are chopped up and used for flavoring.

cho·les·ter·ol (kə les′tər ôl) *n.* a waxy substance found in the body and in certain foods. When there is much of it in the blood, it is thought to cause hardening of the arteries.

chor·us (kôr′əs) *n.* **1** a group of people trained to speak or sing together [Ancient Greek plays usually had a *chorus* which explained what the actors were doing.] **2** singers and dancers who work together as a group and not as soloists, as in a musical show. **3** the part of a song that is repeated after each verse; refrain [The *chorus* of "The Battle Hymn of the Republic" begins "Glory, glory, hallelujah!"] ◆ *v.* to speak or sing together or at the same time [The Senators *chorused* their approval.]

chrome (krōm) *n.* chromium, especially when it is used to plate steel or other metal

chute (shoot) *n.* **1** a part of a river where the water moves swiftly. **2** a waterfall. **3** a long tube or slide in which things are dropped or slid down to a lower place [a laundry *chute*].

cir·cuit (sur′kət) *n.* **1** the act of going around something; course or journey in a circle [The moon's *circuit* of the earth takes about 28 days.] **2** the complete path of an electric current; also, any hookup, wiring, etc. that is connected into this path.

cir·cu·la·tion (sur′kyə lā′shən) *n.* **1** free movement around from place to place [The fan kept the air in *circulation*.] **2** the movement of blood through the veins and arteries. **3** the average number of copies of a magazine or newspaper sent out or sold in a certain period [Our school paper has a weekly *circulation* of 630.]

cir·cum·fer·ence (sər kum′fər əns) *n.* **1** the line that bounds a circle or other rounded figure or area. **2** the length of such a line [The *circumference* of the pool is 70 feet.]

clause (klôz *or* kläz) *n.* a group of words that includes a subject and a verb, but that forms only part of a sentence: in the sentence "She will visit us if she can," "She will visit us" is a clause that could be a complete sentence, and "if she can" is a clause that depends on the first clause.

clean·ly (klen′lē) *adj.* always keeping clean or kept clean. —**clean′li·ness** *n.*

clev·er (klev′ər) *adj.* **1** quick in thinking or learning; smart; intelligent. **2** showing skill or fine thinking [a *clever* move in chess]. —**clev′er·ly** *adv.* —**clev′er·ness** *n.*

close (klōz) *v.* **1** to make no longer open; shut [*Close* the door.] **2** to bring or come to a finish; end [to *close* a speech]. —**closed, clos′ing** ◆ *n.* an end; finish.

clothes (klōz *or* klō*th*z) *n.pl.* cloth or other material made up in different shapes and styles to wear on the body; dresses, suits, hats, underwear, etc.; garments.

Co. or **co.** *abbreviation for* **company**, **county**.

coarse (kôrs) *adj.* **1** made up of rather large particles; not fine [*coarse* sand]. **2** rough or harsh to the touch [*coarse* cloth]. **3** not polite or refined; vulgar; crude [a *coarse* joke]. —**coarse′ly** *adv.* —**coarse′ness** *n.*

co·coa (kō′kō) *n.* **1** a powder made from roasted cacao seeds, used in making chocolate. **2** a drink made from this powder by adding sugar and hot water or milk.

cof·fee (kôf′ē *or* käf′e) *n.* a dark-brown drink made by brewing the roasted and ground seeds of a tropical plant in boiling water.

co·logne (kə lōn′) *n.* a sweet-smelling liquid like perfume, but not so strong.

col·umn (käl′əm) *n.* **1** a long, generally round, upright support; pillar. Columns usually stand in groups to hold up a roof or other part of a building, but they are sometimes used just for decoration. **2** any long, upright thing like a column [a *column* of water; the spinal *column*]. **3** any of the long sections of print lying side by side on a page and separated by a line or blank space [Each page of this book has two *columns*.]

com·bi·na·tion (käm′bi nā′shən) *n.* **1** the act of combining or joining [He succeeded by a *combination* of hard work and luck.] **2** the series of numbers or letters that must be turned to in the right order to open a kind of lock called a ☆**combination lock** [Most safes have a *combination lock*.]

com·bine (kəm bīn′) *v.* to come or bring together; join; unite [to *combine* work with pleasure; to *combine* chemical elements]. —**com·bined′, com·bin′ing**

com·ment (käm′ent) *n.* a remark or note that explains or gives an opinion [The teacher's *comments* on the poem helped us to understand it.] ◆*v.* to make comments or remarks [Doctors should not *comment* on their patients to others.]

com·mo·tion (kə mō′shən) *n.* a noisy rushing about; confusion [There was a great *commotion* as the ship began to sink.]

com·mu·ni·cate (kə myoo′nə kāt′) *v.* to make known; give or exchange information [to *communicate* by telephone; to *communicate* ideas by the written word]. —**com·mu′ni·cat·ed, com·mu′ni·cat·ing**

com·mu·ni·ca·tion (kə myoo′ni kā′shən) *n.* **1** the act of communicating [the *communication* of disease; the *communication* of news]. **2** a way or means of communicating [The hurricane broke down all *communication* between the two cities.] **3** information, message, letter, etc. [They received the news in a *communication* from their lawyer.]

com·pact (kəm pakt′ *or* käm′pakt) *adj.* closely and firmly packed together [Tie the clothes in a neat, *compact* bundle.] ◆*n.* (käm′pakt) ☆a model of automobile smaller and cheaper than the standard model.

com·pa·ny (kum′pə nē) *n.* a group of people; especially, a group joined together in some work or activity [a *company* of actors; a business *company*]. —*pl.* **com′pa·nies**

com·pare (kəm per′) *v.* **1** to describe as being the same; liken [The sound of thunder can be *compared* to the roll of drums.] **2** to examine certain things in order to find out how they are alike or different [How do the two cars *compare* in size and price?] —**com·pared′, com·par′ing**

com·pel (kəm pel′) *v.* to make do something; force [Many men were *compelled* by the draft to serve in the armed forces.] —**com·pelled′, com·pel′ling**

com·pet·i·tor (kəm pet′i tər) *n.* a person who competes; rival [business *competitors*].

com·plaint (kəm plānt′) *n.* **1** the act of complaining or finding fault. **2** something to complain about [The tenants gave a list of their *complaints* to the landlord.]

com·plete (kəm plēt′) *adj.* **1** having no parts missing; full; whole [a *complete* deck of cards]. **2** finished; ended [No one's education is ever really *complete*.] **3** thorough; perfect [I have *complete* confidence in my doctor.] ◆*v.* to make complete; finish or make whole, full, perfect, etc. [When will the new road be *completed*?] —**com·plet′ed, com·plet′ing** —**com·plete′ly** *adv.*

com·po·si·tion (käm′pə zish′ən) *n.* **1** the act, work, or style of composing something. **2** something composed, as a piece of writing or a musical work. **3** the parts or materials of a thing and the way they are put together [We shall study the *composition* of this gas.]

com·po·sure (kəm pō′zhər) *n.* calmness of mind; self-control; serenity.

com·pound (käm′pound) *n.* anything made up of two or more parts or materials; mixture. ◆*adj.* made up of two or more parts ["Handbag" is a *compound* word.]

con·ceal (kən sēl′) *v.* to hide or keep secret; put or keep out of sight [I *concealed* my amusement. The thief *concealed* the stolen jewelry in a pocket.]

con·ceit (kən sēt′) *n.* too high an opinion of oneself; vanity [His *conceit* shows when he talks about how bright he is.] —**con·ceit′ed** *adj.*

con·ces·sion·aire (kən sesh ə ner′) *n.* the owner or operator of a business, such as a refreshment stand.

con·demn (kən dem′) *v.* **1** to say that a person or thing is wrong or bad [We *condemn* cruelty to animals.] **2** to declare to be guilty; convict [A jury tried and *condemned* them.] —**con·dem·na·tion** (kän′dem nā′shən) *n.*

con·fer·ence (kän′fər əns) *n.* a meeting of people to discuss something [A *conference* on education was held in Washington.]

con·fet·ti (kən fet′ē) *pl.n.* [*used with a singular verb*] bits of colored paper thrown about at carnivals and parades [*Confetti* was all over the street.]

column

a	**ask, fat**
ā	**ape, date**
ä	**car, lot**
e	**elf, ten**
ē	**even, meet**
i	**is, hit**
ī	**ice, fire**
ō	**open, go**
ô	**law, horn**
oi	**oil, point**
oo	**look, pull**
oo	**ooze, tool**
ou	**out, crowd**
u	**up, cut**
u	**fur, fern**
ə	**a in ago**
	e in agent
	e in father
	i in unity
	o in collect
	u in focus
ch	**chin, arch**
ŋ	**ring, singer**
sh	**she, dash**
th	**thin, truth**
th	**then, father**
zh	**s in pleasure**

con·fir·ma·tion (kän fər mā′shən) *n.* **1** the act of confirming, or making sure. **2** something that confirms or proves.

con·fuse (kən fyo͞oz′) *v.* **1** to mix up, especially in the mind; put into disorder; bewilder [You will *confuse* us with so many questions.] **2** to fail to see or remember the difference between; mistake [You are *confusing* me with my twin.] —**con·fused′, con·fus′ing** —**con·fus·ed·ly** (kən fyo͞oz′id lē) *adv.*

con·ju·gate (kän′jə gāt) *v.* to list the different forms of a verb in person, number, and tense [*Conjugate* "to be," beginning "I am, you are, he is."] —**con′ju·gat·ed, con′ju·gat·ing** —**con′ju·ga′tion** *n.*

con·science (kän′shəns) *n.* a sense of right and wrong; feeling that keeps one from doing bad things [My *conscience* bothers me after I tell a lie.]

con·scious (kän′shəs) *adj.* aware of one's own feelings or of things around one [*conscious* of a slight noise].

con·sum·er (kən so͞om′ər) *n.* a person or thing that consumes; especially, a person who buys goods for his own needs and not to sell to others or to use in making other goods for sale.

con·tain·er (kən tān′ər) *n.* a thing for holding something; box, can, bottle, pot, etc.

con·trol (kən trōl′) *v.* **1** to have the power of ruling, guiding, or managing [A thermostat *controls* the heat.] **2** to hold back; curb [*Control* your temper!] —**con·trolled′, con·trol′ling** ◆*n.* **1** power to direct or manage [He's a poor coach, with little *control* over the team.] **2** a part or thing that controls a machine [the *controls* of an airplane]. —**con·trol′la·ble** *adj.*

con·ven·tion (kən ven′shən) *n.* a meeting of members or delegates from various places, held every year or every few years [a political *convention*; a national *convention* of English teachers].

con·ver·sa·tion (kän′vər sā′shən) *n.* a talk or a talking together.

con·vert·i·ble (kən vurt′ə bəl) *adj.* that can be converted [Matter is *convertible* into energy.] ◆*n.* ☆an automobile with a top that can be folded back.

con·vey (kən vā′) *v.* **1** to take from one place to another; carry or transport [The cattle were *conveyed* in trucks to the market.] **2** to make known; give [Please *convey* my best wishes to them.]

corps (kôr) *n.* **1** a section or a special branch of the armed forces [the Marine *Corps*]. **2** a group of people who are joined together in some work or organization [a press *corps*].

cor·re·spond·ence (kôr ə spän′dens) *n.* **1** the writing and receiving of letters [to engage in *correspondence*]. **2** the letters written or received [The *correspondence* concerning the new contract is in the file.]

coun·sel (koun′səl) *n.* **1** the act of talking together in order to exchange ideas or opinions; discussion [They took *counsel* before making the decision.] **2** the lawyer or lawyers who are handling a case. ◆*v.* to give advice to; advise [a person who *counsels* students]. —**coun′seled** or **coun′selled, coun′sel·ing** or **coun′sel·ling**

coun·se·lor or **coun·sel·lor** (koun′sə lər) *n.* **1** a person who advises; advisor. **2** a lawyer. **3** a person in charge of children at a camp.

coun·ter·act (koun tər akt′) *v.* to act against; to stop or undo the effect of [The rains will help *counteract* the dry spell.]

coun·ter·at·tack (koun′tər ə tak) *n.* an attack made in return for another attack. ◆*v.* to attack so as to answer the enemy's attack.

coun·ter·bal·ance (koun′tər bal əns) *n.* a weight, power, or force that balances or acts against another.

coun·ter·feit (koun′tər fit) *adj.* made in imitation of the real thing so as to fool or cheat people [*counterfeit* money]. ◆*n.* a thing that is counterfeit. ◆*v.* to make an imitation of in order to cheat [to *counterfeit* money]. —**coun′ter·feit·er** *n.*

coun·ter·part (koun′tər pärt) *n.* **1** a person or thing that is very much like another [He is his father's *counterpart*.] **2** a thing that goes with another thing to form a set [This cup is the *counterpart* to that saucer.]

course (kôrs) *n.* **1** a going on from one point to the next; progress in space or time [the *course* of history; the *course* of a journey]. **2** a way or path along which something moves; channel, track, etc. [a golf *course*; race*course*]. **3** a part of a meal served at one time [The main *course* was roast beef.] **4** a complete series of studies [I took a business *course* in high school.] **5** any of these studies [a mathematics *course*]. —**coursed, cours′ing**

cow·ard (kou′ərd) *n.* a person who is unable to control his fear and so shrinks from danger or trouble.

cram (kram) *v.* **1** to pack full or too full [Her suitcase is *crammed* with clothes.] **2** to stuff or force [He *crammed* the papers into a drawer.] **3** to study many facts in a hurry, as for a test. —**crammed, cram′ming**

cray·on (krā′ən *or* krā′än) *n.* a small stick of chalk, charcoal, or colored wax, used for drawing or writing. ◆*v.* to draw with crayons.

cra·zy (krā′zē) *adj.* **1** mentally ill; insane. **2** very foolish or mad [a *crazy* idea]. **3** very eager or enthusiastic: *used only in everyday talk* [I'm *crazy* about the movies.] —**cra′zi·er, cra′zi·est** —**cra′zi·ly** *adv.* —**cra′zi·ness** *n.*

cre·a·tion (krē ā′shən) *n.* **1** the act of creating. **2** the whole world and everything in it; universe. **3** anything created or brought into being.

cre·a·tive (krē ā′tiv) *adj.* creating or able to create; inventive; having imagination and ability. —**cre·a·tiv·i·ty** (krē′ā tiv′ə tē) *n.*

crepe or **crêpe** (krāp) *n.* **1** a thin, crinkled cloth. **2** (krāp *or* krep) a very thin pancake, rolled up or folded with a filling: *usually* **crêpe**.

cres·cent (kres′ənt) *n.* **1** the shape of the moon in its first or last quarter. **2** anything shaped like this, as a curved bun or roll. ◆*adj.* shaped like a crescent.

croc·o·dile (kräk′ə dīl) *n.* a large lizard like the alligator, that lives in and near tropical rivers. It has a thick, tough skin, a long tail, large jaws, and pointed teeth.

crois·sant (krə sänt′) *n.* a rich, flaky bread roll made in the form of a crescent.

cro·quet (krō kā′) *n.* an outdoor game in which the players use mallets to drive a wooden ball through hoops in the ground.

cru·el (krōō′əl) *adj.* **1** liking to make others suffer; having no mercy or pity [The *cruel* Pharaoh made slaves of the Israelites.] **2** causing pain and suffering [*cruel* insults; a *cruel* winter]. —**cru′el·ly** *adv.*

cruise (krōōz) *v.* **1** to sail or drive about from place to place, as for pleasure or in searching for something. **2** to move smoothly at a speed that is not strained [The airplane *cruised* at 300 miles per hour.] —**cruised, cruis′ing** ◆*n.* a ship voyage from place to place for pleasure.

crumb (krum) *n.* a tiny piece broken off, as of bread or cake.

crutch (kruch) *n.* a support used under the arm by a lame person to help in walking. — *pl.* **crutch′es**

crys·tal (kris′təl) *n.* **1** a clear, transparent quartz that looks like glass. **2** a very clear, sparkling glass. **3** something made of such glass, as a goblet or bowl. **4** any of the regularly shaped pieces into which many substances are formed when they become solids. A crystal has a number of flat surfaces in an orderly arrangement [Salt, sugar, and snow are made up of *crystals*.] ◆*adj.* made of crystal.

cul·ture (kul′chər) *n.* **1** improvement by study or training, especially of the mind, manners, and taste; refinement. **2** the ideas, skills, arts, tools, and way of life of a certain people in a certain time; civilization [the *culture* of the Aztecs]. —**cul′tur·al** *adj.* —**cul′tur·al·ly** *adv.*

cur·few (kur′fyōō) *n.* a time in the evening beyond which certain persons or all people must not be on the streets [Our town has a nine o'clock *curfew* for children.]

cur·ren·cy (kur′ən sē) *n.* ☆ the money in common use in any country; often, paper money. —*pl.* **cur′ren·cies**

cus·tom (kus′təm) *n.* **1** a usual thing to do; habit [It is my *custom* to have tea after dinner.] **2** something that has been done for a long time and so has become the common or regular thing to do [the *custom* of eating turkey on Thanksgiving]. **3 customs,** *pl.* taxes collected by a government on goods brought in from other countries; also, the government agency that collects these taxes. ◆*adj.* made or done to order [*custom* shoes].

cym·bal (sim′bəl) *n.* a round brass plate, used in orchestras and bands, that makes a sharp, ringing sound when it is hit. Cymbals can be used in pairs that are struck together.

cy·press (sī′prəs) *n.* an evergreen tree with cones and dark leaves.

crocodile

Dd

damp (damp) *adj.* slightly wet; moist [*damp* clothes; *damp* weather]. ◆*n.* a slight wetness; moisture [Rains caused *damp* in the basement.] —**damp′ly** *adv.* —**damp′ness** *n.*

dare (der) *v.* **1** to face bravely or boldly; defy [The hunter *dared* the dangers of the jungle.] **2** to call on someone to do a certain thing in order to show courage; challenge [She *dared* me to swim across the lake.] —**dared, dar′ing** ◆*n.* a challenge to prove that one is not afraid [I accepted her *dare* to swim across the lake.]

dar·ing (der′iŋ) *adj.* bold enough to take risks; fearless. ◆*n.* bold courage.

de·bate (dē bāt′) *v.* **1** to give reasons for or against; argue about something, especially in a formal contest between two opposite sides [The Senate *debated* the question of foreign treaties.] **2** to consider reasons for and against [I *debated* the problem in my own mind.] —**de·bat′ed, de·bat′ing** ◆*n.* the act of debating something; discussion or formal argument. —**de·bat′er** *n.*

de·brief (dē brēf′) *v.* to question someone who has ended a mission, to get information [The astronaut was *debriefed* after the space flight.]

debt (det) *n.* **1** something that one owes to another [a *debt* of $25; a *debt* of gratitude]. **2** the condition of owing [I am greatly in *debt* to you.]

de·cay (dē kā′) *v.* **1** to become rotten by the action of bacteria [The fallen apples *decayed* on the ground.] **2** to fall into ruins; become no longer sound, powerful, rich, beautiful, etc. [Spain's power *decayed* after its fleet was destroyed.] ◆*n.* a rotting or falling into ruin.

a	ask, fat
ā	ape, date
ä	car, lot
e	elf, ten
ē	even, meet
i	is, hit
ī	ice, fire
ō	open, go
ô	law, horn
oi	oil, point
oo	look, pull
ōō	ooze, tool
ou	out, crowd
u	up, cut
u	fur, fern
ə	a in ago
	e in agent
	e in father
	i in unity
	o in collect
	u in focus
ch	chin, arch
ŋ	ring, singer
sh	she, dash
th	thin, truth
th	then, father
zh	s in pleasure

de·cent (dē′sənt) *adj.* **1** proper and fitting; not to be ashamed of; respectable [*decent* manners; *decent* language]. **2** fairly good; satisfactory [a *decent* wage]. **3** kind; generous; fair [It was *decent* of you to lend me your car.] —**de′cent·ly** *adv.*

de·cep·tive (dē sep′tiv) *adj.* deceiving; not what it seems to be. —**de·cep′tive·ly** *adv.*

dec·i·bel (des′ə bəl) *n.* a unit for measuring the relative loudness of sound.

de·cline (dē klīn′) *v.* **1** to bend or slope downward [The lawn *declines* to the sidewalk.] **2** to become less in health, power, or value; decay [A person's strength usually *declines* in old age.] **3** to refuse something, especially in a polite way [I am sorry I must *decline* your invitation.] ◆ *n.* **1** the process or result of becoming less, smaller, or weaker; decay [a *decline* in prices]. **2** the last part [the *decline* of life] **3** a downward slope [We slid down the *decline.*]

dec·o·ra·tion (dek′ə rā′shən) *n.* **1** anything used for decorating; ornament [*decorations* for the Christmas tree]. **2** a medal, ribbon, etc. given as a sign of honor.

decoration

de·crease (dē krēs′ *or* dē′krēs) *v.* to make or become gradually less or smaller [She has *decreased* her weight by dieting. The pain is *decreasing.*] —**de·creased′, de·creas′ing** ◆ *n.* a decreasing or growing less [a *decrease* in profits].

ded·i·cate (ded′i kāt) *v.* **1** to set aside for a special purpose [The church was *dedicated* to the worship of God. The doctor has *dedicated* her life to cancer research.] **2** to say at the beginning of a book, etc. that it was written in honor of, or out of affection for, a certain person [He *dedicated* his novel to his wife.] —**ded′i·cat·ed, ded′i·cat·ing** —**ded′i·ca′tion** *n.*

de·fi·cien·cy (dē fish′ən sē) *n.* an amount short of what is needed; shortage [A *deficiency* of vitamin C causes scurvy.] —*pl.* **de·fi′cien·cies**

de·lete (dē lēt′) *v.* to take out or cross out something printed or written [Her name has been *deleted* from the list of members.] —**de·let′ed, de·let′ing** —**de·le·tion** (di lē′shən) *n.*

de·liv·er·y (dē liv′ər ē) *n.* the act of delivering; a transferring or distributing [daily *deliveries* to customers; the *delivery* of a prisoner into custody]. —*pl.* **de·liv′er·ies**

den·im (den′im) *n.* a coarse cotton cloth that will take hard wear and is used for work clothes or play clothes.

de·pend (dē pend′) *v.* **1** to be controlled or decided by [The attendance at the game *depends* on the weather.] **2** to put one's trust in; be sure of [You can't *depend* on the weather.] **3** to rely for help or support [They *depend* on their parents for money.]

de·pos·it (dē päz′it) *v.* **1** to place for safekeeping, as money in a bank. **2** to give as part payment or as a pledge [They *deposited* $500 on a new car.] **3** to lay down [I *deposited* my books on the chair. The river *deposits* tons of mud at its mouth.] ◆ *n.* **1** something placed for safekeeping, as money in a bank. **2** something left lying, as sand, clay, or minerals deposited by the action of wind, water, or other forces of nature.

dept. *abbreviation for* **department**.

depth (depth) *n.* **1** the fact of being deep, or how deep a thing is; deepness [the *depth* of the ocean; a closet five feet in *depth*; the *depth* of a color; the great *depth* of their love]. **2** the middle part [the *depth* of winter].

de·scend (dē send′) *v.* **1** to move down to a lower place [to *descend* from a hilltop; to *descend* a staircase]. **2** to become lesser or smaller [Prices have *descended* during the past month.] **3** to come from a certain source [They are *descended* from pioneers.]

des·ert (dez′ərt) *n.* a dry sandy region with little or no plant life. ◆ *adj.* **1** of or like a desert. **2** wild and not lived in [a *desert* island].

de·serve (də zurv′) *v.* to have a right to; be one that ought to get [This matter *deserves* thought. You *deserve* a scolding.] —**de·served′, de·serv′ing** —**de·serv′ed·ly** *adv.*

de·serv·ing (də zur′ving) *adj.* that ought to get help or a reward [a *deserving* student].

de·sign·er (də zī′nər) *n.* a person who designs or makes original plans [a dress *designer*].

de·sir·a·ble (də zīr′ə bəl) *adj.* worth wanting or having; pleasing, excellent, beautiful, etc. —**de·sir′a·bil′i·ty** *n.* —**de·sir′a·bly** *adv.*

de·spair (də sper′) *n.* a giving up or loss of hope [Sam is in *despair* of ever getting a vacation.] ◆ *v.* to lose or give up hope [The prisoner *despaired* of ever being free again.]

des·sert (də zurt′) *n.* ☆something sweet served at the end of a meal, as fruit, pie, or cake.

de·struc·tive (dē struk′tiv) *adj.* destroying or likely to destroy [a *destructive* windstorm].

de·vel·op (dē vel′əp) *v.* **1** to make or become larger, fuller, better, etc.; grow or expand [The seedling *developed* into a tree. Reading *develops* one's knowledge.] **2** to bring or come into being and work out gradually; evolve [Dr. Salk *developed* a vaccine for polio. Mold *developed* on the cheese.] **3** to treat an exposed photographic film or plate with chemicals, so as to show the picture.

di·ag·o·nal (dī ag′ə nəl) *adj.* **1** slanting from one corner to the opposite corner, as of a square. **2** going in a slanting direction [a tie with *diagonal* stripes]. ◆*n.* a diagonal line, plane, course, or part. —**di·ag′o·nal·ly** *adv.*

dic·tion·ar·y (dik′shə ner′ē) *n.* a book in which the words of a language, or of some special field, are listed in alphabetical order with their meanings, pronunciations, and other information [a school *dictionary*]. —*pl.* —**dic·tion·ar′ies**

die·sel (dē′zəl *or* dē′səl) *n. often* **Diesel 1** a kind of internal-combustion engine that burns fuel oil by using heat produced by compressing air: *also called* **diesel engine or diesel motor**. **2** a locomotive or motor vehicle with such an engine.

dif·fer·ence (dif′ər əns *or* dif′rəns) *n.* **1** the state of being different or unlike [the *difference* between right and wrong]. **2** a way in which people or things are unlike [a *difference* in size]. **3** the amount by which one quantity is greater or less than another [The *difference* between 11 and 7 is 4.]

dif·fuse (di fyoōs′) *adj.* **1** spread out; not centered in one place [This lamp gives *diffuse* light.] **2** using more words than are needed; wordy [a *diffuse* style of writing]. ◆*v.* (di fyoōz′)**1** to spread out in every direction; scatter widely [to *diffuse* light]. **2** to mix together [to *diffuse* gases or liquids].

di·gest (di jest′ *or* dī jest′) *v.* to change food in the stomach and intestines into a form that can be used by the body [Small babies cannot *digest* solid food.] —**di·gest′i·ble** *adj.*

di·no·saur (dī′nə sôr) *n.* any of a group of reptiles that lived millions of years ago. Dinosaurs had four legs and a long, tapering tail, and some were almost 100 feet long.

dis·ap·point (dis ə point′) *v.* to fail to give or do what is wanted, expected, or promised; leave unsatisfied [I am *disappointed* in the weather. You promised to come, but *disappointed* us.]

dis·ap·point·ment (dis′ə point′mənt) *n.* **1** a disappointing or being disappointed [one's *disappointment* over not winning]. **2** a person or thing that disappoints [The team is a *disappointment* to us.]

dis·ci·pline (dis′ə plin) *n.* **1** training that teaches one to obey rules and control one's behavior [the strict *discipline* of army life]. **2** the result of such training; self-control; orderliness [The pupils showed perfect *discipline*.] ◆*v.* **1** to train in discipline [Regular chores help to *discipline* children.] **2** to punish. —**dis′ci·plined, dis′ci·plin·ing**

dis·count (dis′kount) *n.* an amount taken off a price, bill, or debt [He got a 10% *discount* by paying cash, so the radio cost $90 instead of $100.] ◆*v.* to take off a certain amount as a discount from a price, bill, etc.

dis·ease (di zēz′) *n.* a condition of not being healthy; sickness; illness [Chicken pox is a common childhood *disease*. Some fungi cause *disease* in animals and plants.] —**dis·eased′** *adj.*

dis·guise (dis gīz′) *v.* **1** to make seem so different as not to be recognized [to *disguise* oneself with a false beard; to *disguise* one's voice]. **2** to hide so as to keep from being known [She *disguised* her dislike of him by being very polite.] —**dis·guised′, dis·guis′ing** ◆*n.* any clothes, makeup, way of acting, etc. used to hide who or what one is.

dis·may (dis mā′) *v.* to fill with fear or dread so that one is not sure of what to do [We were *dismayed* at the sight of the destruction.] ◆*n.* loss of courage or confidence when faced with trouble or danger [The doctor's report filled her with *dismay*.]

dis·o·bey (dis′ ō bā′) *v.* to fail to obey or refuse to obey.

dis·tort (di stôrt′) *v.* **1** to twist out of its usual shape or look [The old mirror gave a *distorted* reflection.] **2** to change so as to give a false idea [The facts were *distorted*.] —**dis·tor′tion** *n.*

dis·turb·ance (di stur′bəns) *n.* **1** a disturbing or being disturbed. **2** anything that disturbs. **3** noisy confusion; uproar; disorder.

di·vi·sor (də vī′zər) *n.* the number by which another number is divided [In $6 \div 3 = 2$, the number 3 is the *divisor*.]

dom·i·no (däm′ə nō) *n.* a small, oblong piece of wood, plastic, etc. marked with dots on one side. A set of these pieces is used in playing the game called **dominoes**, in which the halves are matched. —*pl.* **dom′i·noes** *or* **dom′i·nos**

doubt (dout) *v.* to think that something may not be true or right; be unsure of; question [I *doubt* that those are the correct facts. Never *doubt* my love.] ◆*n.* a doubting; being unsure of something [I have no *doubt* that you will win.] —**doubt′er** *n.*

dough·nut (dō′nut) *n.* a small, sweet cake fried in deep fat, usually shaped like a ring.

down·stream (doun′strēm) *adv., adj.* in the direction in which a stream is flowing.

draw·back (drô′bak *or* drä′bak) *n.* a condition that acts against one; hindrance; disadvantage.

drought (drout) *or* **drouth** (drouth) *n.* a long period of dry weather, with little or no rain.

drow·sy (drou′zē) *adj.* **1** sleepy or half asleep. **2** making one feel sleepy [*drowsy* music]. —**drow′si·er, drow′si·est** —**drow′si·ly** *adv.* —**drow′si·ness** *n.*

du·ti·ful (doōt′ə fəl *or* dyoōt′ə fəl) *adj.* doing or ready to do one's duty; having a proper sense of duty [a *dutiful* parent]. —**du′ti·ful·ly** *adv.*

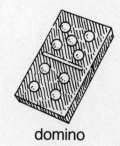

domino

a	ask, fat
ā	ape, date
ä	car, lot
e	elf, ten
ē	even, meet
i	is, hit
ī	ice, fire
ō	open, go
ô	law, horn
oi	oil, point
ơơ	look, pull
o͞o	ooze, tool
ou	out, crowd
u	up, cut
u	fur, fern
ə	a in ago
	e in agent
	e in father
	i in unity
	o in collect
	u in focus
ch	chin, arch
ŋ	ring, singer
sh	she, dash
th	thin, truth
th	then, father
zh	s in pleasure

Ee

ear·nest (ur′nəst) *adj.* not light or joking; serious or sincere [an *earnest* wish]. —**ear′nest·ly** *adv.* —**ear′nest·ness** *n.*

earn (urn) *v.* **1** to get as pay for work done [She *earns* $10 an hour.] **2** to get or deserve because of something done [He *earned* a medal for swimming.] **3** to get as profit [Your savings *earn* 5% interest.] — **earn′ings** *pl. n.*

ear·ring (ir′riŋ) *n.* an ornament worn on or in the lobe of the ear.

earth·en·ware (urth′ən wer) *n.* the coarser sort of dishes, vases, jars, etc. made of baked clay.

ea·sel (ē′zəl) *n.* a standing frame for holding an artist's canvas, a chalkboard, etc.

east·ward (ēst′wərd) *adv., adj.* in the direction of the east [an *eastward* journey; to travel *eastward*].

ech·o (ek′ō) *n.* sound heard again when sound waves bounce back from a surface. —*pl.* **ech′oes** ◆*v.* —**ech′oed, ech′o·ing**

e·clipse (e klips′) *n.* a hiding of all or part of the sun by the moon when it passes between the sun and the earth (called a **solar eclipse**); also, a hiding of the moon by the earth's shadow (called a **lunar eclipse**). ◆*v.* to cause an eclipse of; darken. —**e·clipsed′, e·clips′ing**

e·col·o·gy (ē käl′ə jē) *n.* the science that deals with the relations between all living things and the conditions that surround them. —**e·col′o·gist** *n.*

ed. *abbreviation for:* **1** edition *or* editor. —*pl.* **eds. 2** education.

ed·u·ca·tion (ej′ə kā′shən) *n.* **1** the act or work of educating or training people; teaching [a career in *education*]. **2** the things a person learns by being taught; schooling or training [a high-school *education*].

ef·fec·tive (ə fek′tiv) *adj.* **1** making a certain thing happen; especially, bringing about the result wanted [an *effective* remedy]. **2** in force or operation; active [The law becomes *effective* Monday.] **3** making a strong impression on the mind; impressive [an *effective* speaker]. —**ef·fec′tive·ly** *adv.*

ef·fi·cient (ə fish′ənt) *adj.* bringing about the result or effect wanted with the least waste of time, effort, or materials [an *efficient* method of production; an *efficient* manager]. —**ef·fi′cien·cy** *n.*

E·gyp·tian (ē jip′shən) *adj.* of Egypt, its people, or their culture. ◆*n.* **1** a person born or living in Egypt. **2** the language of the ancient Egyptians. Modern Egyptians speak Arabic.

earring

easel

e·lec·tric·i·ty (ē lek′tris′i tē) *n.* a form of energy that comes from the movement of electrons and protons. It can be produced by friction (as by rubbing wax with wool), by chemical action (as in a storage battery), or by induction (as in a dynamo or generator). Electricity is used to produce light, heat, power, etc. Electricity moving in a stream, as through a wire, is called **electric current**.

em·bank·ment (im baŋk′mənt) *n.* a long mound or wall of earth, stone, etc. used to keep back water, hold up a roadway, etc.

em·bar·go (em bär′gō) *n.* a government order that forbids certain ships to leave or enter its ports.—*pl.* **em·bar′goes** ◆*v.* to put an embargo upon. —**em·bar′goed, em·bar′go·ing**

em·bat·tle (em bat′l) *v.* to prepare for battle. —**em·bat′tled, em·bat′tling**

em·bel·lish (em bel′ish) *v.* to decorate or improve by adding something [to *embellish* a talk with details]. —**em·bel′lish·ment** *n.*

em·bit·ter (em bit′ər) *v.* to make bitter; make feel angry or hurt [He was *embittered* by her remark.]

em·bla·zon (em blā′zən) *v.* **1** to decorate with bright colors or in a rich, showy way [The bandstand was *emblazoned* with bunting.] **2** to mark with an emblem [The shield was *emblazoned* with a golden lion.]

em·broi·der·y (em broi′dər ē) *n.* **1** the art or work of embroidering. **2** an embroidered decoration. —*pl.* **em·broi′der·ies**

em·pha·size (em′fə sīz) *v.* to give special force or attention to; stress [I want to *emphasize* the importance of honesty.] —**em′pha·sized, em′pha·siz·ing**

em·ploy·ment (e ploi′mənt) *n.* **1** the condition of being employed. **2** one's work, trade, or profession.

em·pow·er (em pou′ər) *v.* to give certain power or rights to; authorize [The warrant *empowered* the police to search the house.]

emp·ty (emp′tē) *adj.* having nothing or no one in it; not occupied; vacant [an *empty* jar; an *empty* house]. —**emp′ti·er, emp′ti·est** ◆*v.* **1** to make or become empty [The auditorium was *emptied* in ten minutes.] **2** to take out or pour out [*Empty* the dirty water in the sink.] **3** to flow out; discharge [The Amazon *empties* into the Atlantic.] —**emp′tied, emp′ty·ing** —*pl.* **emp′ties** —**emp′ti·ly** *adv.* —**emp′ti·ness** *n.*

en·com·pass (en kum′pəs) *v.* **1** to surround on all sides; enclose or encircle [a lake *encompassed* by mountains]. **2** to have in it; contain or include [A dictionary *encompasses* much information.]

en·cour·age (en kur′ij) *v.* **1** to give courage or hope to; make feel more confident [Praise *encouraged* her to try harder.] **2** to give help to; aid; promote [Rain *encourages* the growth of plants.] —**en·cour′aged, en·cour′ag·ing** —**en·cour′age·ment** *n.*

en·dan·ger (en dān′jər) *v.* to put in danger or peril [to *endanger* one's life].

en·dow (en dou′) *v.* **1** to provide with some quality or thing [a person *endowed* with musical talent; a land *endowed* with natural resources]. **2** to provide a gift of money to a college, hospital, museum, etc., that will bring a regular income to help support it. —**en·dow′ment** *n.*

en·gage (en gāj′) *v.* **1** to promise to marry [Harry is *engaged* to Grace.] **2** to promise or undertake to do something [She *engaged* to tutor the child after school.] **3** to draw into; involve [She *engaged* him in conversation.] —**en·gaged′, en·gag′ing**

Eng·lish (iŋ′glish) *adj.* of England, its people, language, etc. ◆*n.* **1** the language spoken in England, the U.S., Canada, Australia, New Zealand, Liberia, etc. **2** a course in school for studying the English language or English literature.

en·grave (en grāv′) *v.* **1** to carve or etch letters, designs, etc. on [a date *engraved* on a building]. **2** to cut or etch a picture, lettering, etc. into a metal plate, wooden block, etc. to be used for printing; also, to print from such a plate, block, etc. [an *engraved* invitation]. —**en·graved′, en·grav′ing** —**en·grav′er** *n.*

en·light·en (en līt′n) *v.* to get someone to have knowledge or know the truth; get rid of ignorance or false beliefs; inform. —**en·light′en·ment** *n.*

en·list (en list′) *v.* **1** to join or get someone to join; especially, to join some branch of the armed forces [She *enlisted* in the navy. This office *enlisted* ten new recruits.] **2** to get the support of [Try to *enlist* your parents' help.] —**en·list′ment** *n.*

en·roll or **en·rol** (en rōl′) *v.* **1** to write one's name in a list, as in becoming a member; register [New students must *enroll* on Monday.] **2** to make someone a member [We want to *enroll* you in our swim club.] —**en·rolled′, en·roll′ing**

en·roll·ment or **en·rol·ment** (en rōl′mənt) *n.* **1** the act of enrolling. **2** the number of people enrolled.

en·sure (en shoor′) *v.* **1** to make sure or certain [Good weather will *ensure* a large attendance.] **2** to make safe; protect [Seat belts help to *ensure* you against injury in a car accident.] —**en·sured′, en·sur′ing**

e·qui·lat·er·al (ē′kwi lat′er əl) *adj.* having all sides equal in length.

e·quip (ē kwip′) *v.* to provide with what is needed; outfit [The soldiers were *equipped* for battle. The car is *equipped* with power brakes.] —**e·quipped′, e·quip′ping**

☆**es·ca·la·tor** (es′kə lāt′ər) *n.* a stairway whose steps are part of an endless moving belt, for carrying people up or down.

es·cape (e skāp′) *v.* **1** to break loose; get free, as from prison. **2** to keep from getting hurt, killed, etc.; keep safe from; avoid [Very few people *escaped* the plague.] —**es·caped′, es·cap′ing** ◆*n.* **1** the act of escaping [The prisoners made their plans for an *escape*.] **2** a way of escaping [The fire closed in and there seemed to be no *escape*.]

Es·ki·mo (es′kə mō) *n.* **1** any member of a group of people who live mainly in the arctic regions of the Western Hemisphere. —*pl.* **Es′ki·mos** or **Es′ki·mo 2** the language of the Eskimos. ◆*adj.* of the Eskimos.

es·say (es′ā) *n.* a short piece of writing on some subject, giving the writer's personal ideas.

es·teem (e stēm′) *v.* to have a good opinion of; regard as valuable; respect [I *esteem* his praise above all other.] ◆*n.* good opinion; high regard; respect [to hold someone in high *esteem*].

etc. *abbreviation for* et cetera.

e·vap·o·rate (ē vap′ə rāt) *v.* **1** to change into vapor [Heat *evaporates* water. The perfume in the bottle has *evaporated*.] **2** to disappear like vapor; vanish [Our courage *evaporated* when we saw the lion.] **3** to make thicker by heating so as to take some of the water from [to *evaporate* milk]. —**e·vap′o·rat·ed, e·vap′o·rat·ing** —**e·vap′o·ra′tion** *n.*

☆**ev·er·glade** (ev′ər glād) *n.* a large swamp.

ex. *abbreviation for* **example, extra.**

ex·cel·lence (ek′sə ləns) *n.* the fact of being better or greater; extra goodness [We all praised the *excellence* of their singing.]

ex·cept (ek sept′) *prep.* leaving out; other than; but [Everyone *except* you liked the movie.] ◆*v.* to leave out; omit; exclude [Only a few of the students were *excepted* from her criticism.] ◆*conj.* were it not that; only: *used only in everyday talk* [I'd go with you *except* I'm tired.]

ex·cit·ing (ek sīt′iŋ) *adj.* causing excitement; stirring; thrilling [an *exciting* story].

ex·haust (eg zôst′ *or* eg zäst′) *v.* **1** to use up completely [Our drinking water was soon *exhausted*.] **2** to let out the contents of; make completely empty [The leak soon *exhausted* the gas tank.] **3** to use up the strength of; tire out; weaken [They are *exhausted* from playing tennis.] ◆*n.* the used steam or gas that comes from the cylinders of an engine; especially, the fumes from the gasoline engine in an automobile.

ex·hib·it (eg zib′it) *v.* to show or display to the public [to *exhibit* stamp collections]. ◆*n.* **1** something exhibited to the public [an art *exhibit*]. **2** something shown as evidence in a court of law.

engrave

a	ask, fat
ā	ape, date
ä	car, lot
e	elf, ten
ē	even, meet
i	is, hit
ī	ice, fire
ō	open, go
ô	law, horn
oi	oil, point
͡oo	look, pull
͞oo	ooze, tool
ou	out, crowd
u	up, cut
ʉ	fur, fern
ə	a in ago
	e in agent
	e in father
	i in unity
	o in collect
	u in focus
ch	chin, arch
ŋ	ring, singer
sh	she, dash
th	thin, truth
th	then, father
zh	s in pleasure

ex·ist·ence (eg zis′təns) *n.* **1** the condition of being; an existing. **2** life or a way of life [a happy *existence*]. —**ex·ist′ent** *adj.*

ex·pe·ri·ence (ek spir′ē əns) *n.* **1** the fact of living through a happening or happenings [*Experience* teaches us many things.] **2** something that one has done or lived through [This trip was an *experience* that I'll never forget.] **3** skill that one gets by training, practice, and work [a lawyer with much *experience*]. ◆*v.* to have the experience of [to *experience* success]. —**ex·pe′ri·enced, ex·pe′ri·enc·ing**

ex·pla·na·tion (eks′plə nā′shən) *n.* **1** the act of explaining [This plan needs *explanation*.] **2** something that explains [This long nail is the *explanation* for the flat tire.] **3** a meaning given in explaining [different *explanations* of the same event].

ex·ploit (eks′ploit) *n.* a daring act or bold deed [the *exploits* of Robin Hood]. ◆*v.* (ek sploit′) to use in a selfish way; take unfair advantage of [Children were *exploited* when they had to work in factories.] —**ex′ploi·ta′tion** *n.*

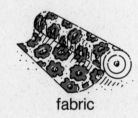

fabric

ex·plore (ek splôr′) *v.* **1** to travel in a region that is unknown or not well known, in order to find out more about it [to *explore* a wild jungle]. **2** to look into or examine carefully [to *explore* a problem]. —**ex·plored′, ex·plor′ing** —**ex′plo·ra′tion** *n.* —**ex·plor′er** *n.*

ex·po·sure (ek spō′zhər) *n.* **1** the fact of being exposed [tanned by *exposure* to the sun]. **2** the time during which film in a camera is exposed to light; also, a section of film that can be made into one picture [Give this film a short *exposure*. There are twelve *exposures* on this film.]

ex·tra·ter·res·tri·al (eks′trə tər res′trē əl) *adj.* being, happening, or coming from a place not the earth [a science fiction story about *extraterrestrial* beings].

ex·treme (ek strēm′) *adj.* **1** to the greatest degree; very great [*extreme* pain]. **2** far from what is usual; also, very far from the center of opinion [She holds *extreme* political views.] ◆*n.* either of two things that are as different or as far from each other as possible [the *extremes* of laughter and tears]. —**ex·treme′ly** *adv.*

eye·sight (ī′sīt) *n.* **1** the ability to see; sight; vision [keen *eyesight*]. **2** the distance a person can see [Keep within *eyesight*!]

fab·ric (fab′rik) *n.* a material made from fibers or threads by weaving, knitting, etc., as any cloth, felt, lace, etc.

fa·cial (fā′shəl) *adj.* of or for the face. ◆☆*n.* a treatment intended to make the skin of the face look better, as by massage and putting on creams and lotions.

faith·ful (fāth′fəl) *adj.* **1** remaining loyal; constant [*faithful* friends]. **2** showing a strong sense of duty or responsibility [*faithful* attendance]. —**faith′ful·ly** *adv.* —**faith′ful·ness** *n.*

fal·low (fal′ō) *adj.* plowed but left unplanted during the growing season [Farmers let the land lie *fallow* at times to kill weeds, make the soil richer, etc.] ◆*n.* land that lies fallow.

fan·ci·ful (fan′si fəl) *adj.* **1** full of fancy; having or showing a quick and playful imagination [*fanciful* costumes for the Halloween party]. **2** not real; imaginary [a *fanciful* idea that horseshoes bring luck].

fas·ci·nate (fas′ə nāt) *v.* to hold the attention of by being interesting or delightful; charm [The puppet show *fascinated* the children.] —**fas′ci·nat·ed, fas′ci·nat·ing** —**fas′ci·na′tion** *n.*

fas·ten (fas′ən) *v.* **1** to join or become joined; attach [The collar is *fastened* to the shirt.] **2** to make stay closed or in place, as by locking or shutting [*Fasten* the door.] —**fas′ten·er** *n.*

fel·low·ship (fel′ō ship′) *n.* **1** friendship; companionship. **2** a group of people having the same activities or interests. **3** money given to a student at a university or college to help him or her study for a higher degree.

fen·der (fen′dər) *n.* a metal piece over the wheel of a car, bicycle, etc. that protects against splashing water or mud.

fes·ti·val (fes′tə vəl) *n.* **1** a day or time of feasting or celebrating; happy holiday [The Mardi Gras in New Orleans is a colorful *festival*.] **2** a time of special celebration or entertainment [Our town holds a maple sugar *festival* every spring.] ◆*adj.* of or for a festival [*festival* music].

fetch (fech) *v.* to go after and bring back; get [The dog *fetched* my slippers.]

fierce (firs) *adj.* **1** wild or cruel; violent; raging [a *fierce* dog; a *fierce* wind]. **2** very strong or eager [a *fierce* effort]. —**fierc′er, fierc′est** —**fierce′ly** *adv.* —**fierce′ness** *n.*

fif·teen (fif′tēn′) *n., adj.* five more than ten; the number 15.

filth·y (fil′thē) *adj.* full of filth; disgusting. **filth′i·er, filth′i·est**

firm (furm) *adj.* **1** that does not easily give way when pressed; solid [*firm* muscles]. **2** that cannot be moved easily; fixed; stable [He stood as *firm* as a rock.] **3** that stays the same; not changing; constant [a *firm* friendship]. —**firm′ly** *adv.* —**firm′ness** *n.*

flash·bulb (flash′bulb) *n.* a light bulb that gives a short, bright light for taking photographs.

flo·rist (flôr′ist) *n.* a person whose business is selling flowers, house plants, etc.

flour·ish (flur′ish) *v.* to grow strongly and well; be successful or healthy; prosper [Daisies *flourish* in full sun.]

fo·li·age (fō′lē ij) *n.* the leaves of a tree or plant, or of many trees or plants.

fol·ly (fä′lē) *n.* a lack of good sense; foolishness.

fore·close (fôr klōz′) *v.* to end a mortgage and become the owner of the mortgaged property [A bank can *foreclose* a mortgage if payments on its loan are not made in time.] —**fore·closed′, fore·clos′ing** —**fore·clo′sure** *n.*

fore·ground (fôr′ground) *n.* the part of a scene or picture that is or seems to be nearest to the one looking at it.

for·eign·er (fôr′in ər *or* fär′in ər) *n.* a person from another country, thought of as an outsider.

fore·knowl·edge (fôr′nä′lij) *n.* knowledge of something before it happens.

fore·most (fôr′mōst) *adj.* first in position or importance [the *foremost* writers of their time]. ◆ *adv.* before all else [to be first and *foremost* a dancer].

fore·sight (fôr′sīt) *n.* **1** a foreseeing. **2** the power to foresee. **3** a looking forward. **4** a looking ahead and planning for the future.

fore·warn (fôr wôrn′) *v.* to warn ahead of time [We were *forewarned* we wouldn't get tickets later.] —**fore·warn′ing** *n.*

foun·da·tion (foun dā′shən) *n.* **1** the part at the bottom that supports a wall, house, etc.; base. **2** the basis on which an idea, belief, etc. rests.

found·er (foun′dər) *n.* a person who founds, or establishes [the *founder* of a city].

fra·grant (frā′grənt) *adj.* having a sweet or pleasant smell.

☆**frank·furt·er** *or* **frank·fort·er** (fraŋk′fər tər) *n.* a smoked sausage of beef or beef and pork; wiener.

freight (frāt) *n.* a load of goods shipped by train, truck, ship, or airplane. ◆ *v.* to carry or send by freight [Cars are often *freighted* by trains or trucks to where they are sold.]

fre·quen·cy (frē′kwən sē) *n.* **1** the fact of being frequent, or happening often. **2** the number of times something is repeated in a certain period [a *frequency* of 1,000 vibrations per second]. The frequency of radio waves is measured in hertz. —*pl.* **fre′quen·cies**

fruit·ful (frōōt′fəl) *adj.* **1** bearing much fruit [a *fruitful* tree]. **2** producing a great deal [Mozart was a *fruitful* composer.] —**fruit′ful·ly** *adv.* —**fruit′ful·ness** *n.*

gal·ax·y (gal′ək sē) ◆*n.* any vast group of stars. —*pl.* **gal′ax·ies**

gal·ler·y (gal′ər ē) *n.* **1** a balcony, especially the highest balcony in a theater, with the cheapest seats. **2** the people who sit in these seats. **3** a place for showing or selling works of art. —*pl.* —**gal′ler·ies**

gawk (gôk *or* gäk) *v.* to stare in a stupid way [The crowd *gawked* at the overturned truck.]

gear (gir) *n.* **1** *often* **gears,** *pl.* a part of a machine consisting of two or more wheels having teeth that fit together so that when one wheel moves the others are made to move [The *gears* pass on the motion of the engine to the wheels of the car.] **2** tools and equipment needed for doing something [My *gear* for fishing consists of a rod, lines, and flies.] ◆*v.* to adjust or make fit [Our new cafeteria is *geared* to handle more students.]

gen·tle (jent′l) *adj.* **1** mild, soft, or easy; not rough [a *gentle* touch]. **2** tame; easy to handle [a *gentle* horse]. **3** gradual; not sudden [a *gentle* slope]. **4** courteous, kindly, or patient [a *gentle* nature]. —**gen′tler, gen′tlest**

gen·u·ine (jen′yōō in) *adj.* **1** really being what it seems to be; not false; true [a *genuine* diamond]. **2** sincere or honest [*genuine* praise]. —**gen′u·ine·ly** *adv.* —**gen′u·ine·ness** *n.*

ge·ol·o·gy (jē ä′lə jē) *n.* the study of the earth's crust and of the way in which its layers were formed. It includes the study of rocks and fossils. —**ge·ol′o·gist** *n.*

gloom·y (glōōm′ē) *adj.* **1** dark or dim [a *gloomy* dungeon]. **2** having or giving a feeling of deep sadness [a *gloomy* mood; a *gloomy* story]. —**gloom′i·er, gloom′i·est** —**gloom′i·ly** *adv.* —**gloom′i·ness** *n.*

glo·ri·fy (glôr′ə fī) *v.* **1** to give glory to; cause to be famous and respected [Our town *glorified* the hero by building a statue.] **2** to praise in worship [to *glorify* God]. **3** to make seem better than is really so [to *glorify* war]. —**glo′ri·fied, glo′ri·fy·ing**

gnarled (närld) *adj.* full of gnarls or knobs; twisted and knotty [a *gnarled* tree; *gnarled* hands].

gnome (nōm)*n.* a dwarf in folk tales who lives inside the earth and guards the treasures there.

govt. *or* **Govt.** *abbreviation for* **government.**

gear

a	ask, fat
ā	ape, date
ä	car, lot
e	elf, ten
ē	even, meet
i	is, hit
ī	ice, fire
ō	open, go
ô	law, horn
oi	oil, point
͞oo	look, pull
o͞o	ooze, tool
ou	out, crowd
u	up, cut
u	fur, fern
ə	a in ago
	e in agent
	e in father
	i in unity
	o in collect
	u in focus
ch	chin, arch
ŋ	ring, singer
sh	she, dash
th	thin, truth
th	then, father
zh	s in pleasure

gra · cious (grā′shəs) *adj.* **1** kind, polite, and charming [a *gracious* host and hostess]. **2** full of grace, comfort, and luxury [*gracious* living].

grad · u · ate (gra′jōō ət) *n.* a person who has finished a course of study at a school or college and has been given a diploma or degree. ◆*v.* (gra′jōō āt′) **1** to make or become a graduate of a school or college. **2** to mark off with small lines for measuring [A thermometer is a tube *graduated* in degrees.] —**grad′u · at · ed, grad′u · at · ing** —**grad′u · a′tion** *n.*

greas · y (grē′sē *or* grē′zē) *adj.* **1** smeared with grease [*greasy* hands]. **2** full of grease [*greasy* food]. **3** like grease; oily [a *greasy* salve]. —**greas′i · er, greas′i · est** —**greas′i · ly** *adv.* —**greas′i · ness** *n.*

greed · y (grēd′ē) *adj.* wanting or taking all that one can get with no thought of what others need [The *greedy* little boy ate all the cookies.] **gredd′i · er, greed′i —est** — **greed′i · ly** *adv.* —**greed′i · ness** *n.*

greet · ing (grēt′iŋ) *n.* **1** the act or words of one who greets. **2** *often* **greetings**, *pl.* a message of regards from someone not present.

growth (grōth) *n.* **1** the act of growing; a becoming larger or a developing. **2** the amount grown; increase [a *growth* of two inches over the summer]. **3** something that grows or has grown [He shaved off the two weeks' *growth* of beard. A tumor is an abnormal *growth* in the body.]

guar · an · tee (ger ən tē′ *or* ger′ən tē) *n.* **1** a promise to replace something sold if it does not work or last as it should [a one-year *guarantee* on the clock]. **2** a promise or assurance that something will be done [You have my *guarantee* that we'll be on time.] ◆ *v.* **1** to give a guarantee or guaranty for. **2** to promise or assure [I cannot *guarantee* that she will be there.] —**guar · an · teed′, guar · an · tee′ing**

guess (ges) *v.* **1** to judge or decide about something without having enough facts to know for certain [Can you *guess* how old he is?] **2** to judge correctly by doing this [She *guessed* the exact number of beans in the jar.] **3** to think or suppose [I *guess* you're right.] ◆*n.* a judgment formed by guessing; surmise [Your *guess* is as good as mine.] —**guess′er** *n.*

guilt · y (gil′tē) *adj.* **1** having done something wrong; being to blame for something [She is often *guilty* of telling lies.] **2** judged in court to be a wrongdoer [The jury found him *guilty* of robbery.] **3** caused by a feeling of guilt [a *guilty* look]. —**guilt′i · er, guilt′i · est** —**guilt′i · ly** *adv.* —**guilt′i · ness** *n.*

gui · tar (gi tär′) *n.* a musical instrument with six strings. It is played by plucking the strings with the fingers or with a plectrum. —**gui · tar′ist** *n.*

gym · na · si · um (jim nā′zē əm) *n.* a building or room with equipment for doing exercises and playing games.

guitar

hand · ker · chief (haŋ′kər chif) *n.* a small piece of cloth for wiping the nose, eyes, or face, or worn as a decoration.

hap · py (hap′ē) *adj.* **1** feeling or showing pleasure or joy; glad; contented [a *happy* child; a *happy* song]. **2** lucky; fortunate [The story has a *happy* ending.] —**hap′pi · er, hap′pi · est** —**hap′pi · ly** *adv.* —**hap′pi · ness** *n.*

hatch · et (hach′ət) *n.* a small ax with a short handle.

haz · ard · ous (haz′ər dəs) *adj.* dangerous; risky.

head · ache (hed′āk) *n.* a pain in the head.

health · y (hel′thē) *adj.* **1** having good health; well [a *healthy* child]. **2** showing good health [a *healthy* appetite]. **3** good for one's health; healthful [a *healthy* climate]. —**health′i · er, health′i · est** —**health′i · ness** *n.*

height (hīt) *n.* **1** the distance from the bottom to the top; tallness [the *height* of a building; a child four feet in *height*]. **2** the highest point or degree [to reach the *height* of fame].

hem · i · sphere (hem′i sfir′) *n.* **1** half of a sphere or globe [The dome of the church was in the shape of a *hemisphere*.] **2** any of the halves into which the earth's surface is divided in geography.

he · ro (hir′ō *or* hē′rō) *n.* **1** a person who is looked up to for having done something brave or noble [Washington was the *hero* of the American Revolution.] **2** the most important person in a novel, play, or movie, especially if the person is good or noble. — *pl.* —**he′roes**

hes · i · ta · tion (hez′i tā′shən) *n.* **1** the act of hesitating, as because of doubt, fear, etc.; unsure or unwilling feeling [I agreed without *hesitation*.] **2** a pausing for a moment [talk filled with *hesitations*].

hex · a · gon (hek′sə gän) *n.* a flat figure with six angles and six sides.

hon · or · a · ble (än′ər ə bəl) *adj.* **1** worthy of being honored [an *honorable* trade]. **2** honest, upright, and sincere [*honorable* intentions]. **3** bringing honor [*honorable* mention]. —**hon′or · a · bly** *adv.*

hor · i · zon · tal (hôr′ə zänt′l) *adj.* parallel to the horizon; not vertical; level; flat [The top of a table is *horizontal*; its legs are vertical.] ◆*n.* a horizontal line, plane, etc. —**hor′i · zon′tal · ly** *adv.*

horse · rad · ish (hôrs′rad′ish) *n.* **1** a plant with a long, white root, that has a sharp, burning taste. **2** a relish made by grating this root.

hexagon

house·hold (hous′hōld) *n.* **1** all the persons who live in one house, especially a family. **2** the home and its affairs [to manage a *household*].

Hud·son (hud′sən) a river in eastern New York. Its mouth is at New York City.

hus·band (huz′bənd) *n.* the man to whom a woman is married.

hwy. *abbreviation for* **highway**.

hymn (him) *n.* **1** a song praising or honoring God. **2** any song of praise.

hy·phen·ate (hī′fənāt) *v.* to join or write with a hyphen. —**hy′phen·at·ed, hy′phen·at·ing** —**hy′phen·a′tion** *n.*

hyp·no·tize (hip′nə tīz) *v.* to put someone into a state of hypnosis or a condition like it. —**hyp′no·tized, hyp′no·tiz·ing** —**hyp′no·tist** *n.*

i·ci·cle (ī′sik əl) *n.* a hanging stick of ice formed by water freezing as it drips down.

I·da·ho (ī′də hō) a State in the northwestern part of the U.S.: abbreviated **Ida., ID**

i·den·ti·fy (ī den′tə fī) *v.* **1** to think of or treat as the same [The Roman god Jupiter is *identified* with the Greek god Zeus.] **2** to show or prove to be a certain person or thing [She was *identified* by a scar on her chin.] —**i·den′ti·fied, i·den′ti·fy·ing**

ig·ni·tion (ig nish′ən) *n.* **1** the act of setting on fire or catching fire. **2** the switch, spark plugs, etc. that set fire to the mixture of gases in the cylinders of a gasoline engine.

il·le·gal (i lē′gəl) *adj.* not legal; not allowed by law; against the law. —**il·le′gal·ly** *adv.*

il·leg·i·ble (il lej′ə bəl) *adj.* hard to read or impossible to read, as because badly written or printed.—**il·leg′i·bly** *adv.*

Il·li·nois (il′ə noi′) a State in the north central part of the U.S.: abbreviated **Ill., IL**

il·lit·er·ate (il lit′ər ət) *adj.* **1** not educated; especially, not knowing how to read or write. **2** showing a lack of education [an *illiterate* letter]. ◆*n.* a person who does not know how to read or write. —**il·lit′er·a·cy** *n.*

il·log·i·cal (il läj′i kəl) *adj.* not logical; showing poor reasoning. —**il·log′i·cal·ly** *adv.*

il·lu·mi·nate (il lōō′mə nāt′) *v.* **1** to give light to; light up [Candles *illuminated* the room.] **2** to make clear; explain [The teacher *illuminated* the meaning of the poem.] —**il·lu′mi·nat′·ed, il·lu′mi·nat′·ing**

im·ma·te·ri·al (im′ə tir′ē əl) *adj.* **1** of no importance [The cost is *immaterial* if the quality is good.] **2** not made of matter; spiritual.

im·ma·ture (im ə toor′ *or* im ə choor′) *adj.* not mature; not fully grown or developed [*immature* fruit; *immature* judgment]. —**im′ma·tu′ri·ty** *n.*

☆**im·mi·grant** (im′ə grənt) *n.* a person who comes into a foreign country to make a new home.

im·mor·tal (im môrt′l) *adj.* **1** never dying; living forever [The Greek gods were thought of as *immortal* beings.] **2** having fame that will last a long time [Shakespeare is an *immortal* poet.] ◆*n.* a being that lasts forever. —**im·mor·tal·i·ty** (i′môr tal′ə tē) *n.* —**im·mor′tal·ly** *adv.*

im·pair (im per′) *v.* to make worse, less, or weaker; damage [The disease *impaired* her hearing.]

im·pa·tient (im pā′shənt) *adj.* **1** not patient; not willing to put up with delay, annoyance, etc. [Some parents become *impatient* when their children cry.] **2** eager to do something or for something to happen [Rita is *impatient* to go swimming.] —**im·pa′tient·ly** *adv.*

im·per·fect (im pur′fikt) *adj.* not perfect; having some fault or flaw [an *imperfect* diamond].

im·po·lite (im pə līt′) *adj.* not polite; rude. —**im·po·lite′ly** *adv.* —**im·po·lite′ness** *n.*

im·prac·ti·cal (im prak′ti kəl) *adj.* not practical; not useful, efficient, etc.

im·print (im print′) *v.* **1** to mark by pressing or stamping [The paper was *imprinted* with the state seal.] **2** to fix firmly [Her face is *imprinted* in my memory.] ◆ *n.* (im′print) a mark made by pressing; print [the *imprint* of a dirty hand on the wall].

im·prop·er (im präp′ər) *adj.* **1** not proper or suitable; unfit [Sandals are *improper* shoes for tennis.] **2** not true; wrong; incorrect [an *improper* street address]. **3** not decent; in bad taste [*improper* jokes]. —**im·prop′er·ly** *adv.*

in·a·bil·i·ty (in′ə bil′ə tē) *n.* the condition of being unable; lack of ability or power.

inc. *abbreviation for* **included, income, incorporated, increase**.

in·ca·pa·ble (in kā′pə bəl) *adj.* **1** not capable; not having the ability or power needed [*incapable* of helping]. **2** not able to undergo; not open to [*incapable* of change]. —**in′ca·pa·bil′i·ty** *n.*

in·cred·i·ble (in kred′ə bəl) *adj.* so great, unusual, etc. that it is hard or impossible to believe [an *incredible* story; *incredible* speed]. —**in·cred′i·bly** *adv.*

Illinois

a	ask, fat
ā	ape, date
ä	car, lot
e	elf, ten
ē	even, meet
i	is, hit
ī	ice, fire
ō	open, go
ô	law, horn
oi	oil, point
oo	look, pull
ōō	ooze, tool
ou	out, crowd
u	up, cut
u	fur, fern
ə	a in ago
	e in agent
	e in father
	i in unity
	o in collect
	u in focus
ch	chin, arch
ŋ	ring, singer
sh	she, dash
th	thin, truth
th	then, father
zh	s in pleasure

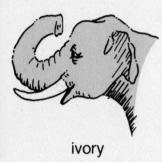

ivory

in·def·i·nite (in def′ə nit) **adj. 1** having no exact limits [an *indefinite* area]. **2** not clear or exact in meaning; vague [*indefinite* instructions]. **3** not sure or positive; uncertain [*indefinite* plans]. —**in·def′i·nite·ly adv.**

in·di·rect (in′də rekt′) **adj. 1** not direct or straight; by a longer way; roundabout [an *indirect* route]. **2** not straight to the point [an *indirect* reply]. —**in′di·rect′ly adv.**

in·dus·try (in′dəs trē) **n. 1** any branch of business or manufacturing [the steel *industry*; the motion-picture *industry*]. **2** all business and manufacturing [Leaders of *industry* met in Chicago.] —*pl.* **in′dus·tries**

in·flate (in flāt′) **v.** to cause to swell out by putting in air or gas; blow up [to *inflate* a balloon]. —**in·flat′a·ble adj.**

in·for·ma·tion (in′fər mā′shən) **n. 1** an informing or being informed [This is for your *information* only.] **2** something told or facts learned; news or knowledge; data [An encyclopedia gives *information* about many things.] **3** a person or service that answers certain questions [Ask *information* for the location of the shoe department.]

in·spec·tion (in spek′shən) **n. 1** the act or process of looking at carefully. **2** an official examination or review [The *inspection* of the troops was postponed.]

in·struc·tor (in struk′tər) **n. 1** a teacher. ☆**2** a college teacher ranking below an assistant professor.

in·stru·ment (in′strə mənt) **n. 1** a tool or other device for doing very exact work, for scientific purposes, etc. [surgical *instruments*]. **2** a device used in making musical sound, as a flute, violin, piano, etc.

in·su·late (in′sə lāt) **v.** to separate or cover with a material that keeps electricity, heat, or sound from escaping [electric wire *insulated* with rubber; a furnace *insulated* with asbestos]. —**in′su·lat·ed, in′su·lat·ing**

in·su·la·tor (in′sə lāt′ər) **n.** anything that insulates; especially, a device of glass or porcelain, for insulating electric wires.

in·sure (in shoor′) **v.** to get or give insurance on [We *insured* our car against theft. Will your company *insure* my house against storms?] —**in·sured′, in·sur′ing** —**in·sur′a·ble adj.**

in·tel·li·gent (in tel′ə jənt) **adj.** having or showing intelligence, especially high intelligence. —**in·tel′li·gent·ly adv.**

in·tol·er·ant (in tä′lər ənt) **adj.** not tolerant; not willing to put up with ideas or beliefs that are different from one's own, or not willing to put up with people of other races or backgrounds. —**in·tol′er·ance n.**

in·trude (in trood′) **v.** to force oneself or one's thoughts on others without being asked or wanted [I don't like to *intrude* when you are so busy.] —**in·trud′ed, in·trud′ing** —**in·tru′sion n.**

in·ven·tion (in ven′shən) **n. 1** the act of inventing [the *invention* of television]. **2** something invented [the many *inventions* of Edison]. **3** the ability to invent [a novelist who shows great *invention* in telling a story].

in·ves·ti·gate (in ves′tə gāt′) **v.** to search into so as to learn the facts; examine in detail [to *investigate* an accident]. —**in·ves′ti·gat·ed, in·ves′ti·gat·ing** —**in·ves′ti·ga′tion n.** —**in·ves′ti·ga′tor n.**

ir·ra·tion·al (ir rash′ən əl) **adj.** that does not make sense; not rational; absurd [an *irrational* fear of the dark]. —**ir·ra′tion·al·ly adv.**

ir·reg·u·lar (ir reg′yə lər) **adj. 1** not regular; not like the usual rule, way, or custom [an *irregular* diet]. **2** not straight, even, or the same throughout [an *irregular* design]. —**ir·reg′u·lar·ly adv.**

ir·rel·e·vant (ir rel′ə vənt) **adj.** having nothing to do with the subject; not to the point [That remark about the candidate's height was *irrelevant* to the issues of the campaign.]

ir·re·spon·si·ble (ir′rē spän′sə bəl) **adj.** not responsible; not showing a sense of duty; doing as one pleases. —**ir′re·spon′si·bly adv.**

is·sue (ish′oo *or* ish′yoo) **n. 1** a thing or group of things sent or given out [the July *issue* of a magazine]. **2** a problem to be talked over [The candidates will debate the *issues*.] ◆**v. 1** to put forth or send out [The city *issues* bonds. The general *issued* an order.] **2** to give or deal out; distribute [The teacher *issued* new books.] —**is′sued, is′su·ing**

i·vo·ry (ī′vər ē *or* ī′vrē) **n. 1** the hard, white substance that forms the tusks of the elephant, walrus, etc. **2** any substance like ivory, as the white plastic used on piano keys. **3** the color of ivory; creamy white. —*pl.* **i′vo·ries** ◆**adj. 1** made of or like ivory. **2** having the color of ivory; creamy-white.

Jj

☆**jack·knife** (jak′nīf) **n. 1** a large pocketknife. **2** a dive in which the diver touches the feet with the hands while in the air. —*pl.* **jack′knives** ◆**v.** to bend at the middle as in a jackknife dive. —**jack′knifed, jack′knif·ing**

Jef·fer·son (jef′ər sən), **Thomas** 1743-1826; the third president of the United States, from 1801 to 1809.

jel·ly (jel′ē) **n. 1** a soft, firm food that looks smooth and glassy, and is easily cut, spread, etc. Jelly is made from cooked fruit syrup, meat juice, or gelatin. **2** any substance like this. —*pl.* **jel′lies** ◆*v.* to become, or make into, jelly. —**jel′lied, jel′ly·ing**

jew·el·er or **jew·el·ler** (jōōl′ər) **n.** a person who makes, sells, or repairs jewelry, watches, etc.

jock·ey (jäk′ē) **n.** a person whose work is riding horses in races.

jour·nal·ism (jur′nəl iz əm) **n.** the work of gathering, writing, or editing the news for publication in newspapers or magazines or for broadcasting on radio or television.

jour·nal·ist (jur′nəl ist) **n.** a person whose work is journalism, as a reporter, news editor, etc. —**jour′nal·is′tic** *adj.*

juic·y (jōō′sē) *adj.* full of juice [a *juicy* plum]. —**juic′i·er, juic′i·est**

ju·ror (joor′ər *or* jur′ər) **n.** a member of a jury.

ju·ven·ile (jōō′və nəl *or* jōō′və nīl) *adj.* **1** young or youthful. **2** of, like, or for children or young people [*juvenile* ideas; *juvenile* books]. ◆*n.* a child or young person.

Kk

kan·ga·roo (kaŋ gə rōō′) **n.** an animal of Australia with short forelegs and strong, large hind legs, with which it makes long leaps. The female carries her young in a pouch in front.—*pl.* **kan·ga·roos′**

Ken·ne·dy (ken′ə dē) **John F.** 1917–1963; the 35th president of the United States, from 1961 to 1963. He was assassinated.

Ken·tuck·y (kən tuk′ē) a state in the eastern central part of the U.S.: abbreviated **Ky., KY**

key·board (kē′bôrd) **n.** the row or rows of keys of a piano, organ, typewriter, etc.

kin·dling (kind′liŋ) **n.** bits of dry wood or the like, for starting a fire.

kitch·en (kich′ən) **n.** a room or place for preparing and cooking food.

kneel (nēl) *v.* to rest on a knee or knees [Some people *kneel* when they pray.] —**knelt** or **kneeled, kneel′ing**

knelt (nelt) *a past tense and past participle of* **kneel.**

☆**knick·ers** (nik′ərz) *n.pl.* short, loose trousers gathered in just below the knees.

knot·hole (nät′hōl) **n.** a hole in a board or tree trunk where a knot has fallen out.

knowl·edge (nä′lij) **n. 1** the fact or condition of knowing [*Knowledge* of the murder spread through the town.] **2** what is known or learned, as through study or experience [a scientist of great *knowledge*]. **3** all that is known by all people.

knuck·le (nuk′əl) **n.** a joint of the finger, especially one connecting a finger to the rest of the hand.

Ko·re·a (kô rē′ə) a country in eastern Asia, divided into two republics, North Korea and South Korea. —**Ko·re′an** *adj., n.*

Ll

lan·guage (laŋ′gwij) **n. 1** human speech or writing that stands for speech [People communicate by means of *language*.] **2** the speech of a particular nation, tribe, etc. [the Greek *language*; the Navaho *language*]. **3** any means of passing on one's thoughts or feelings to others [sign *language*].

laugh·a·ble (laf′ə bəl) *adj.* causing laughter; funny; ridiculous [a *laughable* costume].

launch (lônch *or* länch) *v.* **1** to throw, hurl, or send off into space [to *launch* a rocket]. **2** to cause to slide into the water; set afloat [to *launch* a new ship]. ◆*n.* the act of launching a ship, spacecraft, etc.

laun·dry (lôn′drē *or* län′drē) **n. 1** a place where laundering is done. **2** clothes, linens, etc. that have been, or are about to be, washed and ironed. —*pl.* **laun′dries**

law-a·bid·ing (lô′ə bīd′iŋ *or* lä′ə bīd′iŋ) *adj.* obeying the law [*law-abiding* citizens].

lb. *abbreviation for* **pound.** —*pl.* **lbs.**

lec·ture (lek′chər) **n. 1** a talk on some subject to an audience or class. **2** a long or tiresome scolding. ◆*v.* **1** to give a lecture. **2** to scold. —**lec′tured, lec′tur·ing** —**lec′tur·er** *n.*

leg·is·la·tion (lej′is lā′shən) **n. 1** the act or process of making laws. **2** the laws made.

lei·sure·ly (lē′zhər lē *or* lezh′ər lē) *adj.* without hurrying; slow [a *leisurely* walk]. ◆*adv.* in a slow, unhurried way [We talked *leisurely*.]

light·ning (līt′niŋ) **n.** a flash of light in the sky caused by the passing of electricity from one cloud to another or between a cloud and the earth.

lik·a·ble or **like·a·ble** (līk′ə bəl) *adj.* easy to like because pleasing, friendly, etc.

lim·it·ed (lim′it əd) *adj.* **1** having a limit or limits; restricted in some way [This offer is good for a *limited* time only.] ☆**2** making only a few stops [a *limited* bus].

lim·ou·sine (lim ə zēn′ *or* lim′ə zēn) **n. 1** a large automobile driven by a chauffeur, who is sometimes separated from the passengers by a glass window. ☆**2** a buslike sedan used to carry passengers to or from an airport.

Lin·coln (liŋ′kən) **Abraham** 1809–1865; 16th president of the United States, from 1861 to 1865. He was assassinated.

kangaroo

a	ask, fat
ā	ape, date
ä	car, lot
e	elf, ten
ē	even, meet
i	is, hit
ī	ice, fire
ō	open, go
ô	law, horn
oi	oil, point
oo	look, pull
ōō	ooze, tool
ou	out, crowd
u	up, cut
ʉ	fur, fern
ə	a in ago
	e in agent
	e in father
	i in unity
	o in collect
	u in focus
ch	chin, arch
ŋ	ring, singer
sh	she, dash
th	thin, truth
th	then, father
zh	s in pleasure

lis·ten (lis′ən) **v.** to pay attention in order to hear; try to hear [*Listen* to the rain. *Listen* when the counselor speaks.] —**lis′ten·er n.**

live·li·hood (līv′lē hood′) **n.** a means of living, or of supporting oneself [She earns her *livelihood* as a teacher.]

lock·smith (läk′smith) **n.** a person whose work is making or repairing locks and keys.

lounge (lounj) **v.** to move, sit, or lie in an easy or lazy way; loll. —**lounged, loung′ing** ◆**n.** a room with comfortable furniture where people can lounge. —**loung′er n.**

lunch·eon (lun′chən) **n.** a lunch; especially, a formal lunch with others.

lus·cious (lush′əs) **adj. 1** having a delicious taste or smell; full of flavor [a *luscious* steak]. **2** very pleasing to see, hear, etc. [the *luscious* sound of violins]. —**lus′cious·ly adv.**

lux·u·ry (luk′shər ē or lug′zhər ē) **n. 1** the use and enjoyment of the best and most costly things that give one the most comfort and pleasure [a life of *luxury*]. **2** anything that gives one such comfort, usually something one does not need for life or health [Jewels are *luxuries*.] —*pl.* **lux′u·ries**

Mm

ma·chin·er·y (mə shēn′ər ē) **n. 1** machines in general [the *machinery* of a factory]. **2** the working parts of a machine [the *machinery* of a printing press]. —*pl.* **ma·chin′er·ies**

ma·chin·ist (mə shēn′ist) **n. 1** a person who is skilled in working with machine tools. **2** a person who makes, repairs, or runs machinery.

mag·i·cal (maj′i kəl) **adj.** of or like magic. —**mag′i·cal·ly adv.**

mag·nif·i·cent (mag nif′ə sənt) **adj.** rich, fine, noble, beautiful, etc. in a grand way; splendid [a *magnificent* castle; a *magnificent* idea].

mag·ni·fy (mag′nə fī) **v.** to make look or seem larger or greater than is really so [This lens *magnifies* an object to ten times its size. He *magnified* the seriousness of his illness.] —**mag′ni·fied, mag′ni·fy·ing**

main·stay (mān′stā) **n. 1** the line that runs forward from the upper part of the mainmast, helping to hold it in place. **2** the main or chief support [She was the *mainstay* of her family.]

main·te·nance (mānt′n əns) **n. 1** a maintaining or being maintained; upkeep or support [Taxes pay for the *maintenance* of schools.] **2** a means of support; livelihood [a job that barely provides a *maintenance*].

mallet

mal·let (mal′ət) **n. 1** a wooden hammer made with a short handle for use as a tool. **2** a wooden hammer made with a long handle for playing croquet or with a long, flexible handle for playing polo.

man·age·a·ble (man′ij ə bəl) **adj.** that can be managed, controlled, or done.

man·u·fac·tur·er (man′yōō fak′chər ər) **n.** a person or company that manufactures; especially, a factory owner.

mar·tial (mär′shəl) **adj. 1** having to do with war or armies [*martial* music]. **2** showing a readiness or eagerness to fight [*martial* spirit].

mas·ter·piece (mas′tər pēs) **n. 1** a thing made or done with very great skill; a great work of art. **2** the best thing that a person has ever made or done [*The Divine Comedy* was Dante's *masterpiece*.]

match (mach) **n. 1** any person or thing equal to or like another in some way [Joan met her *match* in chess when she played Joe.] **2** two or more people or things that go well together [That suit and tie are a good *match*.] **3** a game or contest between two persons or teams [a tennis *match*]. ◆**v. 1** to go well together [Do your shirt and tie *match*?] **2** to make or get something like or equal to [Can you *match* this cloth?] **3** to be equal to [I could never *match* that lawyer in an argument.]

may·on·naise (mā ə nāz′ or mā′ə nāz) **n.** a thick, creamy salad dressing made of egg yolks, olive oil, lemon juice or vinegar, and seasoning.

mdse. *abbreviation for* **merchandise.**

meas·ure (mezh′ər) **v. 1** to find out the size, amount, or extent of, as by comparing with something else [*Measure* the child's height with a yardstick. How do you *measure* a person's worth?] **2** to set apart or mark off a certain amount or length of [*Measure* out three pounds of sugar.] —**meas′ured, meas′ur·ing** ◆**n. 1** the size, amount, or extent of something, found out by measuring [The *measure* of the bucket is 15 liters.] **2** a system of measuring [Liquid *measure* is a system of measuring liquids.]

me·chan·ic (mə kan′ik) **n.** a worker skilled in using tools or in making, repairing, and using machinery [an automobile *mechanic*].

med·i·cine (med′ə sən) **n. 1** any substance used in or on the body to treat disease, lessen pain, heal, etc. **2** the science of treating and preventing disease.

mel·low (mel′ō) **adj. 1** soft, sweet, and juicy from ripeness [a *mellow* apple]. **2** having a good flavor from being aged; not bitter [a *mellow* wine]. **3** rich, soft, and pure; not harsh [the *mellow* tone of a cello]. **4** made gentle and kind by age or experience [a *mellow* teacher].

me·men·to (mə men′tō) **n.** an object kept to remind one of something; souvenir [This toy is a *memento* of my childhood.] —*pl.* **me·men′tos** or **me·men′toes**

mem·o·rize (mem′ər īz) *v.* ☆to fix in one's memory exactly or word for word; learn by heart. —**mem′o·rized, mem′o·riz·ing** —**mem′o·ri·za′tion** *n.*

Mex·i·can (mek′si kən) *adj.* of Mexico, its people, their dialect of Spanish, or their culture. ◆*n.* a person born or living in Mexico.

mgr. *abbreviation for* **manager.**

mi·cro·phone (mī′krə fōn) *n.* a device for picking up sound that is to be made stronger, as in a theater, or sent over long distances, as in radio. Microphones change sound into electric waves, which go into electron tubes and are changed back into sound by loudspeakers.

midg·et (mij′ət) *n.* **1** a very small person. **2** anything very small of its kind.

mid·point (mid′point) *n.* a point in the middle or at the center.

mid·sum·mer (mid′sum′ər) *n.* **1** the middle of summer. **2** the period around June 21.

Mid·west·ern (mid′wes′tərn) *adj.* of, in, or having to do with the Middle West.

mil·dew (mil′dōō *or* mil′dyōō) *n.* a fungus that appears as a furry, white coating on plants or on damp, warm paper, cloth, etc. ◆*v.* to become coated with mildew.

mil·lion·aire (mil yə ner′) *n.* a person who has at least a million dollars, pounds, etc.

mi·nor·i·ty (mī nôr′ə tē *or* mi nôr′ə tē) *n.* **1** the smaller part or number; less than half [A *minority* of the Senate voted for the law.] **2** a small group of people of a different race, religion, etc. from the main group of which it is a part. —*pl.* **mi·nor′i·ties**

mis·cal·cu·late (mis kal′kyōō lāt′) *v.* to make a mistake in figuring or planning; misjudge [Our manager *miscalculated* the pitcher's strength and we lost the game.]

mis·cel·la·ne·ous (mis′ə lā′nē əs) *adj.* of many different kinds; mixed; varied [A *miscellaneous* collection of objects filled the shelf.]

mis·chief (mis′chif) *n.* **1** harm or damage [Gossip can cause great *mischief*.] **2** action that causes harm, damage, or trouble. **3** a playful trick; prank. **4** playful, harmless spirits [a child full of *mischief*].

mis·chie·vous (mis′chə vəs) *adj.* **1** causing some slight harm or annoyance, often in fun; naughty [a *mischievous* act]. **2** full of playful tricks; teasing [a *mischievous* child]. **3** causing harm or damage; injurious [*mischievous* slander].

mis·pro·nounce (mis prə nouns′) *v.* to pronounce in a wrong way [Some people *mispronounce* "cavalry" as "calvary."] —**mis·pro·nounced′, mis·pro·nounc′ing** —**mis·pro·nun·ci·a·tion** (mis′prə nun′sē ā′shən) *n.*

mis·tle·toe (mis′əl tō) *n.* an evergreen plant with waxy white, poisonous berries, growing as a parasite on certain trees. People kiss under the mistletoe at Christmas.

mis·un·der·stand (mis′un dər stand′) *v.* to understand in a way that is wrong; give a wrong meaning to. —**mis·un·der·stood** (mis′un der stōōd′), **mis′under·stand′ing**

mo. *abbreviation for* **month.**

mo·bile (mō′bəl *or* mō′bīl *or* mō′bēl) *adj.* that can be moved quickly and easily [a *mobile* army]. ◆*n.* (mō′bēl) a kind of sculpture made of flat pieces, rods, etc. that hang balanced from wires so as to move easily in air currents. —**mo·bil·i·ty** (mō bil′ə tē) *n.*

mod·i·fy (mäd′ə fī) *v.* **1** to make a small or partial change in [Exploration has *modified* our maps of Antarctica.] **2** to make less harsh, strong, etc. [to *modify* a jail term]. **3** to limit the meaning of; describe or qualify [In the phrase "old man" the adjective "old" *modifies* the noun "man."] —**mod′i·fied, mod′i·fy·ing** —**mod′i·fi·ca′tion** *n.* —**mod′i·fi′er** *n.*

mois·ten (mois′ən) *v.* to make or become moist.

mon·o·gram (män′ə gram) *n.* initials, especially of a person's name, put together in a design and used on clothing, stationery, and so on.

mon·o·rail (män′ə rāl) *n.* **1** a railway having cars that run on a single rail, or track, and are hung from it or balanced on it. **2** this track.

mon·o·syl·la·ble (män′ō sil′ə bəl) *n.* a word of one syllable, as *he* or *thought*. —**mon·o·syl·lab·ic** (män′ə si lab′ik) *adj.*

mo·not·o·nous (mə nät′n əs) *adj.* **1** going on and on in the same tone [a *monotonous* voice]. **2** having little or no change; boring or tiresome [a *monotonous* trip; *monotonous* work].

mon·soon (män sōōn′) *n.* **1** a wind of the Indian Ocean and southern Asia, blowing from the southwest from April to October, and from the northeast the rest of the year. **2** the rainy season, when this wind blows from the southwest.

mor·al (môr′əl) *adj.* **1** having to do with right and wrong in conduct [Cheating is a *moral* issue.] **2** good or right according to ideas of being decent and respectable [She was a *moral* woman all her life.] ◆*n.* **1** a lesson about what is right and wrong, taught by a story or event [the *moral* of a fable]. **2 morals,** *pl.* standards of behavior having to do with right and wrong; ethics.

mos·qui·to (mə skēt′ō) *n.* a small insect with two wings. The female bites animals to suck their blood. Some mosquitoes spread diseases, as malaria. —*pl.* **mos·qui′toes** *or* **mos·qui′tos**

mouth·ful (mouth′fool) *n.* **1** as much as the mouth can hold. **2** as much as is usually put into the mouth at one time. —*pl.* **mouth′fuls**

microphone

a	ask, fat
ā	ape, date
ä	car, lot
e	elf, ten
ē	even, meet
i	is, hit
ī	ice, fire
ō	open, go
ô	law, horn
oi	oil, point
ōō	look, pull
ōō	ooze, tool
ou	out, crowd
u	up, cut
u	fur, fern
ə	a in ago
	e in agent
	e in father
	i in unity
	o in collect
	u in focus
ch	chin, arch
ŋ	ring, singer
sh	she, dash
th	thin, truth
th	then, father
zh	s in pleasure

mud·dy (mud′ē) *adj.* full of mud or smeared with mud [a *muddy* yard; *muddy* boots]. —**mud′di·er, mud′di·est** ◆*v.* to make or become muddy. —**mud′died, mud′dy·ing**

mu·ral (myoor′əl) *n.* a picture or photograph, especially a large one, painted or put on a wall. ◆*adj.* of or on a wall [a *mural* painting].

mus·cle (mus′əl) *n.* **1** the tissue in an animal's body that makes up the fleshy parts. Muscle can be stretched or tightened to move the parts of the body. **2** any single part or band of this tissue [The biceps is a *muscle* in the upper arm.] **3** strength that comes from muscles that are developed; brawn.

my·thol·o·gy (mi thäl′ə jē) *n.* **1** myths as a group; especially, all the myths of a certain people [Roman *mythology*]. —*pl.* **my·thol′o·gies 2** the study of myths. —**myth·o·log·i·cal** (mith′ə läj′i kəl) *adj.*

Nn

nar·rate (ner′āt) *v.* to give the story of in writing or speech; tell what has happened [Our guest *narrated* her adventures.] —**nar′rat·ed, nar′rat·ing** —**nar′ra·tor** *n.*

na·tion (nā′shən) *n.* **1** a group of people living together in a certain region under the same government; state; country [the Swiss *nation*]. **2** a group of people sharing the same history, language, customs, etc. [the Iroquois *nation*].

nau·se·a (nô′zhə *or* nä′zhə *or* nô′zē ə) *n.* a feeling of sickness in the stomach that makes a person want to vomit.

ne·go·ti·ate (ni gō′shē āt′) *v.* to talk over a problem, business deal, dispute, etc. in the hope of reaching an agreement [to *negotiate* a contract]. —**ne·go′ti·at·ed, ne·go′ti·at·ing** —**ne·go′ti·a′tion** *n.* —**ne·go′ti·a′tor** *n.*

neigh·bor·ly (nā′bər lē) *adj.* friendly, kind, helpful, etc. [It was very *neighborly* of you to shovel the snow from my walk.] —**neigh′bor·li·ness** *n.*

niece (nēs) *n.* **1** the daughter of one's brother or sister. **2** the daughter of one's brother-in-law or sister-in-law.

No. or **no.** *abbreviation for* **number.**

nois·y (noi′zē) *adj.* **1** making noise [a *noisy* bell]. **2** full of noise [a *noisy* theater]. —**nois′i·er, nois′i·est** —**nois′i·ly** *adv.* —**nois′i·ness** *n.*

no·tice·a·ble (nōt′is ə bəl) *adj.* easily seen; likely to be noticed; remarkable [*noticeable* improvement]. —**no′tice·a·bly** *adv.*

octagon

nour·ish (nur′ish) *v.* to feed; provide with the things needed for life and growth [Water and sunlight *nourished* the plants.] —**nour′ish·ing** *adj.*

nui·sance (nōō′səns *or* nyōō′səns) *n.* an act, thing, or person that causes trouble or bother [It's such a *nuisance* to put on boots just to go next door.]

numb (num) *adj.* not able to feel, or feeling very little [*numb* with cold]. ◆ *v.* to make numb [The cold *numbed* his toes.]

nu·tri·tion (nōō trish′ən *or* nyōō trish′ən) *n.* **1** the process by which an animal or plant takes in food and uses it in living and growing. **2** food; nourishment. **3** the study of the foods people should eat for health and well-being. —**nu·tri′tion·al** *adj.*

Oo

o·boe (ō′bō) *n.* a woodwind instrument whose mouthpiece has a double reed. —**o′bo·ist** *n.*

ob·serv·a·to·ry (äb zurv′ə tôr′ē) *n.* a building with telescopes and other equipment in it for studying the stars, weather conditions, etc. —*pl.* **ob·serv′a·to′ries**

ob·serve (əb zurv′) *v.* **1** to see, watch, or notice [I *observed* that the child was smiling.] **2** to examine and study carefully [to *observe* an experiment]. —**ob·served′, ob·serv′ing** —**ob·serv′er** *n.*

ob·vi·ous (äb′vē əs) *adj.* easy to see or understand; plain; clear [an *obvious* rust stain; an *obvious* danger]. —**ob′vi·ous·ly** *adv.* —**ob′vi·ous·ness** *n.*

oc·ca·sion (ə kā′zhən) *n.* **1** a suitable time; good chance; opportunity [Did you have *occasion* to visit with them?] **2** a particular time [We've met on several *occasions*.] **3** a special time or happening [Independence Day is an *occasion* to celebrate.]

oc·cu·py (äk′yōō pī′) *v.* **1** to live in [to *occupy* a house]. **2** to take up; fill [The store *occupies* the entire building.] **3** to keep busy; employ [Many activities *occupy* his time.] —**oc′cu·pied, oc′cu·py·ing**

oc·cur (ə kur′) *v.* **1** to come into one's mind [The idea never *occurred* to me.] **2** to happen; take place [That event *occurred* years ago.] —**oc·curred′, oc·cur′ring**

oc·ta·gon (äk′tə gän) *n.* a flat figure having eight angles and eight sides.

of·fi·cer (ôf′i sər *or* äf′i sər) *n.* **1** a person holding some office, as in a business, club, or government. **2** a member of a police force. **3** a person who commands others in an army, navy, etc. [Generals and lieutenants are commissioned *officers*.]

oboe

of·fi·cial (ə fish′əl) **n. 1** a person who holds an office, especially in government. ☆**2** a person who sees to it that the rules are followed in a game, as a referee or umpire. ◆**adj. 1** of or having to do with an office [an *official* record; *official* duties]. **2** coming from a person who has authority [an *official* request]. **3** fit for an important officer; formal [an *official* welcome]. —**of·fi′cial·ly adv.**

oint·ment (oint′mənt) **n.** an oily cream rubbed on the skin to heal it or make it soft and smooth; salve.

or·gan·ize (ôr′gə nīz) **v.** to arrange or place according to a system [The library books are *organized* according to their subjects.] —**or′gan·ized, or′gan·iz·ing** —**or′gan·iz′er n.**

o·rig·i·nal·i·ty (ə rij′ə nal′ə tē) **n.** the quality or condition of being fresh, new, or creative.

or·phan·age (ôr′fən ij) **n.** a home for taking care of a number of orphans

out·ra·geous (out rā′jəs) **adj. 1** doing great injury or wrong [*outrageous* crimes]. **2** so wrong or bad that it hurts or shocks [an *outrageous* lie]. —**out·ra′geous·ly adv.**

o·ver·due (ō vər dōō′ *or* ō vər dyōō′) **adj.** delayed past the time set for payment, arrival, etc. [an *overdue* bill; a bus long *overdue*].

o·ver·e·mo·tion·al (ō′vər ē mō′shə nəl) **adj.** too full of emotion or strong feeling [an *overemotional* speech].

o·ver·flow (ō vər flō′) **v. 1** to flow across; flood [Water *overflowed* the streets.] **2** to have its contents flowing over [The sink is *overflowing*.] ◆**n.** (ō′vər flō′) the act of overflowing.

o·ver·grown (ō′vər grōn′) **adj. 1** covered with foliage or weeds [a lawn that is badly *overgrown*]. **2** having grown too large or too fast [an *overgrown* child].

o·ver·joyed (ō vər joid′) **adj.** filled with great joy.

o·ver·pro·tect (ō′vər prə tekt′) **v.** to protect more than is necessary or helpful, especially by trying to keep someone from the normal hurts and disappointments of life.

o·ver·sen·si·tive (ō′vər sn′sə tiv) **adj.** too quick to feel, notice, or respond to.

o·ver·weight (ō′vər wāt′) **n.** more weight than is needed or allowed; extra weight. ◆**adj.** (ō vər wāt′) weighing more than is normal or proper; too heavy.

oys·ter (ois′tər) **n.** a shellfish with a soft body enclosed in two rough shells hinged together. Some are used as food, and pearls are formed inside others.

oz. *abbreviation for* **ounce.** —*pl.* **oz.** or **ozs.**

pain·ful (pān′fəl) **adj.** causing pain; hurting; unpleasant [a *painful* wound]. — **pain′ful·ness n.**

pam·phlet (pam′flət) **n.** a thin booklet with a paper cover.

pap·ri·ka (pə prē′kə) **n.** a red seasoning made by grinding certain peppers.

par·a·chute (par′ə shōōt) **n.** a large cloth device that opens up like an umbrella and is used for slowing down a person or thing dropping from an airplane. ◆**v.** to jump with or drop by a parachute. —**par′a·chut·ed, par′a·chut·ing** —**par′a·chut·ist n.**

par·al·lel·o·gram (par′ə lel′ə gram) **n.** a figure having four sides, with the opposite sides parallel and of equal length.

par·ent (per′ənt) **n. 1** a father or mother. **2** any animal or plant as it is related to its offspring. —**par′ent·hood n.**

pa·ren·the·sis (pə ren′thə sis) **n. 1** a word, phrase, etc. put into a complete sentence as an added note or explanation and set off, as between curved lines, from the rest of the sentence. **2** either or both of the curved lines ( ) used to set off such a word, phrase, etc. —*pl.* **pa·ren·the·ses** (pə ren′thə sēz)

par·tial (pär′shəl) **adj. 1** of or in only a part; not complete or total [a *partial* eclipse of the sun]. **2** favoring one person or side more than another; biased [A judge should not be *partial*.] —**par′tial·ly adv.**

par·tic·i·pate (pär tis′ə pāt) **v.** to take part with others; have a share [Sue *participated* in the school play.] —**par·tic′i·pat·ed, par·tic′i·pat·ing** —**par·tic′i·pa′tion n.** —**par·tic′i·pa′tor n.**

pas·sive (pas′iv) **adj. 1** not active, but acted upon [Spectators have a *passive* interest in sports.] **2** not resisting; yielding; submissive [The *passive* child did as he was told.] —**pas′sive·ly adv.**

pa·tience (pā′shəns) **n.** the fact of being patient or the ability to be patient.

pa·tient (pā′shənt) **adj.** able to put up with pain, trouble, delay, boredom, etc. without complaining [The *patient* children waited in line for the theater to open.] ◆**n.** a person under the care of a doctor. —**pa′tient·ly adv.**

pa·ti·o (pat′ē ō *or* pät′ē ō) **n.** ☆**1** in Spain and Spanish America, a courtyard around which a house is built. ☆**2** a paved area near a house, with chairs, tables, etc. for outdoor lounging, dining, etc. —*pl.* **pa′ti·os**

pa·trol (pə trōl′) **v.** to make regular trips around a place in order to guard it [The watchman *patrolled* the area all night.] —**pa·trolled′, pa·trol′ling** u **n. 1** the act of patrolling. **2** a person or group that patrols.

parachute

a	ask, fat
ā	ape, date
ä	car, lot
e	elf, ten
ē	even, meet
i	is, hit
ī	ice, fire
ō	open, go
ô	law, horn
oi	oil, point
ōō	look, pull
ōō	ooze, tool
ou	out, crowd
u	up, cut
ʉ	fur, fern
ə	a in ago
	e in agent
	e in father
	i in unity
	o in collect
	u in focus
ch	chin, arch
ŋ	ring, singer
sh	she, dash
th	thin, truth
th	then, father
zh	s in pleasure

piccolo

poncho

pause (pôz *or* päz) *n.* a short stop, as in speaking or working. ◆*v.* to make a pause; stop for a short time [He *paused* to catch his breath.] —**paused, paus′ing**

pave (pāv) *v.* to cover the surface of a road, walk, etc., as with concrete or asphalt. —**paved, pav′ing** —**pave the way,** to make the way ready for something; prepare.

pen·al·ty (pen′əl tē) *n.* 1 punishment for breaking a law. 2 a disadvantage, fine, etc. given to one side in a contest for breaking a rule. —*pl.* **pen′al·ties**

per·ceive (pər sēv′) *v.* 1 to become aware of through one of the senses, especially through seeing [to *perceive* the difference between two shades of red]. 2 to take in through the mind [I quickly *perceived* the joke.] —**per·ceived′, per·ceiv′ing**

per·cep·tion (pər sep′shən) *n.* 1 the act of perceiving or the ability to perceive [Jan's *perception* of color is poor.] 2 knowledge or understanding got by perceiving [She has a clear *perception* of her duty.]

per·pen·dic·u·lar (pʉr′pən dik′yoo lər) *adj.* 1 at right angles [The wall should be *perpendicular* to the floor.] 2 straight up and down; exactly upright [a *perpendicular* flagpole]. ◆*n.* a line that is at right angles to the horizon, or to another line or plane [The Leaning Tower of Pisa leans away from the *perpendicular*.]

per·son·al (pʉr′sə nəl) *adj.* of one's own; private; individual [a *personal* opinion; a *personal* secretary].

per·son·nel (pʉr sə nel′) *n.* persons employed in any work, service, etc. [office *personnel*].

per·spec·tive (pər spek′tiv) *n.* 1 the way things look from a given point according to their size, shape, distance, etc. [*Perspective* makes things far away look small.] 2 the art of picturing things so that they seem close or far away, big or small, etc., just as they look to the eye when viewed from a given point. 3 a certain point of view in understanding or judging things or happenings, especially one that shows them in their true relations to one another [Working in a factory will give you a new *perspective* on labor problems.]

pew·ter (pyoot′ər) *n.* 1 a grayish alloy of tin with lead, brass, or copper. 2 things made of pewter, especially dishes, tableware, etc. ◆*adj.* made of pewter.

phe·nom·e·non (fə näm′ə nän) *n.* 1 any fact, condition, or happening that can be seen, heard, and described in a scientific way, such as an eclipse. 2 an unusual or remarkable event or thing [Rain is a *phenomenon* in the desert.] —*pl.* **phe·nom·e·na** (fə näm′ə nə) or (for sense 2 usually) **phe·nom′e·nons**

pho·to·graph (fōt′ə graf) *n.* a picture made with a camera. ◆*v.* 1 to take a photograph of. 2 to look a certain way in photographs [She *photographs* taller than she is.]

phrase (frāz) *n.* a group of words that is not a complete sentence, but that gives a single idea, usually as a separate part of a sentence ["Drinking fresh milk," "with meals," and "to be healthy" are *phrases*.] ◆*v.* to say or write in a certain way [He *phrased* his answer carefully.] —**phrased, phras′ing**

phy·si·cian (fi zish′ən) *n.* a doctor of medicine, especially one who is not mainly a surgeon.

pic·co·lo (pik′ə lō) *n.* a small flute that sounds notes an octave higher than an ordinary flute does.—*pl.* **pic′co·los**

pierce (pirs) *v.* 1 to pass into or through; penetrate [The needle *pierced* her finger. A light *pierced* the darkness.] 2 to make a hole through; perforate; bore [to *pierce* one's ears for earrings]. 3 to make a sharp sound through [A shriek *pierced* the air.] —**pierced, pierc′ing**

pig·ment (pig′mənt) *n.* 1 coloring matter, usually a powder, mixed with oil, water, etc. to make paints. 2 the matter in the cells and tissues that gives color to plants and animals.

pi·ta (pē′tə) *n.* a round, flat bread of the Middle East. It can be split open to form a pocket for a filling of meat, vegetables, etc.

☆**piz·za** (pēt′sə) *n.* an Italian dish made by baking a thin layer of dough covered with tomatoes, spices, cheese, etc.

pkg. *abbreviation for* **package** *or* **packages**.

plain·tiff (plān′tif) *n.* the person who starts a suit against another in a court of law.

plan·et (plan′ət) *n.* any of the large heavenly bodies that revolve around the sun and shine as they reflect the sun's light. The planets, in their order from the sun, are Mercury, Venus, Earth, Mars, Jupiter, Saturn, Uranus, Neptune, and Pluto. —**plan·e·tar·y** (plan′ə ter′ē) *adj.*

plaque (plak) *n.* 1 a thin, flat piece of metal, wood, etc. with decoration or lettering on it. 2 a thin film that forms on the teeth and hardens into tartar if not removed.

play·wright (plā′rīt) *n.* a person who writes plays; dramatist.

pledge (plej) *n.* 1 a promise or agreement [the *pledge* of allegiance to the flag]. 2 something promised, especially money to be given as to a charity. ◆*v.* 1 to promise to give [to *pledge* $100 to a building fund]. 2 to bind by a promise [He is *pledged* to marry her.] —**pledged, pledg′ing**

plumb·er (plum′ər) *n.* a person whose work is putting in and repairing the pipes and fixtures of water and gas systems in a building.

pol·y·gon (päl′i gän′) *n.* a flat, closed figure made up of straight lines, especially one having more than four angles and sides.

pon·cho (pän′chō) *n.* a cloak like a blanket with a hole in the middle for the head. It is worn as a raincoat, etc., originally in South America. —*pl.* **pon′chos**

por·trait (pôr′trit) *n.* a drawing, painting, or photograph of a person, especially of the face.

por·tray (pôr trā′) *v.* **1** to make a picture of, as in a painting. **2** to make a picture in words; describe [The writer *portrays* life in New York.] **3** to play the part of in a play, movie, etc. [The actress *portrayed* a scientist.]

po·si·tion (pə zish′ən) *n.* **1** the way in which a person or thing is placed or arranged [a sitting *position*]. **2** the place where a person or thing is; location [The ship radioed its *position*.] **3** a job or office; post [She has a *position* with the city government.] ◆*v.* to put in a certain position [They *positioned* themselves around the house.]

post·script (pōst′skript) *n.* a note added below the signature of a letter.

post·war (pōst′wôr′) *adj.* after the war.

po·ten·tial (pō ten′shəl) *adj.* that can be, but is not yet; possible [a *potential* leader; a *potential* source of trouble]. ◆*n.* power or skill that may be developed [a baseball team with *potential*]. —**po·ten·tial·ly** *adv.*

poul·try (pōl′trē) *n.* fowl raised for food; chickens, turkeys, ducks, geese, etc.

prac·ti·cal (prak′ti kəl) *adj.* **1** that can be put to use; useful and sensible [a *practical* idea; *practical* shoes]. **2** dealing with things in a sensible and realistic way [Wouldn't it be more *practical* to paint it yourself than pay to have it painted?]

praise (prāz) *v.* **1** to say good things about; give a good opinion of [to *praise* someone's work]. **2** to worship, as in song [to *praise* God]. —**praised, prais′ing** ◆*n.* a praising or being praised; words that show approval.

praise·wor·thy (prāz′wʉr′thē) *adj.* deserving praise; that should be admired.

pre·cau·tion (prē kô′shən *or* prē kä′ shən) *n.* care taken ahead of time, as against danger, failure, etc. [She took the *precaution* of locking the door before she left.] —**pre·cau′tion·ar′y** *adj.*

pre·cede (prē sēd′) *v.* to go or come before in time, order, or rank [She *preceded* him into the room.]

pre·dict (prē dikt′) *v.* to tell what one thinks will happen in the future [I *predict* that you will win.] —**pre·dict′a·ble** *adj.*

pre·fer (prē fʉr′) *v.* to like better; choose first [He *prefers* baseball to football.] —**pre·ferred′, pre·fer′ring**

pre·lude (prel′yōōd *or* prā′lōōd) *n.* a part that comes before or leads up to what follows [The strong wind was a *prelude* to the thunderstorm.]

Pres. *abbreviation for* **President.**

pre·scrip·tion (prē skrip′shən) *n.* **1** an order or direction. **2** a doctor's written instructions telling how to prepare and use a medicine; also, a medicine made by following such instructions.

pre·sume (prē zōōm′ *or* prē zyōōm′) *v.* **1** to be so bold as to; dare [I wouldn't *presume* to tell you what to do.] **2** to take for granted; suppose [I *presume* you know what you are doing.] —**pre·sumed′, pre·sum′ing**

☆**pret·zel** (pret′s'l) *n.* a slender roll of dough, usually twisted in a knot, sprinkled with salt, and baked until hard.

pre·vent (prē vent′) *v.* **1** to stop or hinder [A storm *prevented* us from going.] **2** to keep from happening [Careful driving *prevents* accidents.] —**pre·vent′a·ble** or **pre·vent′i·ble** *adj.*

pre·vi·ous (prē′vē əs) *adj.* happening before in time or order; earlier [at a *previous* meeting; on the *previous* page]. —**pre′vi·ous·ly** *adv.*

prin·ci·pal (prin′sə pəl) *adj.* most important; chief; main [the *principal* crop of a State]. ◆*n.* the head of a school.

prin·ci·ple (prin′sə pəl) *n.* **1** a rule, truth, etc. upon which others are based [the basic *principles* of law]. **2** a rule used in deciding how to behave [It is against her *principles* to lie.]

pro·ceed (prō sēd′) *v.* **1** to go on, especially after stopping for a while [After eating, we *proceeded* to the next town.] **2** to begin and go on doing something [I *proceeded* to build a fire.] **3** to move along or go on [Things *proceeded* smoothly.]

proc·ess (prä′ses) *n.* **1** a series of changes by which something develops [the *process* of growth in a plant]. **2** a method of making or doing something, in which there are a number of steps [the refining *process* used in making gasoline from crude oil]. **3** the act of doing something, or the time during which something is done [I was in the *process* of writing a report when you called.] ◆*v.* to prepare by a special process [to *process* cheese].

pro·duce (prə dōōs′ *or* prə dyōōs′) *v.* **1** to bring forth; bear; yield [trees *producing* apples; a well that *produces* oil]. **2** to make or manufacture [a company that *produces* bicycles]. —**pro·duced′, pro·duc′ing** ◆*n.* (prō′dōōs) something that is produced, especially fruits and vegetables for marketing. —**pro·duc′er** *n.*

pro·found (prō found′) *adj.* **1** showing great knowledge, or thought [the *profound* remarks of the judge]. **2** deeply felt; intense [*profound* grief]. **3** thorough [*profound* changes].

prog·ress (präg′res) *n.* **1** a moving forward [the boat's slow *progress* down the river]. **2** a developing or improving [She shows *progress* in learning French.] ◆*v.* (prō gres′) **1** to move forward; go ahead. **2** to develop or improve; advance [Science has helped us to *progress*.]

pro·jec·tor (prə jek′tər) *n.* a machine for projecting pictures or movies on a screen.

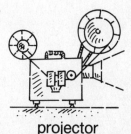
projector

a	ask, fat
ā	ape, date
ä	car, lot
e	elf, ten
ē	even, meet
i	is, hit
ī	ice, fire
ō	open, go
ô	law, horn
oi	oil, point
ೲ	look, pull
ōō	ooze, tool
ou	out, crowd
u	up, cut
ʉ	fur, fern
ə	a in ago
	e in agent
	e in father
	i in unity
	o in collect
	u in focus
ch	chin, arch
ŋ	ring, singer
sh	she, dash
th	thin, truth
th	then, father
zh	s in pleasure

prompt (prämpt) *adj.* **1** quick in doing what should be done; on time [He is *prompt* in paying his bills.] **2** done, spoken, etc. without waiting [We would like a *prompt* reply.] ◆*v.* **1** to urge or stir into action [Tyranny *prompted* them to revolt.] **2** to remind of something that has been forgotten [to *prompt* an actor when a line has been forgotten]. —**prompt′ly** *adv.* —**prompt′ness** *n.*

pro·noun (prō′noun) *n.* a word used in the place of a noun. *I, us, you, they, he, her, it* are some pronouns.

pro·nounce (prə nouns′) *v.* **1** to say or make the sounds of [How do you *pronounce* "leisure"?] **2** to say or declare in an official or serious way [I now *pronounce* you husband and wife.] —**pro·nounced′, pro·nounc′ing**

pro·pel (prə pel′) *v.* to push or drive forward [Some rockets are *propelled* by liquid fuel.] —**pro·pelled′, pro·pel′ling**

pros·e·cute (präs′ə kyōōt) *v.* to put on trial in a court of law on charges of crime or wrongdoing. —**pros′e·cut·ed, pros′e·cut·ing**

pros·e·cu·tor (präs′ə kyōōt′ər) *n.* a person who prosecutes; especially, a lawyer who works for the State in prosecuting persons charged with crime.

pro·te·in (prō′tēn) *n.* a substance containing nitrogen and other elements, found in all living things and in such foods as cheese, meat, eggs, beans, etc. It is a necessary part of an animal's diet.

pro·vi·sion (prō vizh′ən) *n.* **1** a providing or supplying. **2** something provided or arrangements made for the future [Her savings are a *provision* for her old age.] **3** provisions, *pl.* a supply or stock of food.

pro·voke (prō vōk′) *v.* **1** to excite to some action or feeling [to *provoke* a fight]. **2** to annoy or make angry [It *provoked* me to see litter on the lawn.] **3** to stir up [to *provoke* interest].

pt. *abbreviation for* **part, pint, point.** —*pl.* **pts.**

pur·pose (pur′pəs) *n.* **1** what one plans to get or do; aim; goal [I came for the *purpose* of speaking to you.] **2** the reason or use for something [a room with no *purpose*]. —**pur′pose·ful** *adj.* —**pur′pose·less** *adj.*

pur·sue (pər sōō′ *or* pər syōō′) *v.* **1** to follow in order to catch or catch up to [to *pursue* a runaway horse]. **2** to carry out or follow; go on with [She is *pursuing* a career in acting.] **3** to try to find; seek [to *pursue* knowledge]. —**pur·sued′, pur·su′ing** —**pur·su′er** *n.*

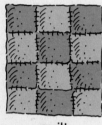

quilt

qt. *abbreviation for* **quart or quarts.**

quad·ri·lat·er·al (kwäd′rə lat′ər əl) *adj.* having four sides. ◆*n.* a flat figure with four sides and four angles.

qual·i·fy (kwôl′ə fī *or* kwä′lə fī) *v.* to make or be fit or suitable, as for some work or activity [Your training *qualifies* you for the job. Does he *qualify* for the team?] —**qual′i·fied, qual′i·fy·ing**

qual·i·ty (kwôl′ə tē *or* kwä′lə tē) *n.* **1** any of the features that make a thing what it is; characteristic [Coldness is one *quality* of ice cream.] **2** degree of excellence [a poor *quality* of paper]. —*pl.* **qual′i·ties**

quan·ti·ty (kwänt′ə tē) *n.* **1** an amount or portion [large *quantities* of food]. **2** a large amount [The factory makes toys in *quantity*.] —*pl.* **quan′ti·ties**

ques·tion·naire (kwes chən ner′) *n.* a written or printed list of questions used in gathering information from people.

quilt (kwilt) *n.* a covering for a bed, made of two layers of cloth filled with down, wool, etc. and stitched together in lines or patterns to keep the filling in place. ◆*v.* **1** to make in the form of a quilt [a *quilted* potholder]. ☆**2** to make quilts.

quiz (kwiz) *n.* a short test given to find out how much one has learned. —*pl.* **quiz′zes** ◆*v.* **1** to ask questions of [The police *quizzed* the suspect.] **2** to test the knowledge of with a quiz [The teacher *quizzed* the class.] —**quizzed, quiz′zing**

quo·ta·tion (kwō tā′shən) *n.* **1** the act of quoting. **2** the words or section quoted [Sermons often have *quotations* from the Bible.]

quo·tient (kwō′shənt) *n.* the number got by dividing one number into another [In 32 ÷ 8 = 4, the number 4 is the *quotient*.]

ra·di·ance (rā′de əns) *n.* the quality or condition of being radiant; brightness.

re·al·ize (rē′ə līz) *v.* to understand fully [I *realize* that good marks depend upon careful work.] —**re′al·ized, re′al·iz·ing** —**re′al·i·za′tion** *n.*

rea·son·a·ble (rē′zən ə bəl) *adj.* **1** using or showing reason; sensible [a *reasonable* person; a *reasonable* decision]. **2** not too high or too low; fair [a *reasonable* price; a *reasonable* salary]. —**rea′son·a·bly** *adv.*

re · ceipt (rē sēt′) **n. 1** the act of receiving [We are in *receipt* of your letter.] **2** a written or printed statement that something has been received [My landlord gave me a *receipt* when I paid my rent.]

re · cent (rē′sənt) **adj.** of a time just before now; made or happening a short time ago [*recent* news]. —**re′cent · ly adv.**

rec·i·pe (res′ə pē) **n.** a list of ingredients and directions for making something to eat or drink [a *recipe* for cookies].

re · cruit (rē krōōt′) **n.** a person who has recently joined an organization, group, or, especially, the armed forces. ◆ **v. 1** to enlist new members in [to *recruit* an army]. **2** to get to join [Our nature club *recruited* six new members.]

re·fer (rē fʉr′) **v. 1** to speak of or call attention; mention [You seldom *refer* to your injury.] **2** to go for facts, help, etc. [Columbus had no accurate maps to *refer* to.] **3** to tell to go to a certain person or place for help, service, information, etc. [Our neighbor *referred* me to a good doctor.] —**re·ferred′, re·fer′ring**

re·frig·er·a·tor (rē frij′ər āt′ər) **n.** a box or room in which the air is kept cool to keep food, etc. from spoiling.

reg·u·la·tion (reg yə lā′shən) **n. 1** the act of regulating or the condition of being regulated [the *regulation* of the sale of alcohol]. **2** a rule or law that regulates or controls [safety *regulations*].

re·hearse (rē hʉrs′) **v. 1** to go through a play, speech, etc. for practice, before giving it in public. **2** to repeat in detail [They *rehearsed* all their troubles to me.] —**re·hearsed′, re·hears′ing** —**re·hears′al n.**

reign (rān) **n.** the rule of a king, queen, emperor, etc.; also, the time of ruling [laws made during the *reign* of Victoria]. ◆ **v.** to rule as a king, queen, etc. [Henry VIII *reigned* for 38 years.]

rein·deer (rān′dir) **n.** a large deer found in northern regions, where it is tamed and used for work or as food. Both the male and female have antlers. —**pl. rein′deer**

re·joice (rē jois′) **v.** to be or make glad or happy [We *rejoiced* at the news.] —**re·joiced′, re·joic′ing** —**re·joic′ing n.**

re · late (rē lāt′) **v. 1** to tell about; give an account of [*Relate* to us what you did.] **2** to connect in thought or meaning; show a relation between [to *relate* one idea to another]. —**re · lat′ed, re · lat′ing**

re · lease (rē lēs′) **v.** to set free or relieve [*Release* the bird from the cage.] ◆ **n.** the act of setting someone or something free [a *release* from prison].

re·li·a·ble (rē lī′ə bəl) **adj.** that can be trusted; dependable [This barometer gives a *reliable* weather forecast.] —**re·li·a·bil·i·ty** (ri lī′ə bil′ə tē) **n.** —**re·li′a·bly adv.**

re·lieve (rē lēv′) **v. 1** to free from pain, worry, etc. [We were *relieved* when the danger passed.] **2** to set free from duty or work by replacing [The guard is *relieved* every four hours.] —**re·lieved′, re·liev′ing**

re·main·der (rē mān′dər) **n.** the part, number, etc. left over [I sold some of my books and gave the *remainder* to the library. When 3 is subtracted from 10, the *remainder* is 7.]

re·mark·a·ble (rē märk′ə bəl) **adj.** worth noticing because it is very unusual [the *remarkable* strength of Hercules]. —**re·mark′a·bly adv.**

rem·e·dy (rem′ə dē) **n. 1** a medicine or treatment that cures, heals, or relieves [a *remedy* for sunburn]. **2** anything that corrects a wrong or helps make things better [a *remedy* for poor education]. —**pl. rem′e·dies** ◆ **v.** to cure, correct, make better, etc. [Some money would *remedy* her situation.] —**rem′e·died, rem′e·dy·ing**

re·peat·ed (ri pēt′əd) **adj.** said, made, or done again or often [*repeated* warnings]. —**re·peat′ed·ly adv.**

re·quire (rē kwīr′) **v. 1** to be in need of [Most plants *require* sunlight.] **2** to order, command, or insist upon [He *required* us to leave.] —**re·quired′, re·quir′ing**

re·search (rē′ sʉrch′ or rē sʉrch′) **n.** careful, patient study in order to find out facts and principles about some subject [to carry on *research* into the causes of cancer]. ◆ **v.** to do research.

re·sem·ble (rē zem′bəl) **v.** to be or look like [Rabbits *resemble* hares but are smaller.] —**re·sem′bled, re·sem′bling**

re·sign (rē zīn′) **v.** to give up one's office, position, membership, etc. [We *resigned* from the club.]

re·sist·ance (rē zis′təns) **n. 1** the act of resisting. **2** the power to resist or withstand [Her *resistance* to colds is low.] **3** the opposing of one force or thing to another [the fabric's *resistance* to wear].

re · solve (rē zälv′ or rē zôlv′) **v. 1** to decide; make up one's own mind [I *resolved* to help them.] **2** to make clear; solve or explain [to *resolve* a problem]. ◆ **n.** firm purpose or determination [her *resolve* to be successful].

re·sound (rē zound′) **v. 1** to echo or be filled with sound [The hall *resounded* with music.] **2** to make a loud, echoing sound; to be echoed [His laughter *resounded* throughout the cave.]

re·trieve (rē trēv′) **v. 1** to get back; recover [to *retrieve* a kite from a tree]. **2** to find and bring back [The spaniel *retrieved* the wounded duck.] —**re·trieved′, re·triev′ing**

re·veal (rē vēl′) **v. 1** to make known what was hidden or secret [The map *revealed* the spot where the treasure was buried.] **2** to show [She took off her hat, *revealing* her golden hair.]

rev·e·nue (rev′ə nōō or rev′ə nyōō) **n.** money got as rent, profit, etc.; income; especially, the money a government gets from taxes, duties, etc.

a	ask, fat
ā	ape, date
ä	car, lot
e	elf, ten
ē	even, meet
i	is, hit
ī	ice, fire
ō	open, go
ô	law, horn
oi	oil, point
ōō	look, pull
ōō	ooze, tool
ou	out, crowd
u	up, cut
ʉ	fur, fern
ə	a in ago
	e in agent
	e in father
	i in unity
	o in collect
	u in focus
ch	chin, arch
ŋ	ring, singer
sh	she, dash
th	thin, truth
th	then, father
zh	s in pleasure

re·vers·i·ble (rē vur′sə bəl) *adj.* that can be reversed; made so that either side can be used as the outer side [a *reversible* coat].

☆**ro·de·o** (rō′dē ō) *n.* a contest or show in which cowboys match their skill in riding horses, roping and throwing cattle, etc. —*pl.* **ro′de·os**

Roo·se·velt, Franklin D. (rō′zə velt) 1882–1945; 32d president of the United States, from 1933 to 1945.

Roo·se·velt, Theodore 1858–1919; 26th president of the United States, from 1901 to 1909.

rough · en (ruf′ən) *v.* to make or become rough [to *roughen* a smooth surface with a coarse file].

row·boat (rō′bōt) *n.* a boat made to be rowed.

Franklin D. Roosevelt

Ss

sauce·pan (sôs′pan *or* säs′pan) *n.* a small metal pot with a long handle, used for cooking.

sau·té (sō tā′) *v.* to fry quickly in a pan with a little fat. **sau·téed** (sō tād′,) **sau·té·ing** (sō tā′ing) ◆*adj.* fried in this way [chicken livers *sauté*].

sax·o·phone (sak′sə fōn) *n.* a woodwind musical instrument with a curved metal body. Its mouthpiece has a single reed.

scald (skôld) *v.* **1** to burn with hot liquid or steam. **2** to use boiling liquid on, as to kill germs. **3** to heat until it almost boils [to *scald* milk for a custard]. ◆*n.* a burn caused by scalding.

scam·per (skam′pər) *v.* to move quickly or in a hurry [squirrels *scampering* through the trees]. ◆*n.* a quick run or dash.

scat·ter (skat′ər) *v.* **1** to throw here and there; sprinkle [to *scatter* seed over a lawn] . **2** to separate and send or go in many directions; disperse [The wind *scattered* the leaves. The crowd *scattered* after the game.]

sce·ner·y (sēn′ər ē) *n.* **1** the way a certain area looks; outdoor views [the *scenery* along the shore]. **2** painted screens, hangings, etc. used on a stage for a play.

sce·nic (sēn′ik) *adj.* **1** having to do with scenery or landscapes [the *scenic* wonders of the Rockies]. **2** having beautiful scenery [a *scenic* route along the river]. —**sce′ni·cal·ly** *adv.*

scent (sent) *n.* **1** a smell; odor [the *scent* of apple blossoms]. **2** the sense of smell [Lions hunt partly by *scent*.] **3** a smell left by an animal [The dogs lost the fox's *scent* at the river.] ◆*v.* to smell [Our dog *scented* a cat.]

saxophone

sched·ule (skej′ool *or* ske′joo əl) *n.* ☆**1** a list of the times at which certain things are to happen; timetable [a *schedule* of the sailings of an ocean liner]. ☆**2** a timed plan for a project [The work is ahead of *schedule*.] ◆*v.* **1** to make a schedule of [to *schedule* one's hours of work]. ☆**2** to plan for a certain time [to *schedule* a game for 3:00 P.M.] —**sched′uled, sched′ul·ing**

scheme (skēm) *n.* **1** a plan or system in which things are carefully put together [the color *scheme* of a painting]. **2** a plan or program, often a secret or dishonest one [a *scheme* for getting rich quick]. ◆ *v.* to make secret or dishonest plans; to plot [Lee is always *scheming* to get out of work.] —**schemed, schem′ing**

schol·ar·ship (skä′lər ship) *n.* a gift of money to help a student continue his or her education.

sci·en·tif·ic (sī′ən tif′ik) *adj.* **1** having to do with, or used in, science [a *scientific* study; *scientific* equipment]. **2** using the rules and methods of science [*scientific* procedure]. —**sci′en·tif′i·cal·ly** *adv.*

scis·sors (siz′ərz) *n.pl.* a tool for cutting, with two blades that are joined so that they slide over each other when their handles are moved: *also used with a singular verb. Also called* **pair of scissors.**

scour (skour) *v.* to clean by rubbing hard, especially with something rough or gritty [The cook *scoured* the greasy frying pan with soap and steel wool.]

scowl (skoul) *v.* to lower the eyebrows and the corners of the mouth in showing displeasure; look angry or irritated [She *scowled* upon hearing the bad news.] ◆ *n.* a scowling look; an angry frown.

scratch (skrach) *v.* **1** to mark or cut the surface of slightly with something sharp [Thorns *scratched* her legs. Our cat *scratched* the chair with its claws.] **2** to rub or scrape, as with the nails, to relieve itching [to *scratch* a mosquito bite]. **3** to cross out by drawing lines through [She *scratched* out what he had written.] ◆*n.* **1** a mark or cut made in a surface by something sharp. **2** a slight wound.

scream (skrēm) *v.* **1** to give a loud, shrill cry, as in fright or pain [They *screamed* as the roller coaster hurtled downward.] **2** to make a noise like this [The sirens *screamed*. We *screamed* with laughter.] ◆*n.* a loud, shrill cry or sound; shriek.

scrimp (skrimp) *v.* to spend or use as little as possible [to *scrimp* to save money].

sculp·ture (skulp′chər) *n.* **1** the art of carving wood, chiseling stone, casting or welding metal, modeling clay or wax, etc. into statues, figures, or the like. **2** a statue, figure, etc. made in this way. ◆*v.* to cut, chisel, form, etc. in making sculptures. —**sculp′tured, sculp′tur·ing** —**sculp′tur·al** *adj.*

seal (sēl) *n.* **1** a piece of paper, wax, etc. with a design pressed into it, fixed to an official document to show that it is genuine. Such wax designs were once also used to seal letters. **2** something that closes or fastens tightly. ◆*v.* to close or fasten tight [to *seal* cracks with putty; to *seal* a letter]. —**seal′er** *n.*

search (surch) *v.* **1** to look over or through in order to find something [We *searched* the house. The police *searched* the thief for a gun.] **2** to try to find [to *search* for an answer]. —**search′er** *n.*

sea·son·al (sē′zən əl) *adj.* of or depending on a season or the seasons [*seasonal* rains; *seasonal* work]. —**sea′son·al·ly** *adv.*

se·cu·ri·ty (si kyoor′ə tē) *n.* **1** the condition or feeling of being safe or sure; freedom from danger, fear, doubt, etc. **2** something that protects [Insurance is a *security* against loss.] **3** something given or pledged as a guarantee [A car may be used as *security* for a loan.] **4 securities**, *pl.* stocks and bonds. —*pl.* **se·cu′ri·ties**

Seine (sān *or* sen) a river in northern France. It flows through Paris into the English Channel.

seize (sēz) *v.* to take hold of in a sudden, strong, or eager way; grasp [to *seize* a weapon and fight; to *seize* an opportunity]. —**seized, seiz′ing**

se·lec·tion (sə lek′shən) *n.* **1** a selecting or being selected; choice. **2** the thing or things chosen; also, things to choose from [a wide *selection* of colors].

sem·i·cir·cle (sem′i sur′kəl) *n.* a half circle. —**sem·i·cir·cu·lar** (sem′i sur′kyə lər) *adj.*

sem·i·co·lon (sem′i kō′lən) *n.* a punctuation mark (;) used to show a pause that is shorter than the pause at the end of a sentence, but longer than the pause marked by the comma [The *semicolon* is often used to separate closely related clauses, especially when they contain commas.]

sem·i·fi·nal (sem′i fī′nəl) *n.* a round, match, etc. that comes just before the final one in a contest or tournament. —**sem′i·fi′nal·ist** *n.*

sem·i·pre·cious (sem′i presh′əs) *adj.* describing gems that are of less value than the precious gems [The garnet is a *semiprecious* gem.]

ses·sion (sesh′ən) *n.* **1** the meeting of a court, legislature, class, etc. to do its work. **2** the time during which such a meeting or series goes on. **3** a school term or period of study, classes, etc.

sham·poo (sham poo′) *v.* to wash with foamy suds, as hair or a rug. —**sham·pooed′, sham·poo′ing** ◆*n.* **1** the act of shampooing. **2** a special soap, or soaplike product, that makes suds.

sharp (shärp) *adj.* **1** having a thin edge for cutting, or a fine point for piercing [a *sharp* knife; a *sharp* needle]. **2** easily seen; distinct; clear [a *sharp* contrast]. **3** very strong; intense; stinging [a *sharp* wind; *sharp* pain]. —**sharp′ly** *adv.* —**sharp′ness** *n.*

sheaf (shēf) *n.* **1** a bunch of cut stalks of wheat, rye, or straw tied up together in a bundle. **2** a bundle of things gathered together [a *sheaf* of papers]. —*pl.* **sheaves**

shoul·der (shōl′dər) *n.* **1** the part of the body to which an arm or foreleg is connected. **2 shoulders**, the two shoulders and the part of the back between them.

shuf·fle·board (shuf′əl bôrd) *n.* a game in which the players use long sticks to slide disks along a smooth lane, trying to get them on numbered sections.

shut·ter (shut′ər) *n.* **1** a cover for a window, usually swinging on hinges. **2** a part on a camera that opens and closes in front of the lens to control the light going in.

siege (sēj) *n.* the act or an instance of surrounding a city, fort, etc. by an enemy army in an attempt to capture it.

sight·see·ing (sīt′sē′iŋ) *n.* the act of going about to see places and things of interest. —**sight′se′er** *n.*

sig·na·ture (sig′nə chər) *n.* **1** a person's name as he or she has written it. **2** a sign in music placed at the beginning of a staff to give the key or the time.

☆**sil·ver·ware** (sil′vər wer) *n.* things, especially tableware, made of or plated with silver.

sim·mer (sim′ər) *v.* to keep at or just below the boiling point, usually forming tiny bubbles with a murmuring sound [*Simmer* the stew about two hours.]

sim·ple (sim′pəl) *adj.* **1** easy to do or understand [a *simple* task; *simple* directions]. **2** without anything added; plain [the *simple* facts; a *simple* dress]. —**sim′pler, sim′plest**

sketch (skech) *n.* **1** a simple, rough drawing or design, usually done quickly and with little detail. **2** a short outline, giving the main points. ◆*v.* to make a sketch of; draw sketches.

☆**sleigh** (slā) *n.* a carriage with runners instead of wheels, for travel over snow or ice.

slop·py (släp′ē) *adj.* not neat or careful; messy [*sloppy* clothes; a *sloppy* piece of work]. —**slop′pi·er, slop′pi·est** —**slop′pi·ly** *adv.* —**slop′pi·ness** *n.*

smear (smir) *v.* **1** to cover with something greasy, or sticky [to *smear* the actor's face with cold cream]. **2** to rub or spread [*Smear* some grease on the axle.] **3** to make a mark or streak that is not wanted on something [He *smeared* the wet paint with his sleeve.] ◆ *n.* **1** a mark or streak made by smearing. **2** the act of smearing or slandering someone.

shutter

a	ask, fat
ā	ape, date
ä	car, lot
e	elf, ten
ē	even, meet
i	is, hit
ī	ice, fire
ō	open, go
ô	law, horn
oi	oil, point
oo	look, pull
o͞o	ooze, tool
ou	out, crowd
u	up, cut
u	fur, fern
ə	a in ago
	e in agent
	e in father
	i in unity
	o in collect
	u in focus
ch	chin, arch
ŋ	ring, singer
sh	she, dash
th	thin, truth
th	then, father
zh	s in pleasure

smooth (smo͞oth) *adj.* **1** having an even surface, with no bumps or rough spots [as *smooth* as marble; *smooth* water on the lake]. **2** even or gentle in movement; not jerky or rough [a *smooth* airplane flight; a *smooth* ride; *smooth* sailing]. **3** with no trouble or difficulty [*smooth* progress]. ◆*v.* **1** to make smooth or even [*Smooth* the board with sandpaper.] **2** to make easy by taking away troubles, difficulties, etc. [She *smoothed* our way by introducing us to the other guests.] ◆*adv.* in a smooth way [The engine is running *smooth* now.] —**smooth′ly** *adv.*

so·cial (sō′shəl) *adj.* **1** of or having to do with human beings as they live together in a group or groups [*social* problems; *social* forces]. **2** liking to be with others; sociable [A hermit is not a *social* person.] ◆*n.* a friendly gathering; party [a church *social*]. —**so′cial·ly** *adv.*

so·di·um (sō′dē əm) *n.* a soft, silver-white metal that is a chemical element. It is found in nature only in compounds. Salt, baking soda, lye, etc. contain sodium.

sof·ten (sôf′ən *or* säf′ən) *v.* to make or become soft or softer. —**sof′ten·er** *n.*

so·lar (sō′lər) *adj.* **1** of or having to do with the sun [a *solar* eclipse; *solar* energy]. **2** depending on light or energy from the sun [*solar* heating].

sol·dier (sōl′jər) *n.* a person in an army, especially one who is not a commissioned officer. ◆*v.* to serve as a soldier. —**sol′dier·ly** *adj.*

soldier

sol·emn (säl′əm) *adj.* serious; grave; very earnest [a *solemn* face; a *solemn* oath]. —**sol′emn·ly** *adv.*

so·lu·tion (sə lo͞o′shən) *n.* **1** the solving of a problem. **2** an answer or explanation [to find the *solution* to a mystery].

soothe (so͞oth) *v.* **1** to make quiet or calm by being gentle or friendly [The clerk *soothed* the angry customer with helpful answers.] **2** to take away some of the pain or sorrow of; ease [I hope this lotion will *soothe* your sunburn.] —**soothed, sooth′ing** —**sooth′ing·ly** *adv.*

so·pra·no (sə pran′ō *or* sə prä′nō) *n.* **1** the highest kind of singing voice of women, girls, or young boys. **2** a singer with such a voice or an instrument with a range like this. —*pl.* **so·pra′nos**

spa·ghet·ti (spə get′ē) *n.* long, thin strings of dried flour paste, cooked by boiling or steaming and served with a sauce.

spear·mint (spir′mint) *n.* a common plant of the mint family, used for flavoring.

spearmint

spe·cies (spē′shēz *or* spē′sēz) *n.* a group of plants or animals that are alike in certain ways [The lion and tiger are two different *species* of cat.] —*pl.* **spe′cies**

spec·ta·tor (spek′tātər) *n.* a person who watches something without taking part; onlooker [We were *spectators* at the last game of the World Series.]

sports·man (spôrts′mən) *n.* **1** a man who takes part in or is interested in sports. **2** a person who plays fair and does not complain about losing or boast about winning. —*pl.* **sports′men** —**sports′man·like** *adj.* —**sports′man·ship** *n.*

square (skwer) *n.* **1** a flat figure with four equal sides and four right angles. **2** anything shaped like this [Arrange the chairs in a *square*.] ◆*adj.* **1** having the shape of a square. **2** forming a right angle [a *square* corner]. —**squar′er, squar′est** ◆*v.* to mark off in squares, as a checkerboard. —**squared, squar′ing**

squawk (skwôk *or* skäwk) *n.* a loud, harsh cry such as a chicken or parrot makes. ◆*v.* to let out a squawk. —**squawk′er** *n.*

squeeze (skwēz) *v.* **1** to press hard or force together [*Squeeze* the sponge to get rid of the water.] **2** to get by pressing or by force [to *squeeze* juice from an orange; to *squeeze* money from poor people]. —**squeezed, squeez′ing** ◆*n.* a squeezing or being squeezed; hard press. —**squeez′er** *n.*

stair·way (ster′wā) *or* **stair·case** (ster′kās) *n.* a flight of steps, usually with a handrail.

sta·tion·ar·y (stā′shə ner′ē) *adj.* **1** staying in the same place; not moving; fixed [A *stationary* bicycle is pedaled for exercise, but does not move from its base.] **2** not changing in condition or value; not increasing or decreasing [*stationary* prices].

stead·y (sted′ē) *adj.* not changing or letting up; regular [a *steady* gaze; a *steady* worker]. —**stead′i·er, stead′i·est** —**stead′ied, stead′y·ing** —**stead′i·ly** *adv.* —**stead′i·ness** *n.*

ster·e·o (ster′ē ō′) *n.* a stereophonic record player, radio, sound system, etc. —*pl.* **ster′e·os′**

stew·ard (sto͞o′ərd *or* styo͞o′ərd) *n.* **1** a person, especially on a ship or airplane, whose work is to look after the passengers' comfort.

stiff (stif) *adj.* **1** that does not bend easily; firm [*stiff* cardboard]. **2** not able to move easily [*stiff* muscles]. —**stiff′ly** *adv.* —**stiff′ness** *n.*

stitch (stich) *n.* one complete movement of a needle and thread into and out of the material in sewing. —*pl.* **stitch′es** ◆*v.* to sew or fasten with stitches [to *stitch* a seam].

stow·a·way (stō′ə wā) *n.* a person who hides aboard a ship, plane, etc. for a free or secret ride.

strain·er (strān′ər) *n.* a thing used for straining, as a sieve, filter, etc.

stretch (strech) **v.** **1** to draw out to full length, to a greater size, to a certain distance, etc.; extend [She *stretched* out on the sofa. Will this material *stretch*? *Stretch* the rope between two trees. The road *stretches* for miles through the hills.] **2** to pull or draw tight; strain [to *stretch* a muscle]. ◆**n.** **1** a stretching or being stretched [a *stretch* of the arms]. **2** an unbroken space, as of time or land; extent [a *stretch* of two years; a long *stretch* of beach].

strict (strikt) **adj.** **1** keeping to rules in a careful, exact way [a *strict* supervisor]. **2** never changing; rigid [a *strict* rule]. —**strict′ly adv.** —**strict′ness n.**

style (stīl) **n.** **1** the way in which anything is made, done, written, spoken, etc.; manner; method [pointed arches in the Gothic *style*]. **2** the way in which people generally dress, act, etc. at any particular period; fashion; mode [*Styles* in clothing keep changing.] **3** a fine, original way of writing, painting, etc. [This author lacks *style*.] —**styled, styl′ing**

sub · con · tract (sub′kän′trakt) **n.** a contract in which a company hires a second company to do part of a job that the first company has agreed to complete. ◆ **v.** to make a subcontract [to *subcontract* for plumbing and electrical work].

subj. *abbreviation for* **subject, subjunctive.**

sub · ma · rine (sub′mə rēn) **n.** a kind of warship that can travel under the surface of water. ◆**adj.** (sub mə rēn′) that lives, grows, happens, etc. under the surface of the sea [Sponges are *submarine* animals.]

sub · scrip · tion (səb skrip′shən) **n.** **1** the act of subscribing or something that is subscribed. **2** an agreement to take and pay for a magazine, theater tickets, etc. for a particular period of time.

sub · stan · tial (səb stan′shəl) **adj.** **1** of or having substance; material; real or true [Your fears turned out not to be *substantial*.] **2** strong; solid; firm [The bridge didn't look very *substantial*.] **3** more than average or usual; large [a *substantial* share; a *substantial* meal]. **4** wealthy or well-to-do [a *substantial* farmer]. —**sub · stan′tial · ly adv.**

sub · sti · tute (sub′stə tōōt *or* sub′stə tyōōt) **n.** a person or thing that takes the place of another [He is a *substitute* for the regular teacher.] ◆**v.** to use as or be a substitute [to *substitute* vinegar for lemon juice; to *substitute* for an injured player]. —**sub′sti · tut · ed, sub′sti · tut · ing** —**sub′sti · tu′tion n.**

suc · ceed (sək sēd′) **v.** **1** to manage to do or be what was planned; do or go well [I *succeeded* in convincing them to come with us.] **2** to come next after; follow [Carter *succeeded* Ford as president.]

suc · cess · ful (sək ses′fəl) **adj.** **1** having success; turning out well [a *successful* meeting]. **2** having become rich, famous, etc. [a *successful* architect]. —**suc · cess′ful · ly adv.**

su · crose (sōō′krōs) **n.** a sugar found in sugar cane, sugar beets, etc.

suf · fi · cient (sə fish′ənt) **adj.** as much as is needed; enough [Do you have *sufficient* supplies to last through the week?] —**suf · fi′cient · ly adv.**

suit · a · ble (sōōt′ə bəl) **adj.** right for the purpose; fitting; proper [a *suitable* gift]. —**suit′a · bil′i · ty n.** —**suit′a · bly adv.**

su · per · fi · cial (sōō′pər fish′əl) **adj.** of or on the surface; not deep [a *superficial* cut; a *superficial* likeness]. —**su · per · fi · ci · al · i · ty** (sōō′pər fish′ē al′ə tē) **n.** —**su′per · fi′cial · ly adv.**

su · per · son · ic (sōō′pər sän′ik) **adj.** **1** of or moving at a speed greater than the speed of sound. **2** *another word for* **ultrasonic.**

su · per · vise (sōō′pər vīz) **v.** to direct or manage, as a group of workers; be in charge of. —**su′per · vised, su′per · vis · ing**

sur · round (sər round′) **v.** to form or arrange around on all or nearly all sides; enclose [The police *surrounded* the criminals. The house is *surrounded* with trees.]

sur · vey (sər vā′) **v.** to measure the size, shape, boundaries, etc. of a piece of land by the use of special instruments [to *survey* a farm]. ◆**n.** (sur′vā) **1** a general study covering the main facts or points [The *survey* shows that we need more schools. This book is a *survey* of American poetry.] **2** the act of surveying a piece of land, or a record of this [He was hired to make a *survey* of the lake shore.] —*pl.* **sur′veys**

sur · vey · ing (sər vā′iŋ) **n.** the act, work, or science of one who surveys land.

Swede (swēd) **n.** a person born or living in Sweden.

Swiss (swis) **adj.** of Switzerland or its people. ◆**n.** a person born or living in Switzerland. —*pl.* **Swiss**

sym · me · try (sim′ə trē) **n.** **1** an arrangement in which the parts on opposite sides of a center line are alike in size, shape, and position [The human body has *symmetry*.] **2** balance or harmony that comes from such an arrangement.

syn · the · siz · er (sin′thə sī zər) **n.** ☆an electronic musical instrument that makes sounds that cannot be made by ordinary instruments.

submarine

a	ask, fat
ā	ape, date
ä	car, lot
e	elf, ten
ē	even, meet
i	is, hit
ī	ice, fire
ō	open, go
ô	law, horn
oi	oil, point
೦೦	look, pull
ōō	ooze, tool
ou	out, crowd
u	up, cut
ʉ	fur, fern
ə	a in ago
	e in agent
	e in father
	i in unity
	o in collect
	u in focus
ch	chin, arch
ŋ	ring, singer
sh	she, dash
th	thin, truth
th	then, father
zh	s in pleasure

tab·u·late (tab′yo͞o lāt′) **v.** to arrange in tables or columns [to *tabulate* numbers]. —**tab′u·lat·ed, tab′u·lat·ing** —**tab′u·la′tion** **n.** —**tab′u·la′tor** **n.**

tam·bou·rine (tam bə rēn′) **n.** a small, shallow drum with only one head and with jingling metal disks in the rim. It is shaken, struck with the hand, etc.

tar·iff (ter′if) **n.** 1 a list of taxes on goods imported or, sometimes, on goods exported. 2 such a tax or its rate.

taught (tôt *or* tät) *past tense and past participle of* **teach.**

teach (tēch) **v.** 1 to show or help to learn how to do something; train [She *taught* us to skate.] 2 to give lessons to or in [Who *teaches* your class? He *teaches* French.] 3 to make or help to know or understand [The accident *taught* her to be careful.] —**taught, teach′ing** —**teach′a·ble adj.**

tech·ni·cal (tek′ni kəl) **adj.** 1 having to do with the useful or industrial arts or skills [A *technical* school has courses in mechanics, welding, etc.] 2 of or used in a particular science, art, profession, etc. [*technical* words; *technical* skill]. —**tech′ni·cal·ly adv.**

tech·nique (tek nēk′) **n.** a way of using tools, materials, etc. and following rules in doing something artistic, in carrying out a scientific experiment, etc. [a violinist with good bowing *technique*].

tech·nol·o·gy (tek näl′ə jē) **n.** 1 the study of the industrial arts or applied sciences, as engineering, mechanics, etc. 2 science as it is put to use in practical work [medical *technology*]. 3 a method or process for dealing with a technical problem. —**tech·no·log·i·cal** (tek′nə läj′i k'l) **adj.** —**tech′no·log′i·cal·ly adv.** —**tech·nol′o·gist n.**

tex·tile (teks′tīl *or* teks′təl) **n.** a fabric made by weaving; cloth. ◆**adj.** 1 having to do with weaving or woven fabrics [He works in the *textile* industry.] 2 woven [Linen is a *textile* fabric.]

tex·ture (teks′chər) **n.** 1 the look and feel of a fabric as caused by the arrangement, size, and quality of its threads [Corduroy has a ribbed *texture*.] 2 the general look and feel of any other kind of material; structure; makeup [Stucco has a rough *texture*.] ◆**v.** to cause to have a particular texture. —**tex′tured, tex′tur·ing**

the·ol·o·gy (*th*ē äl′ə jē) **n.** 1 the study of God and of religious beliefs. 2 a system of religious beliefs. —*pl.* (for sense 2 only) —**the·ol′o·gies**

the·o·ry (thē′ə rē *or th*ir′ē) **n.** 1 an explanation of how or why something happens, especially one based on scientific study and reasoning [Charles Darwin's important *theory* of evolution]. 2 the general principles on which an art or science is based [music *theory*]. 3 an idea, opinion, guess, etc. [My *theory* is that the witness lied.] —*pl.* **the′o·ries**

the·sau·rus (thi sôr′əs *or th*i sï′ əs) **n.** a book containing lists of synonyms or related words. —*pl.* **the·sau·ri** (thi sôr′ī) or **the·sau′rus·es**

thick (thik) **adj.** 1 great in width or depth from side to side; not thin [a *thick* board]. 2 as measured from one side through to the other [a wall ten inches *thick*]. ◆**adv.** in a thick way. —**thick′ly adv.**

thief (thēf) **n.** a person who steals, especially secretly. —*pl.* **thieves** (thēvz)

thirst·y (thʉrs′tē) **adj.** 1 wanting to drink; feeling thirst [The spicy food made me *thirsty*.] 2 needing water; dry [*thirsty* fields]. —**thirst′i·er, thirst′i·est** —**thirst′i·ly adv.** —**thirst′i·ness n.**

this·tle (*th*is′əl) **n.** a plant with prickly leaves and flower heads of purple, white, pink, or yellow.

thor·ough (thʉr′ō) **adj.** 1 complete in every way; with nothing left out, undone, etc. [a *thorough* search; a *thorough* knowledge of the subject]. 2 very careful and exact [a *thorough* worker]. —**thor′ough·ly adv.**

threw (thro͞o) *past tense of* **throw.**

through (thro͞o) **prep.** 1 in one side and out the other side of; from end to end of [The nail went *through* the board. We drove *through* the tunnel.] 2 from the beginning to the end of [We stayed in Maine *through* the summer.] ◆**adv.** 1 from the beginning to the end [to see a job *through*]. 2 in a complete and thorough way; entirely [We were soaked *through* by the rain.] ◆**adj.** finished [Are you *through* with your homework?]

through·out (thro͞o out′) **prep.** all the way through; in every part of [The fire spread *throughout* the barn.] ◆ **adv.** in every part; everywhere [The walls were painted white *throughout*.

throw (thrō) **v.** 1 to send through the air by a fast motion of the arm; hurl, toss, etc. [to *throw* a ball]. 2 to make fall down; upset [to *throw* someone in wrestling]. —**threw, thrown, throw′ing** ◆**n.** the act of throwing [The fast *throw* put the runner out at first base.]

tight (tīt) **adj.** 1 put together firmly or closely [a *tight* knot]. 2 fitting too closely [a *tight* shirt]. —**tight′ly adv.** —**tight′ness n.**

ti·ny (tī′nē) **adj.** very small; minute. —**ti′ni·er, ti′ni·est**

tip·toe (tip′tō) **n.** the tip of a toe. ◆**v.** to walk on one's tiptoes in a quiet or careful way. —**tip′toed, tip′toe·ing**

tambourine

ti·tle (tīt′l) *n.* **1** the name of a book, chapter, poem, picture, piece of music, etc. **2** a word showing the rank, occupation, etc. of a person ["Baron," "Ms.," and "Dr." are *titles.*] **3** a claim or right; especially, a legal right to own something, or proof of such a right [The *title* to the car is in my name.] ◆ *v.* to give a title to; name. —**ti′tled, ti′tling**

tol·er·ate (täl′ə rāt) *v.* to let something be done or go on without trying to stop it [I won't *tolerate* such talk.] —**tol′er·at·ed, tol′er·at·ing**

tomb·stone (tōōm′stōn) *n.* a stone put on a tomb telling who is buried there; gravestone.

tough·en (tuf′ən) *v.* to make or become tough or tougher.

trans·ac·tion (tran zak′shən *or* tran sak′shən) *n.* **1** the act or an instance of transacting **2** something transacted [The *transaction* was completed when all parties signed the contract.]

trans·fer (trans fur′ *or* trans′fər) *v.* **1** to move, carry, send, or change from one person or place to another [He *transferred* his notes to another notebook. Jill has *transferred* to a new school.] **2** to move a picture, design, etc. from one surface to another, as by making wet and pressing. —**trans·ferred′, trans·fer′ring** ◆ *n.* (trans′fər) a thing or person that is transferred [They are *transfers* from another school.] —**trans·fer′a·ble** *or* **trans·fer′ra·ble** *adj.*

trans·form·er (trans fôr′mər) *n.* **1** a person or thing that transforms. **2** a device that changes the voltage of an electric current.

☆**tran·sis·tor** (tran zis′tər *or* tran sis′tər) *n.* an electronic device, made up of semiconductor material, that controls the flow of electric current. Transistors are small and last a long time.

trans·mis·sion (trans mish′ən *or* tranz mish′ən) *n.* **1** the act of transmitting or passing something along [the *transmission* of messages by telegraph]. **2** the part of a car that sends the power from the engine to the wheels.

trans·par·ent (trans per′ənt) *adj.* so clear or so fine it can be seen through [*transparent* glass; a *transparent* veil].

trans·por·ta·tion (trans pər tā′shən) *n.* **1** the act of transporting. **2** a system or business of transporting things.

treas·ur·y (trezh′ər ē) *n.* **1** the money or funds of a country, company, club, etc. **2** **Treasury**, the department of a government in charge of issuing money, collecting taxes, etc. **3** a place where money is kept. —*pl.* **treas′ur·ies**

tri·an·gu·lar (trī aŋ′gyə lər) *adj.* of or shaped like a triangle; having three corners.

tri·col·or (trī′kul′ər) *n.* a flag having three colors, especially the flag of France. ◆*adj.* having three colors. —**tri′col′ored** *adj.*

tri·lin·gual (trī liŋ′gwəl) *adj.* **1** of or in three languages [a *trilingual* region]. **2** using or able to use three languages, especially with equal or nearly equal ability [a *trilingual* child].

tril·o·gy (tril′ə jē) *n.* a set of three plays, novels, etc. which form a related group, although each is a complete work [Louisa May Alcott's "Little Women," "Little Men," and "Jo's Boys" make up a *trilogy.*] —*pl.* **tril′o·gies**

tri·ple (trip′əl) *adj.* **1** made up of three [A *triple* cone has three dips of ice cream.] **2** three times as much or as many. ◆*n.* ☆a hit in baseball on which the batter gets to third base. ◆*v.* to make or become three times as much or as many. —**tri′pled, tri′pling**

trip·li·cate (trip′lə kət) *adj.* made in three copies exactly alike [a *triplicate* receipt].

tri·um·phant (trī um′fənt) *adj.* **1** having won victory or success; victorious [Our team was *triumphant.*] **2** happy or joyful over a victory [We could hear their *triumphant* laughter.] —**tri·um′phant·ly** *adv.*

trol·ley (trä′lē) *n.* ☆**1** a device that sends electric current from a wire overhead to the motor of a streetcar, trolley bus, etc. ☆**2** an electric streetcar: also **trolley car.** —*pl.* **trol′leys**

trou·sers (trou′zərz) *n.pl.* an outer garment with two legs, especially for men and boys, reaching from the waist usually to the ankles; pants.

Tru·man (trōō′mən) **Harry S.** 1884–1972; the 33d president of the United States, from 1945 to 1953.

trust·wor·thy (trust′wur′thē) *adj.* deserving to be trusted; reliable. —**trust′wor′thi·ness** *n.*

truth·ful (trōōth′fəl) *adj.* **1** telling the truth; honest [a *truthful* person]. **2** that is the truth; accurate [to give a *truthful* report]. —**truth′ful·ly** *adv.* —**truth′ful·ness** *n.*

tsp. *abbreviation for* **teaspoon** *or* **teaspoons.**

tur·moil (tur′moil) *n.* a noisy or confused condition.

☆**tux·e·do** (tuk sē′dō) *n.* **1** a man's jacket worn at formal dinners, dances, etc. It was often black, with satin lapels and no tails. Now tuxedos have many patterns and colors. **2** a suit with such a jacket, worn with a dark bow tie. —*pl.* **tux·e′dos**

twitch (twich) *v.* to move or pull with a sudden jerk [A rabbit's nose *twitches* constantly.] ◆ *n.* a sudden, quick motion or pull, often one that cannot be controlled [a *twitch* near one eye]. —*pl.* **twitch′es**

ty·phoon (tī fōōn′) *n.* any violent tropical cyclone that starts in the western Pacific.

typ·ist (tīp′ist) *n.* a person who uses a typewriter; especially, one whose work is typing.

tombstone

a	ask, fat
ā	ape, date
ä	car, lot
e	elf, ten
ē	even, meet
i	is, hit
ī	ice, fire
ō	open, go
ô	law, horn
oi	oil, point
oo	look, pull
ōō	ooze, tool
ou	out, crowd
u	up, cut
u	fur, fern
ə	a in ago
	e in agent
	e in father
	i in unity
	o in collect
	u in focus
ch	chin, arch
ŋ	ring, singer
sh	she, dash
th	thin, truth
th	then, father
zh	s in pleasure

ul·tra·son·ic (ul′trə sän′ik) *adj.* describing or having to do with sounds too high for human beings to hear.

ul·tra·vi·o·let (ul′trə vī′ə lət) *adj.* lying just beyond the violet end of the spectrum [*Ultraviolet* rays are invisible rays of light that help to form vitamin D in plants and animals and can kill certain germs.]

un- **1** *a prefix meaning* not *or* the opposite of [An *unhappy* person is one who is not happy, but sad.] **2** *a prefix* meaning to reverse or undo the action of [To *untie* a shoelace is to reverse the action of tying it.]

un·a·void·a·ble (unə void′ə bəl) *adj.* that cannot be avoided; inevitable [an *unavoidable* accident]. —**un′a·void′a·bly** *adv.*

un·a·ware (un ə wer′) *adj.* not aware; not knowing or noticing [We were *unaware* of the danger in going there.]

un·be·liev·a·ble (unbə lēv′ə bəl) *adj.* that cannot be believed; astounding; incredible.

un·con·di·tion·al (un′kən dish′ən 'l) *adj.* not depending on any conditions; absolute [an *unconditional* guarantee]. —**un′con·di′tion·al·ly** *adv.*

un·due (un dōō′ *or* un dyōō′) *adj.* more than is proper or right; too much [Don't give *undue* attention to your appearance.]

un·fair (un fer′) *adj.* not fair, just, or honest. —**un·fair′ly** *adv.* —**un·fair′ness** *n.*

☆**u·ni·cy·cle** (yōōn′ə sī′kəl) *n.* a riding device that has only one wheel and pedals like a bicycle.   It is used for trick riding, as in a circus.

unicycle

u·ni·form (yōōn′ə fôrm) *adj.* **1** always the same; never changing [Driving at a *uniform* speed saves gas.] **2** all alike; not different from one another [a row of *uniform* houses]. ◆*n.* the special clothes worn by the members of a certain group [a nurse's *uniform*]. —**u′ni·form·ly** *adv.*

un·i·lat·er·al (yōōn′ə lat′ər əl) *adj.* done by or involving only one of several nations, sides, or groups a *unilateral* decision].

u·nique (yōō nēk′) *adj.* **1** that is the only one; having nothing like it [Mercury is a *unique* metal in that it is liquid at ordinary temperatures.] **2** unusual; remarkable [It is a very *unique* motion picture.]

u·ni·son (yōōn′ə sən) *n.* sameness of musical pitch, as of two or more voices or tones.

u·ni·ver·sal (yōōn′ə vur′səl) *adj.* **1** of, for, or by all people; concerning everyone [a *universal* human need]. **2** present everywhere [*universal* pollution of the air we breathe]. —**u·ni·ver·sal·i·ty** (yōō′nə vər sal′ə tē) *n.*

u·ni·ver·si·ty (yōōn′ə vur′sə tē) *n.* a school of higher education, made up of a college or colleges and, usually, professional schools, as of law and medicine. —*pl.* **u′ni·ver′si·ties**

u·su·al (yōō′zhōō əl) *adj.* such as is most often seen, heard, used, etc.; common; ordinary; normal. —**as usual,** in the usual way. —**u′su·al·ly** *adv.*

U·tah (yōō′tô *or* yōō′tä) a state in the southwestern part of the U.S.: abbreviated **Ut., UT**

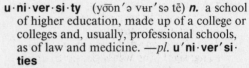

veil (vāl) *n.* a piece of thin cloth, as net or gauze, worn especially by women over the face or head to hide the features, as a decoration, or as part of a uniform [a bride's *veil*; a nun's *veil*]. ◆*v.* to cover, hide, etc. with or as if with a veil.

ven·ture·some (ven′chər səm) *adj.* **1** ready to take chances; daring; bold [a *venturesome* explorer]. **2** full of risks or danger; risky [a *venturesome* trip through a swamp].

ver·sion (vur′zhən) *n.* **1** something translated from the original language [an English *version* of the Bible]. **2** a report or description from one person's point of view [Give us your *version* of the accident.] **3** a particular form of something [an abridged *version* of a novel; the movie *version* of a play].

ver·tex (vur′teks) *n.* **1** the highest point; top. **2** any corner point of a triangle, square, cube, etc. —*pl.* **ver·tex·es** *or* **ver·ti·ces** (vur′tə sēz)

ver·ti·cal (vur′i kəl) *adj.* straight up and down; perpendicular to a horizontal line [The walls of a house are *vertical*.] ◆*n.* a vertical line, plane, etc. —**ver′ti·cal·ly** *adv.*

vi·bra·tion (vī brā′shən) *n.* rapid motion back and forth; quivering [The *vibration* of the motor shook the bolts loose.] —**vi·bra·to·ry** (vī′brə tôr′ē) *adj.*

vid·e·o (vid′ē ō′) *adj.* **1** having to do with television.   **2**having to do with the picture portion of a television broadcast. **3** having to do with the display of data or graphics on a computer screen. ◆ *n.* **1** *the same as* **television   2** *a short form of* **videocassette   3** *a short form of* **videotape   4**a program recorded on film or videotape for viewing on television or with a videocassette recorder.

vid·e·o·tape (vid′ē ō tāp′) *n.* a thin magnetic tape on which both the sound and picture signals of a TV program can be recorded by electronics.

veil

vir·tu·ous (vur′choo wəs *or* vur′ chyoo əs) *adj.* having virtue; good, moral, chaste, etc. —**vir′tu·ous·ly** *adv.*

vi·sion (vizh′ən) *n.* **1** the act or power of seeing; sight [She wears glasses to improve her *vision.*] **2** something seen in the mind, or in a dream, trance, etc. ["while *visions* of sugarplums danced in their heads"].

vis·u·al (vizh′oo wəl) *adj.* **1** having to do with sight or used in seeing [*visual* aids]. **2** that can be seen; visible [*visual* proof]. —**vis′u·al·ly** *adv.*

void (void) *adj.* **1** having nothing in it; empty; vacant [A vacuum is a *void* space.] **2** being without; lacking [a heart *void* of kindness]. u *n.* **1** an empty space. **2** a feeling of loss or emptiness [His death left a great *void* in our hearts.]

vol. *abbreviation for* **volume.** —*pl.* **vols.**

voy·age (voi′ij) *n.* **1** a journey by water [an ocean *voyage*]. **2** a journey through the air or through outer space [a *voyage* by rocket]. ◆*v.* to make a voyage. —**voy′aged, voy′ag·ing** —**voy′ag·er** *n.*

vs. *abbreviation for* **versus.**

Ww

wait (wāt) *v.* **1** to stay in a place or do nothing while expecting a certain thing to happen [*Wait* for the signal. I *waited* until six o'clock, but they never arrived.] **2** to remain undone for a time [Let it *wait* until next week.] **3** to serve food at a meal [He *waits* on table. She *waits* on me.] ◆*n.* the act or time of waiting [We had an hour's *wait* for the train.]

wan·der (wän′dər) *v.* **1** to go from place to place in an aimless way; ramble; roam [to *wander* about a city]. **2** to go astray; drift [The ship *wandered* off course. The speaker *wandered* from the subject.] — **wan′der·er** *n.*

wash·a·ble (wôsh′ə bəl *or* wäsh′ə bəl) *adj.* that can be washed without being damaged.

Washington (wôsh′iŋ tən *or* wäsh′iŋ tən), **George** (jorj) 1732–1799; first president of the United States, from 1789 to 1797. He was commander in chief of the American army in the Revolutionary War.

wa·ter·way (wôt′ər wā) *n.* **1** a channel through which water runs. **2** any body of water on which boats or ships can travel, as a canal or river.

wel·fare (wel′fer) *n.* **1** health, happiness, and so on; well-being. **2** aid by government agencies for the poor or those out of work.

weath·er (weth′ər) *n.* the conditions outside at any particular time with regard to temperature, sunshine, rainfall, etc. [We have good *weather* today for a picnic.]

weight (wāt) *v.* **1** heaviness; the quality a thing has because of the pull of gravity on it. **2** amount of heaviness [What is your *weight*?] **3** a piece of metal used in weighing [Put a two-ounce *weight* on the balance.] **4** any solid mass used for its heaviness [to lift *weights* for exercise; a paper *weight*].

weird (wird) *adj.* **1** strange or mysterious in a ghostly way [*Weird* sounds came from the cave.] **2** very odd, strange, etc. [What a *weird* hat! What *weird* behavior!] —**weird′ly** *adv.* —**weird′ness** *n.*

wheth·er (hweth′ər *or* weth′ər) *conj.* **1** if it is true or likely that [I don't know *whether* I can go.] **2** in either case that [It makes no difference *whether* he comes or not.]

whis·tle (hwis′l *or* wis′əl) *v.* **1** to make a high, shrill sound as by forcing breath through puckered lips or by sending steam through a small opening. **2** to produce by whistling [to *whistle* a tune]. —**whis′tled, whis′tling** ◆*n.* **1** a device for making whistling sounds. **2** the act or sound of whistling. —**whis′tler** *n.*

with·draw·al (with drô′əl *or* with drô′əl) *n.* the act or fact of withdrawing, as money from the bank.

wit·ness (wit′nəs) *n.* **1** a person who saw, or can give a firsthand account of, something that happened [A *witness* told the police how the fire started.] **2** a person who gives evidence in a law court. ◆*v.* to be present at; see [to *witness* a sports event].

woe·ful (wō′fəl) *adj.* full of woe; mournful; sad.

wrath (rath) *n.* great anger; rage; fury.

wreck·age (rek′ij) *n.* **1** the act of wrecking. **2** the condition of being wrecked. **3** the remains of something that has been wrecked.

wrench (rench) *n.* **1** a sudden, sharp twist or pull [With one *wrench,* he loosened the lid.] **2** a tool for holding and turning nuts, bolts, or pipes. ◆ *v.* to twist or pull sharply [She *wrenched* the keys from my grasp.]

wres·tle (res′əl) *v.* to struggle with, trying to throw or force to the ground without striking blows with the fists. —**wres′tled, wres′tling** ◆*n.* **1** the action or a bout of wrestling. **2** a struggle or contest. —**wres′tler** *n.*

wring (riŋ) *v.* **1** to squeeze and twist with force [to *wring* out the wet clothes]. — **wrung, wring′ing**

wrist·watch (rist′wäch *or* rist′wôch) *n.* a watch worn on a strap or band that fits around the wrist.

George
Washington

a	ask, fat
ā	ape, date
ä	car, lot
e	elf, ten
ē	even, meet
i	is, hit
ī	ice, fire
ō	open, go
ô	law, horn
oi	oil, point
oo	look, pull
oo	ooze, tool
ou	out, crowd
u	up, cut
ʉ	fur, fern
ə	a in ago
	e in agent
	e in father
	i in unity
	o in collect
	u in focus
ch	chin, arch
ŋ	ring, singer
sh	she, dash
th	thin, truth
th	then, father
zh	s in pleasure

xy·lo·phone (zī′lə fōn) **n.** a musical instrument made up of a row of wooden bars of different sizes, that are struck with wooden hammers.

yearn (yʉrn) **v.** to be filled with longing or desire [to *yearn* for fame].

yel·low (yel′ō) **adj.** having the color of ripe lemons, or of an egg yolk. ◆**n.** a yellow color. ◆**v.** to make or become yellow [linens *yellowed* with age]. —**yel′low·ish adj.**

yield (yēld) **v.** **1** to give up; surrender [to *yield* to a demand; to *yield* a city]. **2** to give or grant [to *yield* the right of way; to *yield* a point]. **3** to give way [The gate would not *yield* to our pushing.] **4** to bring forth or bring about; produce; give [The orchard *yielded* a good crop. The business *yielded* high profits.] ◆**n.** the amount yielded or produced.

zo·ol·o·gy (zō·äl′ə jē) **n.** the science that studies animals and animal life.